Islam and the Drive to Global Justice

Faith and Politics: Political Theology in a New Key

Series Editors: Lori Brandt Hale, Augsburg University; W. David Hall, Centre College

"Political Theology" is a theme which straddles two major areas of inquiry: political philosophy and theology, or differently phrased: the realms of secular politics and the sacred. The relationship is marked by difference, sometimes by tension or conflict. During the past century, such conflict reached a boiling point when the Nazi regime sought to co-opt or integrate the Christian population. In opposition to this attempt, a "Confessing Church" was formed which, under the leadership of Karl Barth, issued the Barmen Declaration (May 31st, 1934). The declaration insisted on the independence of faith from political power structures while, at the same time, guarding against the pure "privatization" of faith.

In our time, the relation between religion and politics is still fraught. This tension holds true across religious traditions and political structures. This series launches new investigations into political theology on a global level. Its guiding question is "how do theology and religion provide analytical and constructive lenses to make sense of perennial and current political issues and problems?"

Recent Titles

Islam and The Drive to Global Justice: Principles of Justice Beyond Dominant Ethnic and Religious Communities, edited by Louay M. Safi

The Future of Christian Realism: International Conflict, Political Decay, and the Crisis of Democracy, edited by Dallas Gingles, Joshua Mauldin, and Rebekah L. Miles

Islamic Political Theology, Edited by Massimo Campanini and Marco Di Donato

Dietrich Bonhoeffer, Theology, and Political Resistance, Edited by Lori Brandt Hale & W. David Hall

Political Life in Dark Times: A Call for Renewal, By Fred Dallmayr

The Legacy of the Barmen Declaration: Politics and the Kingdom, By Fred Dallmayr

Islam and the Drive to Global Justice

Principles of Justice Beyond Dominant Ethnic and Religious Communities

Edited by
Louay M. Safi

LEXINGTON BOOKS
Lanham • Boulder • New York • London

Rowman & Littlefield
Bloomsbury Publishing Inc, 1359 Broadway, New York, NY 10018, USA
Bloomsbury Publishing Plc, 50 Bedford Square, London, WC1B 3DP, UK
Bloomsbury Publishing Ireland, 29 Earlsfort Terrace, Dublin 2, D02 AY28, Ireland
www.bloomsbury.com

Published by Lexington Books
An imprint of The Rowman & Littlefield Publishing Group, Inc.
4501 Forbes Boulevard, Suite 200, Lanham, Maryland 20706
www.rowman.com
86-90 Paul Street, London EC2A 4NE

Copyright © 2024 by The Rowman & Littlefield Publishing Group, Inc.

All rights reserved. No part of this publication may be: i) reproduced or transmitted in any form, electronic or mechanical, including photocopying, recording or by means of any information storage or retrieval system without prior permission in writing from the publishers; or ii) used or reproduced in any way for the training, development or operation of artificial intelligence (AI) technologies, including generative AI technologies. The rights holders expressly reserve this publication from the text and data mining exception as per Article 4(3) of the Digital Single Market Directive (EU) 2019/790.

British Library Cataloguing in Publication Information available

Library of Congress Cataloging-in-Publication Data
Names: Ṣāfī, Lu'ayy, editor.
Title: Islam and the drive to global justice : principles of justice beyond dominant ethnic and religious communities / Louay M. Safi.
Description: Lanham : Lexington Books, 2023. | Series: Faith and politics: political theology in a new key | Includes bibliographical references and index. |
Summary: "This book focuses on the tradition of Islamic rationalism articulating a conceptually and ethically inclusive global framework that broadens the call for the exercise of justice beyond dominant ethnic and religious communities. It argues for replacing the power-centered approach to global order with human-centered approach that privilege shared values and interests"— Provided by publisher.
Identifiers: LCCN 2023046350 (print) | LCCN 2023046351 (ebook) |
 ISBN 9781666954029 (cloth) | ISBN 9781666954036 (ebook)
Subjects: LCSH: Islam and justice. | Justice, Administration of (Islamic law)
Classification: LCC BP173.43 .I856 2023 (print) | LCC BP173.43 (ebook) |
DDC 297.2/7—dc23/eng/20231023
LC record available at https://lccn.loc.gov/2023046350
LC ebook record available at https://lccn.loc.gov/2023046351

Contents

Introduction   1

PART I: REEVALUATING THE GROUNDS FOR A JUST GLOBAL ORDER   7

1. Islamic Rational Idealism and the Universalization of Justice   9
   Louay M. Safi

2. Justice in the Qur'an: Interpretations of a Universal Value in a Globalizing World   31
   Asma Afsaruddin

3. Sensory Aesthetics of Belief and Unbelief in the Qur'an and Its Impact on Interreligious and Intersocietal Relations   57
   Abdulkader Tayob

4. The Islamic Inflection of Connective Justice: Between Cosmopolitan Civility, Institutional Relationality, and Intellectual Reflexivity   79
   Armando Salvatore

5. Sharia and Freedom: A Reassessment   101
   Mustafa Akyol

6. Toward a Civilizational Ethos: From the *Homo Moralis* to the *Homo Ethicus*   125
   Mohammed Hashas

PART II: GLOBAL CONFLUENCE IN THE MUSLIM SOUTH   153

7. Muṣlim Intellectuals and Global Justice: A View from Southeast Asia   155
   Khairudin Aljunied

8	Toward a Justice-Based Foreign Policy *Farid Senzai*	171
9	Religious Diversity in Arab Society: Myth, Conspiracy, and Reality *Mohammed Abu-Nimer*	193
10	Arab Authoritarianism and Western Complacency *Louay M. Safi*	209

Conclusion	227
Index	231
About the Contributors	239

Introduction

Justice has always been the bedrock of any sociopolitical order that uplifts the lives of those who are part of it and must therefore be the bedrock of the emerging global order that continues to take shape before our eyes. As an intuitive value and sentiment, justice is cherished across a wide spectrum of religions and cultures. People often demand that justice be done every time they encounter a violation of civic and human rights. People, however, continually disagree over what constitutes justice and how justice can best be realized. *Islam and the Drive to Global Justice* aims to contribute to the debate over global justice by drawing on the contemporary and historical justice discourse within the Islamic traditions and by exploring Islamically inspired critique of the policies and practices of world powers toward Muslim populations. The discussion does not necessarily aim at negating ideas and practices currently advanced to promote global justice but to bring insights from Islamic sources and literature relevant to the debate over the universality of religious values and the interconnectivity of Islamic traditions to global challenges. To achieve this goal, I invited eight prominent scholars of Islam to address two key questions: What does Islamic scholarship have to say about global justice? And how do Muslims approach the institutionalization of justice in diverse post-modern society?

This volume explores the relevance of Islamic values and traditions to the advancement of global justice by examining Islam's capacity to overcome three interrelated challenges facing the dispensation of justice in contemporary society: inclusivity, disparity, and selectivity. Inclusivity is particularly acute in multireligious and multiethnic societies, and for a while secularism and multiculturalism became the anecdotes for religious and ethnic exclusivism. But with the transformation of secularism from a principle to separate religious and political authorities to an ideology desiring to combat the transcendental foundation of modern society, and with the rejection of multiculturalism by the increasingly emboldened nationalist groups, the ability of multicultural and multireligious society to survive and prosper is ever more in jeopardy.

In responding to the serious deterioration of the ethics of inclusivity even in societies where significant progress was achieved in combating discrimination and social injustice, the book draws on the Islamic rational tradition to articulate a conceptually and ethically inclusive global framework that broadens the exercise of justice beyond dominant ethnic and religious communities. It also draws on the humanity-oriented teachings of Islam and on the multiethnic and multireligious experience of historical Islamic societies in the Middle Ages. The book also focuses on the ongoing intellectual and political debate among Muslim scholars and intellectuals about the need to free the essentially transcendental values and principles of monotheistic traditions from the exclusivist sociopolitical models in which they were historically cast.

The book comprises ten chapters organized into two parts. Part I covers the first six chapters that deal with conceptual and theoretical elements of justice in the Islamic sources and traditions and the way they relate to the concept of global justice. In addition to contrasting the power-based Grego-Roman realism with the transcendental idealism advanced by the early Hebrew and Christian traditions, and later systematized by Islamic rationalism, this part challenges conventional views of justice in both the Western and Islamic rational traditions. It also outlines more inclusive models for advancing global peace and justice. Part II sheds light on exclusivist practices in the global order that create disparity and double standards, focusing on the impact of the nation-centric approach by global powers towards foreign policy and international relations.

Chapter 1 contrasts the Grego-Roman ethical order, which elevates power to the top of the moral hierarchy and promotes a stratified sociopolitical order, with the transcendental values that grew within the monotheistic tradition. It further illuminates the role played by Islamic rationalism in overcoming the moral realism advanced by ancient paganistic societies that privileged power over ethical demands, and in advancing, as early as the seventh century, an open-society model as it embraced religious and ethnic diversity and contributed to the universalization of the principle of equal dignity.

Chapter 2 develops a typology of the different forms of justice by engaging the Qur'anic text and then proceeding to discuss two notions of justice in greater detail: interpersonal and social justice. This chapter pays special attention to justice within the family and justice among nations and religious communities. The chapter also contemplates the importance of incorporating Islamic perspectives into a global conversation on justice and the idea of responsible stewardship of the globe and global resources and on the recognition of the equal dignity of every human being and the reconciliation of intercultural and interreligious tensions through civil dialogue.

Chapter 3 engages Islamic sources and scholarly literature as it reflects on the religious Other. It explores the way the Qur'an reveals the impact of the notion of beauty on human choices and suggests that religious beliefs are mediated in the Qur'anic discourse through the notion of beauty. The chapter proposes that a universal sensory perception mediates belief and disbelief and thus reinforces an ethic of empathy toward the religious Other. Recognizing the connection between sensory perception and the way people are able to perceive transcendental truth, the author stresses the need to maintain an ethic of tolerance and empathy without giving up truth. Such formulation of religious truth is powerful as it allows a deeper understanding of differences in beliefs and a better appreciation of the complexity of religious truth.

Chapter 4 examines the nexus between civility, cosmopolitanism, and justice within Islamic traditions by looking beyond the surface of the hermeneutics of sharia and contrasts the corporal and sacramental nature of Western institutions with the emphasis on relational and civil in historical Islam, focusing on the institution of waqf (charitable endowment). It also shows how the difference in approaches impacts state–society relationship in the two traditions, allowing historical Islamic society to water down the rigid distinction between the private and public spheres that originates from Westphalian. It ultimately calls into question the rigid distinction between state and society.

Chapter 5 further explores the notion of sharia, recognizing the important role it played historically as both the moral and legal foundation of society. It points out that sharia was historically developed by independent jurists who were the custodian of law. The failure to recognize its complete independence from the state led modern scholars, both Muslims and Orientalists, to confuse the moral and legal. This chapter strives therefore to engage, contrast, and redefine key concepts, including sharia and Qur'an, sharia and law, and sin and crime.

Chapter 6 provides a critical reading of key concepts, such as faith and religion, morality and ethics, sharia and law, spiritualism and spirituality, and idealism and realism. It further argues that rational idealism is crucial for engaging in profound "spiritual self-criticism" and for nurturing moral practices in both the private and public spheres. The author argues that transcendental faith traditions, as repository of moral and ethical energies, have a major role to play in guiding world affairs, currently dominated by utilitarianism and realism alone. Political Islam as known and practiced today is nothing but a fading shadow in comparison with the Islamic rational tradition and the energies it could muster to uplift the human spirit. It is the energies that emanates from the classical spirit of the Islam that produced the Islamic civilization, and which ensure the relevance of transcendental ethos and safeguard its vibrance now and in the future.

Chapter 7 introduces the work of a leading Southeast Asian Muslim thinker, Hamka (1908–1981), who profoundly engaged in the idea of global justice and argues that his unique view of global justice is borne out of his experiences as a social movement activist, politician, and intellectual committed to the reformation of global and local societies. Hamka's ideas on global justice have also shaped his acute engagements and critique of various dominant conceptions of global justice in his time. This chapter argues that Hamka, by creatively redefining the practical concepts of *khalifatullah fil'ard* (vicegerents of God on earth), *amanah* (sacred trust), *shura* (mutual consultation), and *maslahah* (general welfare), has formulated an innovative vision of global justice that pushes the frontiers of contemporary thinking over inequalities and inequities which characterize the world we live in today.

Chapter 8 looks critically at the United States' support of authoritarian regimes in the Middle East and describes it as the norm rather than the exception. It insists that the U.S. foreign policy is rooted in "power-politics" and focuses exclusively on narrow "self-interest," describing such an approach as counterproductive and short-sighted. The U.S. invasion of Iraq and Afghanistan and its continual support of autocratic regimes are carefully analyzed to illustrate this point. Such ill-informed invasions, subsequent occupations, and the continued support of authoritarian regimes throughout the Middle East have had disastrous long-term consequences on the Middle Eastern societies. The chapter calls for the adoption of a value-based approach to foreign policy that focuses on the ethics of dignity and on justice. Such an approach, the author insists, would inevitably bring a vigorous debate over how—or even whether—values, morality, and ethics should factor into U.S. foreign policy. The chapter further argues that the United States should pursue a much more "principled," value-based foreign policy that is ethical and morally grounded.

Chapter 9 examines the various approaches adopted by Arab governments to protect religious pluralism and diversity in postcolonial Arab society. It explores the wide-range cases of denial, accommodation, and integration in response to religious diversity and points to the many challenges and obstacles facing local and international agencies that promote religious diversity. The chapter outlines several anxieties and concerns expressed by various social, religious, and political agencies when dealing with religious diversity and identifies effective models and examples of introducing religious diversity in Arab societies.

Finally, chapter 10 exposes the connection between European powers and autocratic regimes in the MENA region and illustrates how this misguided approach has contributed to the rise of religious extremism and produced failed states in Syria, Lebanon, Iraq, and Yemen that undermine both national and global peace and stability. The chapter is critical of the modernization approach to the MENA region and argues that it is rooted in European political realism that places the exercise of power, national interests, and dominance over the values of freedom, equality, and democracy. Using case studies that illustrate the role of the social secularization strategy in Syria, Iran, and Egypt in undermining democratic and reformist movements in those countries, the chapter calls for adopting a different approach rooted in liberal and democratic values rather than cultural practices and lifestyle. The chapter illustrates how Islamic values, as articulated by reform movements, support a democratic and pluralist political order, and emphasizes the need to legitimize and support both secular and Islamic social forces that advocate democracy and human rights.

Part I

REEVALUATING THE GROUNDS FOR A JUST GLOBAL ORDER

Chapter 1

Islamic Rational Idealism and the Universalization of Justice

Louay M. Safi

The concept of justice, anchored in transcendental ethics, is often studied under the rubric of the ethics of deontology or the ethics of duty. Transcendental ethics, central to all monotheistic traditions, received its intellectual articulation first in the work of Islamic rationalism. Islamic ethics demands that people pursue meaningful and responsible living by adhering to a set of universal principles, including justice, equality, and compassion. Acting in the world in a meaningful way requires the alignment of the values the individual holds with the universal values that reside in the transcendent, regarded in Islam as the source of being and value. We examine, in this chapter, the principles of Islamic ethics and explore its evolution and relevance to the globalizing society of late modernity. We begin by examining how the idea of justice was understood in ancient societies by focusing on the meaning of justice in ancient Greece and Rome. This examination provides us with the background for understanding the role played by the monotheistic religions in general and the tradition of rational idealism in particular—a tradition that evolved under Islam but was later adopted by Kant. This chapter aims at shedding light on the transformation of the concept of justice from being an instrument for maintaining social stratification to one that calls humanity to embrace the principle of equal dignity. We focus particularly on the centrality of the idea of equal justice and the project of subordinating the exercise of power to the rules of justice undertaken by Islamic rationalism. We conclude by discussing justice in the public sphere and the subordination of power to ethical demands, the development of social pluralism, and the protection of moral autonomy.

Islamic normative sources locate Islamic ethics within the Abrahamic tradition and consider justice, equality, and freedom of religion to be intrinsic to all monotheistic traditions. The transcendental ethics that underscores the call for public duty is traced back in Islamic sources to Abraham's rejection of the rigid social hierarchy of pagan kingdoms and the subjugation of the public to the worship of man-made idols. The current chapter is divided into five sections that explore Islamic principles and trace their roots and their historical evolution to the Abrahamic traditions. To better understand the impact of Islamic ethics on modern public ethics, we focus, in section 1, on contrasting the transcendental ethics founded in monotheistic traditions with that of ancient Greece and Rome. This section is quite central for appreciating the extent to which modern public values are at odds with Greek ethics, as we shed light on the inequality at the core of the Greco-Roman perception of justice and on the exclusivity of their concept of virtue. We turn, in section 2, to examine the place of Islamic ethics within the broader system of monotheistic ethics as we explore the emergence of monotheistic values in the Hebrew prophetic traditions. Again, this section is quite essential for locating Islamic ethics within the broader scheme of ethical teachings and practices. In section 3, we visit the thesis advanced by the nineteenth-century German philosopher Hegel, who credits Islam as being the first to subordinate political power to ethical judgment. We shed light, in this section, on the question suggested by Hegel regarding the inability of early Christianity to demand ethical limitations on the exercise of power by the Roman emperors even though it shared the same monotheistic values with Islam. Section 4 is devoted to understanding what the Islamic normative sources, particularly the Qur'anic ethical pronouncements and the prophetic moral example, have to say about public ethics and moral agency. Finally, in section 5, we examine the role of Islamic rationalism in articulating the principles of public ethics. Finally, we discuss, in section 5, the system of social pluralism historically developed within Islam that ensured the moral autonomy of confessional communities.

We examine, in the subsequent sections, the historical evolution of Islamic ethics, focusing particularly on Islam's contribution to the rise of public ethics that requires the subordination of political power to ethical judgment. The first step to unpack the various dimensions of Islamic ethics and its relevance to global justice is to understand the great transformation of humanity from social stratification under the pagan view of the world to the monotheistic worldview that stresses the idea of the equal dignity of all people.

FROM SOCIAL STRATIFICATION TO EQUAL DIGNITY

Modern scholars trace the values that govern personal and public behaviors, such as justice, equality, and accountability, to the Greek ethical philosophy. A closer examination of how these values are internalized and practiced today shows that they evolved within the ancient monotheistic traditions before they were given their rational articulation in the schools of Islamic rational idealism between the seventh and eleventh centuries. The ethics of rational idealism was later adopted by Immanuel Kant in the late eighteenth century and was further expounded in the work of Fichte, Schelling, and Hegel, who are often subsumed under the rubric of German Idealism.

Table 1.1 compares the most essential values advanced by the Greek, and later by the Roman, philosophers with those emphasized in the monotheistic traditions. The Greek virtues were considered by both Plato and Aristotle as befitting to the Greek citizenry, and most notably to the Greek aristocracy. They were at the core of their power-centered view of reality. Greek virtues share a little with the transcendental values that lay the foundation of the ethics of dignity. The Greco-Roman virtues essentially reflect the leadership qualities the nobility class must possess to be able to rule the Greek nation-state and the Roman Empire; they were grounded in the notion of manliness suited for the ruling class in Athens and Rome. Indeed, the word "virtue" in English is the translation of the Latin word "virtus" which means manliness.

The Greek nobility cared about justice but not equal justice. Plato for instance thought that a just city required a stratified public order in which the population is divided into three permanent social strata: the guardians, the axillaries, and the partisans. The guardians will be raised from a young age to be rulers; the auxiliaries will be raised to become soldiers; and the craftsman, or the people as Plato referred to them, will be the producers and those who provide the services to meet societal needs. He associated justice with the division of social responsibility among these three social strata that were based on family heritage rather than individual competence.[1] Furthermore, Plato suggested that the division of society into three classes must be supported with a fictitious tale, a sort of a "noble" or "magnificent" lie. As he put it:

> Citizens, we shall say to them in our tale, you are brothers, yet God has framed you differently. Some of you have the power of command, and in the composition of these he has mingled gold, wherefore also they have the greatest honour; others he has made of silver, to be auxiliaries; others again who are to be husbandmen and craftsmen he has composed of brass and iron; and the species will generally be preserved in the children. But as all are of the same original stock,

Table 1.1 The Highest Values in the Greco-Roman and Monotheistic Traditions

Ethics of Virtue (Greco-Roman)	*Ethics of Dignity (Monotheism)*
1. Wisdom	1. Equal dignity
2. Courage	2. Social accountability
3. Justice among equals	3. Universal justice
4. Temperance	4. Compassion

> a golden parent will sometimes have a silver son, or a silver parent a golden son. And God proclaims as a first principle to the rulers, and above all else, that there is nothing which they should so anxiously guard, or of which they are to be such good guardians, as of the purity of the race. Such is the tale; is there any possibility of making our citizens believe in it? Not in the present generation, he replied; there is no way of accomplishing this; but their sons may be made to believe in the tale, and their sons'' sons, and posterity after them.[2]

The class-based justice advanced by Plato not only promotes inequality and social hierarchy but is also based on dishonesty masked as a "magnificent lie." For Plato, truth is not the foundation of reality but rather the other way around. For him, real power is the determinant of social interactions, and the truth must therefore be subordinated to power.

Aristotle's justice is hierarchical and completely oblivious to the notion of equal dignity that many of us take today for granted. For him, justice is "proportional" rather than "reciprocal."[3] It lies in treating equal people equally and unequal people unequally. The equality and inequality referred to here were reflected in the structure of the Athenian society. Only the citizens, who constituted 10% of the residents of Athens, were equal.[4] No member of the Athenian society could seek justice by invoking the principle of reciprocity or equal dignity. Reciprocity and equal justice were not notions that the Greek would ever consider in any dispute that crossed the boundaries of social class and status. A Greek citizen who "unjustifiably" took the life of a slave or a partisan did not have to worry about issues of equality, and hence reciprocity would have never been brought to bear on the crime. Aristotle considers, in his *Nicomachean Ethics*, the concept of justice only in relation to men who are free and relatively equal to each other, and he also shares Plato's conviction that the notion of equal justice is relevant only within the order of rank. Hierarchical orders take precedence over any consideration of equality and reciprocity. In *Book V*, he likes the equality of "men" to the equality of "objects." He goes on to argue that as the objects that are not equal in values are evaluated and judged on the basis of "proportion" rather than equality, so do people. "If they are not equal, they will not have what is equal, but this is the origin of quarrels and complaints—when either equals have and are awarded unequal shares or unequals equal shares." Furthermore, the idea that "unequals" should be treated unequally is accepted today in connection with the notion of merit, but Aristotle and other Greek philosophers did not limit unequal treatment to matters of merit as understood in modern literature. What is often equivocated when a reference is made to Greek ethics is the fact that the notion of merit for Greek philosophers does not relate to the modern sense of merit which is influenced by the arguments of the equal dignity Middle-Age Europeans learned from the translated works of Islamic rational idealism. For the Greeks, the notion of merit was always attached to "class" and "race," as Aristotle reveals in the following passage:

> [F]or all men agree that what is just in distribution must be according to merit in some sense, though they do not all specify the same sort of merit, but democrats identify it with the status of freeman, supporters of oligarchy with wealth (or with noble birth), and supporters of aristocracy with excellence.[5]

So, the concept of merit, according to Aristotle, is grounded in the structure of governance and the nature of state. It acquires different meanings under different forms of government. As the Greeks moved from the mode of aristocracy to oligarchy to democracy, so did the basis of "merit" changed accordingly to that of excellence, wealth, and the status of freemen. Aristotle is not equivocal about the inequality of people and does not consider the principle of reciprocity to be appropriate for bringing justice to an officer of the state who inflicted a wound on a commoner. In such a case, the appropriate way to resolve such conflict is to appeal to what he calls "certificatory justice."[6] As he puts it: "For in many cases reciprocity and certificatory justice are not in accord; e.g. (1) if an official has inflicted a wound, he should don't be wounded in return."[7] Clearly, maintaining the power structure and preserving the positive law that safeguard this structure are more important than addressing issues of inequality and social stratification.

> Therefore the justice or injustice of citizens is not manifested in these relations; for it was as we saw according to law, and between people naturally subject to law, and these as we saw' are people who have an equal share in ruling and being ruled.[8]

The order of rank to the Greeks and later to the Romans was not only intra-societal but also inter-societal and global. On the inter-societal front, ancient Greeks and Romans used the term barbarian (barbarous) in reference to either people who stand in opposition to them or those fighting back against their imperial expansion to bring other people under their dominance, an imperial domain the Romans called Pax-Roman or the Roman peace. By the time Augustus assumed power, it became a common term to refer to all people outside Rome's dominion, including the Germanic tribes, the Persians, the Gauls, and the Carthaginians.[9] Ancient Greece and Rome maintained a system of social stratification and used the term barbarians to describe the people who did not share Greek and Roman heritage. The Roman reserved the most horrific punishment to those who challenged the policies of the ruling class or their established laws. The individual who challenged the state or state laws was punished by crucifixion. Similarly, the city of Palmira was visited with unsparing ruins when it challenged the absolute dominance of Rome.

In short, the Greco-Roman ethics of virtue was grounded in a power-centered realism that promoted social hierarchy as the approximation of the "truth" even though it was based on a "noble" lie. Interestingly, social hierarchy and the stratification of the Greek and Roman societies were never questioned by the Greek philosophers or by the Enlightenment scholars who claimed to draw modern philosophy and ethics from the Greek sources.

THE UNIVERSALIZATION OF THE ETHICS OF DIGNITY

Modern philosophy traces the ethics of equal dignity to leading Enlightenment philosophers, most notably to Locke and Kant. The ethics of dignity we encounter in the work of the Enlightenment philosophers did not emerge within European modernity but is as old as the monotheistic tradition could go. Locke's and Kant's ethical philosophy is squarely anchored in the monotheistic demands that individual action should be aligned with universal truth. The Kantian ethics is epitomized in his categorical imperative: "Act only according to that maxim whereby you can . . . will, that it should become a universal law of nature."[10] This statement underlines the hallmark of the Kantian ethics. Ethical behavior must be consistent and should be applied equally to all people because people share the same sense of humanity and have therefore equal dignity. Kant reveals the monotheistic ground of his ethics when he writes:

> [W]ithout a God and a world that is now not visible to us but is hoped for, the majestic ideas of morality are, to be sure, objects of approbation and admiration but not incentives for resolve and realization.[11]

It's important to realize that the ethics of dignity was not born in the Kantian philosophy but in the Abrahamic faith before they were further developed in the Hebrew prophetic tradition and early Christianity and were later articulated in rational terms by Islamic rationalism. The ethics of duty has been historically epitomized in the principle of "speaking truth to power" which we all are familiar with today. The principle was a novelty to the ancient mind when it appeared as the Abrahamic act of rebellion against idol worshiping. At the level of public ethics, the ethics of duty is rooted in the principle that constituted the Abrahamic act of "speaking truth to power." Speaking truth to power is the principle that liberated humanity from its servitude to powerful individuals and groups. It is the very principle that subordinated power to truth, and which was gradually matured into the principle of equal dignity of all human beings. Placing truth above power was from day one at the core of the Abrahamic tradition. Abraham's rebellion against idol worshiping was simply a rejection of the elevation of man-made idols to the level of truth, and an affirmation that truth must be placed above the demands of powerful kings and rulers who claim kinship with the divine.

The Abrahamic tradition of "speaking truth to power" was given a communal expression under the leadership of Moses, who led the Hebrew tribes out of their servitude in Egypt by demanding freedom and justice for his people. The first transcendental ethical code prescribed to the Israelites was at the heart of the Saini Covenant and took the form of the Ten Commandments. In addition to the first four commandments that require the utmost fidelity to be given to the creator and sustainer of the universe, the covenant demanded an utmost respect for human life and property and required that people act with honesty and without greed and deception. The covenant gave common people a moral agency on par with the most powerful in their community.

This moral agency was exemplified by the Hebrew prophets who upheld the ideals of moral responsibility and equal dignity. They did that by speaking truth to power and by siding with the poor and weak against unrestrained power, as they for centuries pushed against the excesses committed by Hebrew kings and high priests. All Hebrew prophets, from Amos, Elijah, Hosea, and Nathan down to the time of John the Baptist and Jesus Christ, stood against the "cult" of the king who placed power at the top of the hierarchy of values, even above the value of truth. The cult of the King included the high priests who often subordinated their religious knowledge to the power of the king.

The covenant of Saini was not between God and Moses but between God and the people. This was quite a revolutionary idea in antiquity. The idea that all human beings must be judged by the same set of values regardless of their power and wealth was a novelty in ancient society. Everywhere in the ancient world, the king was not only the source of the law but was above the law—not so among the Jewish tribes. For them, everyone was under the law, including kings, prophets, and priests.

ISLAM AND THE RECONCILIATION OF POWER AND TRUTH

With the death of Prophet Muhammad, who Muslims believe to be the final prophet, the reformist role previously undertaken by the biblical prophets was assumed by Islamic scholars and jurists. Islamic rationalism managed, in the first three centuries of Islam, to develop an ethical and legal system that subordinated the exercise of power to the demands of a transcendental law that stood above the state. The German philosopher Hegel recognized this important contribution of Islam to the development of public ethics and the reconciliation of temporal power to ethical demands. Here is what he had to say about the emergence of public ethics.

> The Reconciliation presented in Christianity, but only in the germ, without national or political development. We must therefore regard it as commencing rather with the enormous contrast between the spiritual, religious principle, and the barbarian Real World. For Spirit as the consciousness of an inner World is, at the commencement, itself still in an abstract form. All that is secular is consequently given over to rudeness and capricious violence. The Mohammedan principle—the enlightenment of the Oriental World—is the first to contravene this barbarism and caprice. We find it developing itself later and more rapidly than Christianity; for the latter needed eight centuries to grow up into a political form.[12]

In this condensed passage of the *Philosophy of History*, Hegel underscores the nature of politics in polytheistic societies where power was the highest public value and where truth took a back seat. Hegel sheds light, in the same passage, on the role played by Islam and Christianity in subjecting power to ethical demands. To unpack the profound observation that Hegel succinctly introduced in this passage, I will focus first on the first part that deals with the power exercised by Rome before turning to the role of Islamic public ethics in reconciling the secular with the ethical. In this insightful passage, Hegel asserts the brutal nature of the secular power in ancient societies, such as that of Greece and Rome and recognizes the fact that these societies showed no interest in reconciling secular power with ethical demands. He recognizes that early Christianity possessed the spiritual and ethical values for developing a social and political order anchored in the notions of justice and equality. But these notions, as we all know today, remained at the level of spirituality as the Roman Empire succeeded in molding Christianity to respond to its power structure, therefore postponing the institutionalization of its values for at least eight centuries until the religious reformation reclaimed, in Europe, the values of justice, equality, and freedom.

Meanwhile, reconciling power and ethics remained elusive for premodern European. The inability of Roman Christianity to restrain the way Rome exercised power is evident in St. Augustine's most important work: *The City of God*. Augustine believed that justice is necessary for ensuring that kingdoms are organized in accordance with the behavior expected of ethical humanity. "Justice being taken away, then, what are kingdoms but great robberies? For what are robberies themselves, but little kingdoms?"[13] Augustine recognizes that justice is necessary for kingdoms, but he had little faith in the human ability to bring power under the rule of justice. Yet, at the same time, he seems to be convinced that the subordination of the exercise of power to ethical demands is untenable. Augustine believed that the kingdoms created by the natural man are shrouded in sin. He argues that the rise of powerful kingdoms and the use of coercive power are a result of human sinfulness. Institutions of power are a divinely sanctioned remedy and punishment for human sin. He therefore concludes that political power is intended as an instrument of punishing sinful humanity. For him, the City of God, where Christian values can be practiced, and the City of Man, where brutal power is exercised under the Roman hierarchy, were irreconcilable.[14]

Real politics and ethical values were completely divorced from the imagery of pre-Christian Rome and remained separate under Roman Christianity as the Roman emperors embraced Christianity, beginning with Constantine, who succeeded in taming the Christian demands for social equality by early Christians. As Hegel rightly observed, it was under Islam that the secular order of the state was brought under ethical judgment. He credits Islam for developing a set of ideas and institutions that placed ethical limits on the exercise of power and political authority. Rome exercised power without any ethical restraints as the Romans used every tool of power to maintain supremacy over the populations that scummed to their brutal force. The Roman way of ruling other nations was vividly described by Rome's greatest poet Virgil in *Book VI* of the Aeneid: "O Roman! Remember by your strength to rule Earth's peoples. . . . To spare the conquered and crush the proud."[15] The only place in Europe that escaped the Roman rule was in the Northwest region, or the Occident region, where the movement to reform Roman Christianity originated, leading to the Protestant Reformation in the fifteenth and sixteenth centuries and to the Catholic Reformation in the nineteenth and twentieth centuries.

The nineteenth and twentieth centuries brought a profound transformation to the modern West, particularly in public institutions and practices. By the middle of the twentieth century, the Eurocentric view of the world began to give way to movements that championed equal dignity and universal human rights. What has been lost though in this important transformation is the role played by the transcendental ethics that harbored the values at the root of modern social and political reforms. These are studied today under the rubric of deontological ethics without any reference to their spiritual and ethical source. Lost too has been the place of Islam and Islamic rationalism in paving the way to European scholarship that benefited from the expansive translations of the works of Islamic philosophers and Kalam scholars to Latin and other European languages between the eleventh and seventeenth centuries. We return, in the next section, to explore how the schools of Islamic rationalism succeeded in reconciling the secular with the ethical and in bringing power under the rule of law.

THE ROOTS OF PUBLIC ETHICS IN ISLAMIC SOURCES

In the seventh century, Islam took the principle of speaking truth to power that evolved under Judaism and early Christianity to a new height. As Hegel pointed out, Muslim scholars were the first to transform the moral demands for equality, justice, and accountability from being elements of individual subjectivity and made them a central part of public discourse and social and political practices. In doing so, Muslim scholars and jurists were inspired by the Qur'an's pronouncements on the necessity of organizing public life in accordance with ethical principles. The Qur'an identifies various ethical principles with direct implications on public ethics. For example, verse 13 of chapter 49 stresses the equal dignity of all human beings, regardless of their ethnicity and heritage, and sheds light on the wisdom behind the division of humanity to nations and tribes.[16] They stress that humanity is divided into people and tribes for facilitating mutual recognition and social solidarity. Elsewhere in the Qur'an, we are told that the grouping of people helps create checks and balances among various groups to prevent the perpetuation of corruption in any particular group.

Similarly, verse 135 of chapter 4 advocates justice without fear or favor,[17] while verse 140 of chapter 3 calls on the believers to speak truth to power, a principle that the Qur'an traces back to Prophet Abraham.[18] The Islamic scriptures clearly call on people of faith to commit themselves to the principles of justice and equality and demand that people exercise moral agency in the public by promoting the common good and ensuring that the right is upheld, and corrupt practices are prevented from dominating public interaction.

The Qur'anic pronouncements were taken to heart by early Muslims, as they strove to develop public institutions. The prophet translated the Qur'anic injunctions that stress the equal dignity of all people by establishing a pluralistic political community in Medina through the instrument of the Covenant of Medina, considered by contemporary scholars of Islam as the first written constitution. The covenant, as we will see below, stressed the principles of equal dignity of all socio-religious components of the City of Medina, including the Jewish tribes. Similarly, the first political successor elected to the office of Caliphate after Prophet Muhammad, was aware of the limitations placed on power and the ethical demands of his office, as the following quote from his inaugural address reveals.[19] Speaking after his election, Abu Bakr, the first caliph, had this to say:

> I have been given authority over you even though I am not the best of you. Help me, if I am in the right; set me right if I am in the wrong. Truthfulness is in honesty and falsehood is in treachery. The weak among you is strong in my eyes until I restore him his right, God willing, and the strong among you is a weak

with me till, if the Lord wills, I have taken what is due from him. Obey me as long as I obey God and His Prophet, and when I disobey Him and His Prophet, you own me no obedience.[20]

The above statement shows awareness by the first caliph of the obligations of his office: to serve the public, to be held accountable by the lager community that elected him and to ensure that justice is served for all members of the community, particularly those who lack the power to confront the powerful. The statement asserts the equal dignity of all people and the fact that being elected to public office does not bestow the holder of political office with superiority. It directly links the legitimacy of holding public office to the ability of the power holder to act in the public interests and to listen to the critical views of the public.

The ethical demands placed on the holders of public office began, however, to gradually fade away, as the political accountability of the office of the caliph became less potent with the expansion of the city-state of Medina into Persia, Syria, and Egypt and the rise of the dynastic form of government under Islam. Dynastic rule did not however go unchallenged as the scholarly and juristic communities found a way to limit the power of the caliph and the sultan, a question we explore in the next section.

ISLAMIC RATIONALISM AND THE ETHICS OF DIGNITY

The rise of Islamic rationalism in the second century of Islam, or the eighth century of the Common Era, was quite subsequential as it led to the systematization of the law and the development of Islamic philosophy and science. Islamic rationalists asserted that the values emphasized in the Qur'an were both innate and universal to humanity. Their innateness and universality were later expressed in rational terms in the work of the Kalam scholars. As I argue below, Kalam scholars developed a new approach to analyzing normative sources and social practices, as I discuss under the rubric of rational idealism. Rational idealism advanced first by the Mutazilites, and later by the Asharites, opposed the power-centered realism-espoused traditional jurists. Mutazilites in particular advanced the following five Principles of Faith:

1. Unity of Being (Tawhid),
2. Justice,
3. Moral Agency,
4. Social Accountability,
5. Speaking Truth to Power.

Over the first three centuries of Islam, the Mutazilites developed five doctrines that revolved around the above five principles they all shared, regardless of any other disagreements they may have had. These principles focused on ensuring that all members of society were socially responsible for the quality of life in their communities. Tawhid meant that the believers should live by the same values that God ordained as worthy of humanity. These values, they argued, are not only innate to human beings but also inherent in the cosmos. The values that define Islamic ethics are derived by Islamic rationalists from what the Qur'an refers to as "the beautiful Names of God."

Table 1.2 illustrates a list of God's most repeated names that are mentioned in the Qur'an, which the Qur'an calls the "beautiful names of God." They are obviously adjectives or qualities related to God which are familiar to humans, as they are also used to describe the qualities of human beings. For Muslim scholars, these qualities, or values, provide the spiritual connection between human beings and the divine, even though they are present at different levels of magnitude. They are present at the level of absolute order in transcendence, but their presence is limited in the human forms. A-Ghazali argued in his work *The Sublime Purpose* (*al maqsid al athna*) that one important implication of exploring the beautiful names of God is to make them the ideals for human behavior and the guide for character formation. These values were seen as moral obligations to be embraced and defended by the believers and were identified by Islamic rationalism as the overall purposes of revelation. Muslim scholars couched these values or purposes in rational discourse. The Mutazilites, the pioneers of Islamic rationalism, asserted the moral agency of every believer and rejected the arguments made by the Umayyad rulers, the first Muslim dynasty, that their ability to defeat other power contenders was a clear sign that their dynastic rule received the divine approval. Kalam scholars rejected these arguments and worked collectively to anchor political legitimacy in subordinating the power of caliph to the rule of Islamic law.

Table 1.2 The Beautiful Names of God

God's Beautiful Names	Ethical Values
Compassionate	Compassion
Merciful	Mercy
Peaceful	Peace
Just	Justice
Forgiver	Forgiveness
Provider	Providence
Knowledgeable	Knowledge
Wise	Wisdom
Loving	Love

Abu al-Hassan al-Mawardi (972–1058 CE) for instance described the relationship between the head of the state (the Imam) and the people as one of contractual agreement, through which the caliph would have to maintain ten duties in exchange for the people's recognition of the legitimacy of his rule. Under the title "The Contract of Imamate," al-Mawardi says the following:

> Imamate is established for the succession of the prophet in guarding the religion and the ordering of the affairs of the world, and entering the contract by those who can carry it is a solemn duty.[21]

Al-Mawardi wrote, as early as the tenth century, the textbook on power limitations and political accountability, as he identified ten duties of the Imam, including the following four principal duties:

1. The dispensation of justice,
2. Maintenance of law and order,
3. Defense against foreign invasions,
4. Collection of taxes (Kharaj) in accordance with the Shari'ah laws.

The fourth point in the above list illustrates the sort of limitations placed on the power of the holder of public office in historical Muslim society, including the power to decide the amount of tax that could be levied on the general population. It is worth mentioning here that the tax code was written by Islamic jurists—rather than the caliph or sultan—who were independent in both their legislative authority and financial resources, from the ruling dynasty. The caliph and sultan could only claim the executive power of the state but were unable to legislate. For example, the amount of tax that the state was able to levy was limited by the tax code that was promulgated by Muslim jurists as part of the Jurist law, and tax was differentiated to various categories pursuant to how income was generated (table 1.3)—2.5% on income tax, 10% on productive property, and 20% on minerals.[22]

Similarly, the manner by which treasury money could be spent was codified by the jurists and could not be changed by the holders of political office. Indeed, Muslim jurists, most of whom were trained in the schools of rational idealism, were successful in separating their legislative authority from the

Table 1.3 Limitation Imposed on Taxation by Islamic Jurists

Tax Type	Tax (%)
Income Tax	2.5
Productive Property Tax	10
Mineral Tax	20

executive powers of the caliph and the sultan. They did that by deriving the principles of the law that governed public institutions from the revealed text, making it hard for those who assumed public office to challenge their authority.

SOCIAL PLURALISM AND MORAL AUTONOMY

Another remarkable contribution of Islamic ethics is the unprecedented stress it places, from the time of Prophet Mohammad, on religious freedom, not only at the level of confessional doctrines but also at the level of institutional practices. The sensitivity of Islamic ethos to the principle of religious freedom stems from the Qur'anic message and the prophetic model. The Qur'an declares that human beings are free moral agents and that no one should compel them to accept a faith other than what they feel deep in their own hearts. The Qur'an warns repeatedly against forcing people into a religion not of their own choosing.[23]

Prophet Muhammad translated the Qur'anic commandments into a political constitution as he proclaimed the covenant of Medina that was declared in the multireligious and multiethic community that invited him to assume political leadership that extended beyond the followers of Islam. Upon arriving in the city, he authored a document that established political partnership among the tribes of Medina and guaranteed justice and the freedom of religion and movement to all members of the community. Following the Qur'anic call on the faithful to respect and uphold freedom of religion, the prophet amplified it by institutionalizing it in the restructured practices of City of Medina, as he produced a covenant for organizing the life of an ethnically and religiously diverse population. The covenant makes it crystal clear that Jewish tribes that claimed Medina as their home are fully recognized members of the political society of Medina and that they are fully empowered to profess and practice their faith on par with Muslims.

> The Jews of Banu Auf are one community with the believers. The Jews have their religion and the Muslims theirs.[24]

As recognized members of the newly established polity, they are entitled to equal dignity and protection extended to all members of the polity. The covenant declares them as equal members entitled to equal justice and equal protection.

> To the Jew who follows us belongs help and equality. He shall not be wronged, nor shall his enemies be aided.[25]

As full citizens of the City of Medina, they are expected to share in public expenses, the defense of the city against breach of security, and engage in consultation about all issues relevant to the city's affairs.

> The Jews must bear their expenses and the Muslims theirs. Each must help the other against anyone who attacks the people of this Compact. They must seek mutual advice and consultation.[26]

With the expansion of Islam into the Roman and Persian territories in the North of Arabia, the same privileges extended to the Jews of Medina were granted to the Christian and Zoroastrian communities through a similar contract fashioned after the Medina covenant that was known as the dhimmi covenant. By doing so, Islam created the first pluralist society in modern history whereby people of different religions and ethnicity enjoined equal dignity and equal protection under the law. This new reality that was for long ignored and overlooked by Western Orientalism was acknowledged by Marshall Hodgson, the author of the *Venture of Islam*. Marshall Hodgson describes the multireligious society created in the seventh century on the base of the dhimmi covenant.

> At the time of the Arab conquest, the several religious groups which were to form protected dhimmi communities, gained equality of status among themselves and protection against each other's interference; for instance, against proselytizing from one dhimmi community to another, which the Muslims discouraged.[27]

The equal protection under the law extended to all people regardless of their religious affiliation was not a rhetorical assertion but was backed by the Muslim judiciary under the Abbasid Caliphate. When a Muslim village in northern Iraq demanded that their Christian neighbors cease brewing wine and raising pigs, practices that violate Islamic law, the Christian filed a judicial complaint with office of the caliph in Baghdad and the case was placed before a senior judge with the name of Muhammad bin al-Hasan al-Shaybani, an eighth-century judge, who ruled for the Christian villagers and grounded his ruling in the equal protection extended to Christian by the dhimmi covenant. His ruling on the case states, in unequivocal terms, the moral autonomy extended to non-Muslims who chose to enter into a peace covenant with Muslims.

> Muslims should not appropriate any of the non-Muslims' houses and lands, nor should they intrude into any of their dwellings, because they have become party to a covenant of peace, and because on the day of the Peace of Khaybar, the prophet's spokesman announced that none of the property of the covenanters is permitted to the Muslim. Also, because the non-Muslims have accepted the peace covenant so as they may enjoy their properties and rights on par with Muslims.[28]

For sure, the system of law created by the historical Muslim society was far from perfect, and one could point to instances over the long history of Islam where people were abused by powerful individuals or groups at one time or another. This should not however detract from the fact that the Islamic ethics played a leading role in setting the bar high and demonstrating that a multireligious and multiethnic society can exist under ethical and legal systems that cherish the principle of equal dignity and equal protection of the law.

THE RETURN TO POWER-CENTERED REALISM

While the Greek philosophy was secondary to Islamic rationalism in influencing Western rational thought during the Middle Ages and early modernization, it began to exert greater influence by the close of the nineteenth century with the rise of rational realism. By the middle of the twentieth century, Greek realism began to dominate modern thinking. The rational idealism embraced by Kantian philosophy that was rooted in transcendental ethics peculiar to the monotheistic traditions was rejected by two powerful philosophers: Marx, the father of historical materialism, and Nietzsche, the guru of postmodernism. Like the Greek rationalists, both put emphases on power and placed it at the top of the hierarchy of values. As we saw earlier, Greek philosopher, even the most idealists of them like Plato, subordinated truth to power and therefore gave more attention to the need of the powerful ones: the aristocrats, the oligarchs, or the freeman who never believed in equal dignity of human beings. Idealism and realism competed during the Renaissance and the early years of the Enlightenment, but the balance began to tip toward power with the rise of positivism and materialism in Western Europe. Marx dismissed idealism completely as false consciousness and as an instrument of the bourgeois society, and the religious establishment aligned with it:

> The ruling ideas are nothing more than the ideal expression of the dominant material relationships, the dominant material relationships grasped as ideas; hence of the relationships which make the one class the ruling one, therefore, the ideas of their dominance.[29]

Power rather than ethical principles, Marx concluded, is the deciding value in arranging society. Marx expanded this cynical observation to the entire human history, declaring that the perversion has been the dynamo of historical change and not just a symptom of power relations under feudalism and capitalism. Nietzsche agreed with Marx that the ruling ideas are the ideas of the ruling class and that morality and religion were nothing but social devices to keep the weak and meek content with appalling social conditions. He took this cynicism even further as he reduced all human relations to one explanatory factor, the will to power: "This world is the will to power—and nothing besides!"[30] For him, power was not only an important value to be desired for transforming society but also the only real value the world has ever known. However, while Marx envisaged an end of social stratification in what he argued would be the end of history in the communist society, Nietzsche went in the opposite direction calling for the establishment of a stratified society ruled by the powerful ones. "I feel impelled," he proclaimed, "to reestablish order of rank in an age of suffrage universal, this is, in an age when everyone may judge everyone and everything."[31]

Modern society continues to drift away from the transcendental ethos that produced the very values that transformed it from a feudal society to an advanced civilization in the first place. The gradual rise of exclusivism in Western society that a few centuries ago embraced the egalitarian spirit of rational idealism has reached a worrying level in the last decade. The rise of white nationalism in Europe and the United States is a warning of the growing rejection of egalitarian conditions and the embracement of ethnic and religious centralism. The wrangle of Trump Republicans against Muslims and Latinos in the United States and attacks against minorities by the ultra-nationalist party of Marine Le Pen in France are ominous signs of the return of exclusivist mindsets to the society that pride itself on protecting the equal dignity of citizens. This new trend in Western democracy has encouraged far right movements in other democratic societies, most notably India. On April 4, 2022, Isobel Yeung interviewed Subramanian Swamy, a leader of India's ruling party BJP and a close ally of Modi, India's prime minister. Yeung questioned the ruling party's discriminatory policies against Muslims and the failure of the Indian government to extend equal protection of the law to Muslim citizens. Subramanian denied that his government had done anything wrong to Muslims. When Yeung read Article 14 of India's Constitution that states, "The State shall not deny any person's equality before the law or the equal protection of the laws within the territory of India," he told her that she was misinterpreting that article and that "Article 14 guarantee the equality of the equals," insisting that the 200 million Muslims are not the equals of the Hindu population. He went on to say, "[T]here is no such thing as equal rights; they [the Muslims] are not in an equal category."[32]

CONCLUSION

Transcendental ethics grew within the monotheistic traditions for millennia as a condition of faith before it was given its rational grounding along with its faith foundation in the work of Islamic rationalists. Muslim rational idealism argued that transcendental ethics is a religious requirement for not only revealed traditions but also intrinsic human values. Islam in particular took the requirement of acting ethically from the limitation of sectarian and national society to the expansion of universal humanity. Such commitment is essential for nurturing a healthy global society and for ensuring that people are judged on their character and merits rather than the ethnic affiliations or religious claims. Nurturing just a global order requires an unwavering commitment to the principle of equal humanity that affirms equal human dignity; and they must therefore be treated as deserving partners of global justice.

While modern society made important headways toward creating more egalitarian conditions among citizens, this has not been the case with regard to greater humanity. Exclusivist principles are used to curtail the application of international law equally and prolong the struggle toward equal humanity. The global order is still far away from applying the principles of human rights equally across the board, and world power continue to use the human rights traditions that evolved within monotheistic ethos as an instrument for global control. Indeed, the last two decades have seen significant deterioration of human rights and global justice, as global stratification has been on the rise. Inequality is no more an element of the global conditions but is increasingly threatening equality and justice within national borders, with the advent of exclusivist movements around the world. The worldwide decline in public ethics is increasingly contributing to the breakdown in public trust at both the national and global levels. I attributed, in this chapter, this breakdown to the modern society's gradual drift away from the transcendental traditions that produced the very values that allowed it to rise in the first place. The current thrust could lead to a complete breakdown in the global order unless the stress on the values at the core of the rise of modern civilization, and indeed all civilizations, is restored, and Islamic rationalism can play an important role in such restoration.

NOTES

1. Plato, *The Republic* (Moscow, Idaho: Roman Road Media, 2013), pp. 110–125.
2. Ibid., p. 125.
3. Aristotle, Nicomachean Ethics, Book V, p. 55. Trans. by W. D. Ross (Global Grey 2021). Available at: https://www.globalgreyebooks.com/nicomachean-ethics-ebook.html
4. D. Kamen, *Status in Classical Athens* (Princeton University Press, 2013), p. 9. See also J.A. Rothchild, *Introduction to Athenian Democracy of the Fifth and Fourth*

Centuries BCE; and M.D. Dixon, *Late Classical and Early Hellenistic Corinth: 338–196 BC* (Routledge, 2014), p. 44.

5. Ibid.

6. Ibid., p. 57.

7. Ibid.

8. Ibid., p. 60.

9. Charlton T. Lewis and Charles Short, *A Latin Dictionary* (Oxford: Clarendon Press, 1879). See also 'Freund's Latin dictionary, Online Edition: https://www.perseus.tufts.edu/hopper/text?doc=Perseus%3Atext%3A1999.04.0059%3Aentry%3Dbarbarus

10. Immanuel Kant, *The Groundwork of the Metaphysic of Morals. Trans. Mary Gregor* (Cambridge University Press, 1997), p. 44.

11. Ibid., p. 137.

12. G.W.F. Hegel, *The Philosophy of History*, trans. John Sibree (Kitchener: Batoche Books, 2001), p. 127.

13. Augustine of Hippo, *The City of God*. Translation by William Babcock, notes by Boniface Ramsey. Hyde Park, NY: New City Press, 2012. (Books XV–XVIII).

14. Ibid, Books XI and XIX.

15. Virgil, *The Aeneid*, Trans. by Robert Fitzgerald. Random House, 1983. Book VI.

16. O mankind! We have created you from male and female and made you peoples and tribes that you may know one another (Qur'an 49:13).

17. O believers! Stand firm for justice as witnesses for God even if it is against yourselves, your parents, or close relatives. Be they rich or poor, God is best to ensure their interests (Qur'an 4:135).

18. And from among you must a group must arise who invite people to all that is good and enjoin the doing of all that is right and forbid the doing of all that is wrong. It is they who will attain true success (Qur'an 3:140).

19. See for example, W. Montgomery Watt, *Mohammad: Prophet and Statesman* (Oxford University Press, 1961).

20. Ibn Hisham, *Sirat* (Biography of the Prophet), Abridged by Abdus-Salam M. Hart. Al-Falah Foundation, 2000, p. 292.

21. Abul-Hasan Al-Mawardi, *Al-Ahkam as-Sultaniyyah* [The Laws of Islamic Governance], trans. Asadullah Yate (London: Ta-Ha Publishers, 1996), p. 10.

22. For in depth discussion of taxation in classical Islam, see Abu Yusuf, *Kitab al-kharaj*. Trans. A. Ben Shemesh (Leiden: E.J. Brill, 1969).

23. "No compulsion in religion, truth stand out clear from deviance." (Qur'an 2:256) also: "If your Lord had so willed, all who are on the earth would surely have believed, all of them. Would you, then, force people until they become believers?" (Qur'an 10:99)

24. Ibn Hisham, *Biography of the Prophet* (Sirat Ibn Hisham), trans. Abdus-Salam M. Hart (Cairo, Egypt: Al-Falah Foundation, 2000), p. 108. For an extended analysis of the constitution of Medina, see M. Watt Montgomery, *Islamic Political Thought* (Edinburgh, 1998).

25. Ibn Hisham, *Biography of the Prophet*, p. 110.

26. Ibid.
27. Marshall G. S. Hodgson, *The Venture of Islam*, vol. 1 (Chicago, IL: University of Chicago Press, 1974), p. 306.
28. Muhammad bin Ahmad al-Sarakhsi, *Sharh Kitab al-Siyar al-Kabir*, vol. 4 (Pakistan: Nasrullah Mansur, 1405 A.H.), 1530.
29. Karl Marx and Frederick Engels, "Introduction to a Critique of Political Economy," in *The German Ideology*, Part I, New York: International Publishers, 2001.
30. Nietzsche, *The Will to Power*. Trans. by Walter Kaufmann and R.J. Hollingdale. Vintage Books, 1967. p. 550.
31. Ibid., p. 457.
32. India Clarion, "Muslims Are Not Equal to Hindus, Declares BJP Leader Subramanian Swamy," published on April 3, 2020. https://clarionindia.net/muslims-are-not-equal-to-hindus-declares-bjp-leader-subramanian-swamy/ (Accessed on March 19, 2023).

REFERENCES

Abul-Hasan Al-Mawardi, Al-Ahkam as-Sultaniyyah [The Laws of Islamic Governance], trans. Asadullah Yate. London: Ta-Ha Publishers, 1996.
Aristotle, *Nicomachean Ethics*, Book V, p. 55. Trans. W. D. Ross. Global Grey, 2021.
Briffault, Robert. *The Making of Humanity*. London: George Allen & Unwin House, 1919.
Bruxvoort, Benjamin J. Lipscomb and James Krueger (eds.), *Kant's Moral Metaphysics: God, Freedom, and Immortality*. Berlin: De Gruyter, 2010.
Bulliet, Richard. *The Case for Islamo-Christian Civilization*. Columbia University Press, 2006.
Dixon, M.D. *Late Classical and Early Hellenistic Corinth: 338–196 BC*. Routledge, 2014.
Feiler, Bruce. Abraham A Journey to the Heart of Three Faiths Perfect Bound, n.d.
Feldman, Noah. *The Fall and Rise of the Islamic State*. Princeton University Press, 2008.
Griffel, Frank. "al-Ghazali," The Stanford Encyclopedia of Philosophy, ed. Edward N. Zalta (Summer 2020 Edition), https://plato.stanford.edu/archives/sum2020/entries/al-ghazali/ (accessed July 19, 2020).
Griffel, Frank. *Al-Ghazali's Philosophical Theology*. New York: Oxford University.
Hegel, G.W.F. *Philosophy of Right*. Trans. S.W. Dyde. Batoche Books Kitchener, 2001.
Hegel, G.W.F. *The Philosophy of History*. Trans. John Sibree. Kitchener: Batoche Books, 2001.
Hodgson, Marshall G. S. *The Venture of Islam*, vol. 1. Chicago, IL: University of Chicago Press, 1974, 306.
Hodgson, Marshall G. S. *Venture of Islam: The Classical Age of Islam*, Vol. 1. Chicago, IL: University of Chicago Press, 1974.

Ibn Hisham, Biography of the Prophet (Sirat Ibn Hisham). Trans. Abdus-Salam M. Hart. Cairo, Egypt: Al-Falah Foundation, 2000, p. 108. For an extended analysis of the constitution of Medina, see M. Watt Montgomery, *Islamic Political Thought*. Edinburgh, 1998. Abu Yusuf's Kitab al-kharaj. Trans. A. Ben Shemesh. Leiden: E.J. Brill; London: Luzac, 1969.

Jaspers, Karl. *The Origin and Goal of History*. New Haven, CT: Yale University Press, 1953.

Kamen, D. *Status in Classical Athens*. Princeton University Press, 2013.

Kant, Immanuel. *Groundwork of the Metaphysics of Morals*. Trans. Mary Gregor. Cambridge University Press, 1997.

Kant, Immanuel. *Groundwork of the Metaphysics of Morals*. Trans. Mary Gregor. New York: Cambridge University Press, 1997, 44.

Kant, Immanuel. *The Critique of Pure Reason*. Trans. Werner S. Pluhar. Indianapolis, IN: Hackett Publishing Company, 1996.

Locke, John. *Two Treatises of Government and a Letter Concerning Toleration*. New Haven, CT: Yale University Press, 2003.

Martin, Richard C. and Mark R. Woodward with Dwi S. Atmaja. *Defenders of Reason in Islam: Mutazilism from Medieval School to Modern Symbol*. Oxford: Oneworld Publications, 1997.

Marx, Karl and Frederick Engels. "Introduction to a Critique of Political Economy." In *The German Ideology, Part I*. New York: International Publishers, 2001.

Mawardi, Abul-Hasan al. *Al-Ahkam as-Sultaniyyah the Laws of Islamic Government*. Trans. Asadullah Yate. London, UK: Ta-Ha Publishers, 1996.

Mohammad Ma'ruf Al-Dawalibi. *The Individual and Society in Islam*. UNESC Pub. 1998.

Muhammad bin Ahmad al-Sarakhsi. *Sharh Kitab al-Siyar al-Kabir*, vol. 4. Pakistan: Nasrullah Mansur, 1405 A.H., 1530.

Nietzsche, Friedrich Wilhelm. *The Gay Science*. New York: Random House, 1974.

Nietzsche, Friedrich Wilhelm. *The Will to power*. Trans. Walter Kaufmann. New York: Vintage Books, 1967.

Plato, *The Republic*. Moscow, Idaho: Roman Road Media, 2013.

Rothchild, John A., Introduction to Athenian Democracy of the Fifth and Fourth Centuries BCE (October 9, 2007). Wayne State University Law School Research Paper No. 07-32, Available at SSRN: https://ssrn.com/abstract=1020397 [Accessed June 5, 2023].

Roy, Olivier. *Holy Ignorance When Religion and Culture Part Ways*. Trans. Ros Schwartzn. Oxford University Press, 2013.

Salvatore, Armando. *The Wiley Blackwell History of Islam*. Hoboken, NJ: Wiley Blackwell, 2018.

Sarakhsi, Muhammad bin Ahmad al. *Sharh Kitab al-Siyar al-Kabir*, Vol. 4. Pakistan: Nasrullah Mansur, 1405 A.H.

St. Augustine, The City of God.

Supriyanto, Abdi. "Islam and (Political) Liberalism: A Note on An Evolving Debate in Indonesia." *Journal of Indonesian Islam*, Vol. 3, No. 2 (2009): 378–379.

Virgil, Book VI, Aeneid.

W. Montgomery Watt. *Mohammad: Prophet and Statesman*. Oxford University Press, 1961.
Waldron, Jeremy. *God, Locke, and Equality: Christian Foundations in Locke's Political Thought*. New York: Cambridge University Press, 2002.
Weber, Max. *The Sociology of Religion*. Trans. Talcott Parsons. Beacon Press, 1992.
Wenk, Matthias. "What Is Prophetic about Prophecies: Inspiration or Critical Memory?" *Journal of Pentecostal Theology*, Vol. 26 (2017).

Chapter 2

Justice in the Qur'an

Interpretations of a Universal Value in a Globalizing World

Asma Afsaruddin

Justice is a universal principle that may be assumed to be practically revered, at least in theory, by every society and culture. Although a general desideratum, the concept of justice can be difficult to pin down, and there is no universal definition of what constitutes justice in every time or place. This chapter will explore the meanings of justice within Islamic thought and praxes. Justice is, after all, a pervasive theme in the foundational Islamic texts of Islam. The concept of "justice," encompassed by the Arabic terms *'adl/'adala* and *qist*, suffuses the Qur'anic discourse and must be considered one of Islam's bedrock principles meant to guide human thinking, ethics, morality, and actions.

This chapter will begin by discussing a typology of justice based on a quick survey of some of the most relevant Qur'anic verses concerning this topic. It will then proceed to first discuss in greater detail the concept of interpersonal and social justice, with a special focus on justice within the family, and second, justice among nations and religious communities. Both these issues are very much in the foreground in our contemporary world as the intersectionality of justice with gender, socio-political enfranchisement, and citizenship increasingly occupies our attention. This chapter will conclude with a reflection on the importance of incorporating these Islamic perspectives into a global conversation on justice that focuses on the topics of responsible stewardship of the earth and its resources, recognition of the dignity of every human being, and reconciliation and peacemaking, especially through civil dialogue. The Qur'an after all is a text that is very global in its outlook; God is frequently referred to as "the Lord of the worlds." The Arabic expression is *rabb al-'alamin*; *'alamin* can also be translated as "all creation" underscoring the universality of the Qur'anic message. This chapter concludes by observing that although Islamic perspectives have yet to become predominant on the world stage, the Qur'an's own global orientation and ethics of justice create a mandate for Muslims to contribute more vigorously to these conversations already underway in a rapidly globalizing world.

TYPOLOGY OF JUSTICE[1]

Justice (*'adl, qist*) is a multi-layered concept in the Qur'an whose various inflections invite reflection on how to implement this concept in different spheres of life. Careful study of the Qur'an allows us to develop a typology of justice along the broad lines indicated below.

Justice as a General, Universal Principle

Several verses in the Qur'an refer to justice as a general guiding principle in the lives of believers and exhort Muslims to apply this cardinal principle in every facet of their lives in order to thrive as moral and spiritual human beings. This becomes particularly evident in the verses highlighted below:

> Qur'an 5:8: "O you who believe, be upright for God, and (be) bearers of witness with justice!"

> Qur'an 7:29: "My Lord commands justice/fairness (*qist*)."

> Qur'an 16:90: "God commands justice and fair dealing . . ."

> Qur'an 57:25: "We sent our messengers with clear signs, the Scripture and the Balance, so that people might uphold justice."

The hadith literature similarly extols the virtues of justice and promises abundant rewards in the hereafter for those who practice it in every sphere of their lives. One report contained in the famous hadith compilation known as *Sahih Muslim* quotes the Prophet Muhammad as saying:

> Indeed, those who were just in their conduct will be in the presence of God upon pulpits of light, near the right hand of the Merciful, the Exalted—and both His hands are right; these are they who were just in their rulings and with their families and in everything they undertook.[2]

Personal, Interpersonal, and Social Justice

Personal justice: The principle of justice extends to everyone, beginning with oneself. The importance of personal justice—that is, being just to oneself—is often overlooked in discussions of justice in the Islamic milieu, but the Qur'an is adamant on this point. Being unjust to oneself is often expressed in the Qur'an as "self-oppression" or "wronging oneself/one's soul" (*zulm al-nafs*). This "wronging oneself" is perpetrated either by harboring erroneous beliefs regarding the oneness of God and thereby proceeding to associate false deities with Him or by committing misdeeds in direct contravention of divinely revealed injunctions, or both together.

According to the Qur'an, humans may not be coerced into adopting any belief or faith tradition (Qur'an 2:256). But the Qur'an cajoles humans to ponder the wonders of nature and the world around them and contemplate the smooth functioning of the cosmos. Such reflection allows them to arrive at the conclusion that there can be only one beneficent and magnanimous Creator who is able to will such a state of affairs into existence. Such a thoughtful, rational conclusion is buttressed through divine revelation in which God discloses His nature and invites humans to enter into a personal, nurturing relationship with Him. When humans spurn this invitation and display fealty to what the Qur'an describes as erroneous beliefs and false gods, they are described as having harmed themselves and subjected their souls to torment by denying their *fitra*—their primordial natural inclination to worship the one universal God. The Qur'an laments this state of affairs and counsels instead:

> Turn toward religion in sincere allegiance to the primordial nature of God in accordance with which He has created humans. There is no change in God's creation. That is the upright, established religion, but most of the people are not aware.

With regard to the second form of injustice to oneself, Qur'an 3:117 warns:

> The likeness of what they spend in the life of this world is that of a wind laden with frost which lays waste the harvest of a people who have wronged themselves (*zalamu anfusahum*). It is not God who wronged them; rather it is they who wrong themselves.

Social Justice

The Qur'an exhorts Muslims to unrelentingly and uncompromisingly be just and fair in their dealings with others—family members, friends, and fellow human beings in general, even when this may be detrimental to themselves and/or their loved ones. The following verses emphasize this point:

Qur'an 4:58: "Indeed God commands you to render trusts to whom they are due and when you judge between people to render judgement with justice. Excellent is that which God instructs you. Indeed, God hears and sees all."

Qur'an 4:135: "O you who believe, be firm in upholding justice and bear witness to God, even if it be against yourselves, your parents, or your close relatives. Whether one is rich or poor, God is the best caretaker of both. Do not follow mere desire so that you may act justly- if you undermine justice or turn away from it, God is fully aware of what you do."

The Qur'an furthermore urges believers to show solicitude for the poor and the vulnerable in society and to take care of them through charity. Thus, Qur'an 70: 19–25 proclaims:

Indeed, humans were created impatient; when touched by affliction, they are anxious; when touched by good, they fail to be generous. Except for the prayerful who are constant in their prayers, and those in whose wealth is a recognized share for the beggar and the deprived.

Similarly Qur'an 2:83 commands, "Worship only God. Treat with kindness your parents and kinsfolk, the orphans and the needy; speak in a fair manner with the people; be steadfast in prayer; and practice regular charity."

A special subsection under the rubric of interpersonal and social justice is justice within marriage and the family. The Qur'an recognizes marriage and the family as constituting the bedrock of a well-ordered society, in which wives and husbands are expected to live in mutual harmony, love, and respect, and together care for their children, as discussed in greater detail below.

Criminal Justice

Justice in criminal matters receives considerable attention within the Islamic ethos. The wronged person deserves a hearing before the judicial authorities who must adjudicate the case fairly and impartially. The lex talionis of the ancient biblical world is recognized within the Qur'an; at the same time, its limits are clearly recognized, and the concerned parties are allowed considerable moral discretion in resolving their disputes more magnanimously. Two verses that illustrate this point are as follows:

Qur'an 2:178: Believers! Retribution is prescribed for you in cases of killing: if a freeman is guilty then the freeman; if a slave is guilty then the slave; if a female is guilty, then the female.

Qur'an 5:45: In the Torah We prescribed for them a life for a life, an eye for an eye, a nose for a nose, an ear for an ear, a tooth for a tooth, an injury for an injury; however, the one who pardons [the offense], it will serve as atonement for him.

The Qur'an takes a dim view of those who cause corruption and tumult on earth by committing violent aggression against the rights of ordinary people. Such offences include brigandage, highway robbery, and unjustified acts of sedition, which fall under the rubric of *hiraba* ("unjustified violence," "terrorism") as well as unjustified oppression of the common people and usurpation of their rights, generally designated as *baghy*. These constitute grave acts of injustice, roundly castigated in Qur'an 5:33–34, which specifically proscribes *hiraba*. More generally, *baghy* is denounced as the very antithesis of just and moral conduct in Qur'an 16:90, which proclaims: "God commands justice (*'adl*), the practice of beauty and virtue (*ihsan*), generosity toward relatives while He forbids what is morally reprehensible, unjust, and oppressive (*al-baghy*)."

Other crimes proscribed in the Qur'an which incur punishment after meeting a high evidentiary bar include stealing (Qur'an 5:38–39), adultery (Qur'an 17:32; 24:2), and slander (*qadhf*; Qur'an 49: 11–12; cf. 104:1), unless the perpetrators repent and promise to mend their ways.

Economic Justice and Equitable Market Ethics

The public marketplace is expected to be regulated by a strict code of ethics governing commercial transactions of various kinds. In the premodern world, the *muhtasib/a*[3] (market inspector) played an important role in ensuring that ethical business practices were observed and implemented in the marketplace. Usury (*riba*)—the charging of exorbitant interest on loans—is forbidden. These ethical practices were based on injunctions derived from key Qur'anic verses, as selectively indicated below.

Qur'an 3:130: "O believers, do not partake of usury, doubled and redoubled."

Qur'an 4:29: "O those who believe, do not wrongfully devour each other's wealth but trade with mutual consent."

Qur'an 6:152: "Give full measure and weight in fairness (*bi'l-qist*)."

Qur'an 17:35: "Give full measure when you measure, and weigh with accurate scales; that is the best and fairest course of action."

Qur'an 30:39: "Whatever you lend out in usury to gain value through other people's wealth will not increase in the sight of God, but whatever you give in charity in your desire for God's approval, will earn multiple rewards."

Justice between Religious Communities and Nations

Exclusivist religious identities can foster strong partisan sentiment that more often than not leads to discrimination against members of another religious group. A heightened sense of ethnic belonging can similarly foster discriminatory behavior toward a less privileged ethnic group and lead to social injustice and abuse of human rights. The Qur'an declares that an unwavering commitment to justice should override partisan sentiments and help curb the reflexive human desire to retaliate against people who cause one harm. Furthermore, peaceful groups of people cannot be the objects of aggression under any circumstance. The Qur'an creates common ground between people of righteousness and good will on the basis of their shared values and upright deeds and regardless of their religious affiliations. These perspectives are conveyed in a number of verses, a selection of which is listed below.

Qur'an 2:62: "Those who believe, those who are Jews and Christians and Sabeans, whoever believes in God and the Last Day and does good deeds, surely their reward is with their Lord, and no fear shall come upon them, neither shall they grieve."

Qur'an 2:90: "Fight in the way of God against those who fight you but do not commit aggression, for God does not love aggressors."

Qur'an 5:8: "O believers! Stand firmly for God and give truthful testimony. Do not let the hatred of a people lead you to injustice. Be just! That is closer to righteousness. And be mindful of God; surely God is fully aware of what you do."

Qur'an 60:8 "God does not forbid you from dealing kindly and fairly with those who have neither fought against you nor driven you out of your homes. Surely God loves those who are fair."

Each of these types of justice merits detailed treatment, and Muslim scholars indeed had plenty to say on this large, complex topic. Given length constraints, I am focusing on two main types of justice and discussing some of the predominant themes associated with each: (1) interpersonal and social justice, with a special focus on justice within the family and (2) justice among nations and religious communities.

INTERPERSONAL, FAMILY, AND SOCIAL JUSTICE

One may arguably state that Qur'an 5:8 referenced above epitomizes the very nature of interpersonal and social justice that Muslims are expected to realize in their private and public lives. A quick survey of the commentaries on this verse by major exegetes is revealing of the extent to which justice is emphasized by Muslim scholars for the creation of societies that treat its members fairly and equitably.

The famous exegete from the Abbasid period Muhammad ibn Jarir al-Tabari (d. 310/923) understands God in Qur'an 5:8 to be instructing Muslims as follows:

> let your characters and dispositions be of the kind that makes you stand up for justice (*al-'adl*) with regard to your allies and your enemies; do not be unjust in your regulations (*la tajuru fi ahkamikum*) and your deeds and do not exceed the limits (of proportionality) in your response to their aggression against you; do not violate the boundaries I have set for you in regard to my commands and in regard to your allies on account of their alliance with you; observe my limit with regard to all of them and implement it according to my command.[4]

Al-Tabari emphasizes that the Arabic imperative *wa-la yajrimanna shan'anu qawm* ("do not let the hatred of a people cause you to act wrongly") means that Muslims should not let the aggression of a people cause them to deviate from justice; if they were to do that, then they would succumb to wrongdoing motivated by the enmity of adversaries.[5] Despite their malevolent intent and actions, Muslims are counseled not to give in to anger and treat the offenders with the justice that is due to everyone.

The rest of the verse means, according to al-Tabari, that when Muslims deal with their enemies justly and resist giving into their impulse to retaliate reflexively, they are counted among the *ahl al-taqwa* ("people of piety"). The *ahl al-taqwa*, he says, are those who are vigilant about carrying out God's commands and desist from disobeying Him. This is ultimately the definition of "a just person."[6]

The late sixth-/twelfth-century exegete Fakhr al-Din al-Razi (606/1210) says that Qur'an 5:8 concerns itself with the obligations and responsibilities (*takalif*) of the worshipper. The effects of these responsibilities are primarily twofold: they glorify God's commands and evince compassion for all of God's creation. As for bearing witness (*shahada*), al-Razi quotes 'Ata' ibn Abi Rabah's[7] counsel, "do not show preference in your testimony only for those people who are close to you and who love you; do not withhold your witness from those who are your enemies and are hostile to you."[8]

As for *wa-la yajrimanna shan'anu qawm*, al-Razi offers an explanation very similar to al-Tabari that one should not allow the hostility of the enemy to cause Muslims to deviate from just behavior. Al-Razi says that this part of the verse can be understood to have both a general and particular meaning. Its general meaning is that the hostility of the enemy should not cause Muslims to deviate from just behavior and transgress against the boundaries set up by God. Rather, Muslims should behave in an upright manner even when others behave badly toward them and treat them fairly even when the aggression of their adversary knows no bounds. In other words, the general message to be derived from this verse is that God has commanded humans to behave with everyone justly and fairly, without resorting to partiality or tyrannical behavior or coercion.

The second particular meaning is that the verse was revealed specifically concerning the pagan Quraysh when they prevented Muslims from entering the Sacred Precinct in Mecca in 6/628. Adherence to just and equitable behavior in the face of wrongdoing and oppression is a marker of the truly pious, as the verse goes on to inform. This is further corroborated in Qur'an 2:237 which exhorts the faithful to forgive others who do them wrong "for that is closer to piety."[9]

In the modern period, the famous Egyptian reformer and exegete Muhammad Abduh (d. 1905) in his well-known Qur'an commentary (as recorded by his devoted disciple Rashid Rida) lays great stress, as did his predecessors, on the obligatory nature of behaving justly even with one's own worst enemies. He comments that this injunction to be just is a comprehensive one and applicable to all the duties and tasks that the believer has to carry out in regard to this world and the next. These duties should be carried out without causing any harm to others and without any regard for considerations of blood-kinship, wealth, one's reputation, and standing in society. In the absence of this single-minded commitment to justice, corruption will prevail, and social bonds will become frayed. This, Abduh says, is "the way of God" (*sunnat Allah*), as we witness throughout history. The rancor and hostility of others should not provide the pretext for resorting to injustice. The commandment to observe fairness (*qist*) in one's dealings with everyone without exception means that one must transcend one's proclivity to favor one's allies and friends over those who are not, especially in matters of legislation.[10] The description of *'adl* as being close to piety means that it is an essential element of righteousness which cannot ever be abandoned. This principle must be strictly applied even in the case of non-Muslims, for the prophet reminds us in a hadith: "If one of the protected people (*ahl al-dhimma*; a reference to mainly Jews and Christians) is mistreated then the state becomes an aggressor state" (*kanat al-dawla dawlat al-'uduww*).[11]

Abduh notes that a similar injunction to be resolute in being just under all circumstances exists in Qur'an 4:135; this verse further reminds that this injunction applies even if it means bearing witness against oneself or against one's parents and relatives and without regard for wealth or lack thereof. One should therefore transcend the human inclination to favor one's loved ones because the divine commandment to be just under all circumstances means one should overcome these partisan inclinations.[12] By reading the Qur'an cross-referentially in this manner, Abduh emphasizes the categorical nature of the obligation to be just under all circumstances and the essential connection between faith, piety, and justice.

JUSTICE WITHIN THE FAMILY

When it comes to relations between women and men in the Islamic context, it is casually assumed, even by Muslims, that there is a disparity in the status between the two, especially within the family. Although the spiritual equality of women and men is readily conceded by Muslims based on powerful verses within the Qur'an (33:35, 9:71), their social and legal inequality is more often than not taken for granted and assumed to be based on Qur'anic prescriptions themselves. The gendered hierarchy that results from such assumptions—with men constituted as the dominant group and women occupying the bottom rungs of the socioeconomic ladder—is then deemed to be normative, resulting in the adoption of patriarchy as the organizational principle of society.

As is well-known, patriarchy refers to the structure of society that is literally based upon the "rule of the father." Patriarchy, as simply defined by the Canadian sociologist Dorothy E. Smith, refers to "men's political and personal domination over women."[13] This overarching definition of patriarchy should lead Muslims to question whether such a view could be considered consonant with the Qur'anic vision of a well-ordered harmonious society, in which the family is an essential building block. There is no doubt that male legal scholars from the classical period progressively endorsed a highly patriarchal vision of the family that, arguably, stands in sharp contrast to foundational principles within the Qur'an, including justice and the equality and dignity of all human beings.[14] As particularly modern and contemporary Muslim feminists and modernists have argued and continue to argue, patriarchy in itself is oppressive as a system of domination in which men are allowed to subordinate women at various levels by promoting masculine values and institutional structures to maintain male privilege. The key criticisms of patriarchy advanced by these groups are that (1) women are subordinated simply on the basis of their gender; (2) masculine values are considered intrinsically superior or more valuable; and (3) societies' structures are designed so as to maintain male privilege. Feminist and modernist critiques of patriarchal positions are based on the premise that, given this understanding of patriarchy, its endorsement should be morally and ethically problematic for Muslims because they undermine the basic, core principles of justice and equality derived from the Qur'an. Included among the Qur'anic verses they cite in order to challenge patriarchal views are the following:

a. Qur'an 2:187: "They [wives] are your garments and you [husbands] are their garments."
b. Qur'an 4:1: "O humankind! Be careful of your duty to your Lord Who created you from a single soul and from it created its mate and from them the two has spread abroad a multitude of men and women."
c. Qur'an 9:71: "The believers, men and women, are partners/allies of one another; they command the good and forbid wrong and they perform prayer, give the obligatory alms, and obey God and His messenger. They are those upon whom God has mercy; indeed God is Almighty, Wise."
d. Qur'an 30:21: "And among His signs is this, that He has created for you mates from among yourselves, that you may dwell in tranquility with them; and He has put love and mercy between you."
e. Qur'an 33:35: Those who have surrendered to God among males and females; those who believe among males and females; those who are devout among males and females; those who are truthful among males and females; those who are patient among males and females; those who fear God among males and females; those who give in charity among males and females; those who fast among males and females; those who remember God often among males and females—God has prepared for them forgiveness and great reward.
Qur'an 49:13: "O humankind, verily We have created you from a single (pair) of a male and a female, and have made you into nations and tribes, that you may know each other. Indeed the most honored of you in the sight of God is the most righteous."

With the rise of patriarchal, hierarchical societies, many of these just and liberating teachings of the Qur'an began to be compromised, especially as Muslims came into increasing contact with non-Arab, non-Muslim cultures, whose hierarchical values, such as those of Persia and Byzantium, began to seep into Muslim societies.[15] These changes were then justified through a hermeneutical process that tended to read gendered inequality into scripture.

Why such a process could have occurred over time can be understood when we consider the hows and wherefores of the interpretation of sacred texts. Practically without exception in every faith tradition and community, the interpretation of scripture—the Qur'an, the Bible, and the Bhagavad Gita—has primarily been undertaken by men through the centuries. It is their interpretations that have become authoritative and widely disseminated. In the first generation of Islam, there were women exegetes, notably 'A'isha, the prophet's wife, whose disciples, like her nephew 'Urwa b. al-Zubayr, transmitted her interpretations that have been preserved for us in various commentaries. But after the first generation of Muslims, we rarely, if ever, hear of women commentators on the Qur'an, as a result of which only men's perspectives have become codified in exegetical works.

A common complaint on the part of Muslim feminist scholars is that despite the verses listed above with their prima facie endorsement of parity and partnership between women and men, scriptural exegesis undertaken almost exclusively by men in the pre-modern period has all but occluded this gender egalitarianism of the Qur'an and undermined the impact of its gender-inclusive language. This has led to the creation of a moral and religious paradigm which privileges the male over the female and accords to the former "guardianship" over the latter. As examples of such androcentric exegesis, they point to commentaries generated by male exegetes on specific verses that refer to male–female relations and cast them as one of overlordship exercised by men over subjugated women. Such views became highly influential and authoritative over the centuries.[16]

These dramatic transformations become evident in the exegesis of a highly important cluster of verses that refer to the creation of Adam and his wife before their earthly existence (Qur'an 2:30–39; 7:11–27; 15:26–43; 20: 115–124; and 38:71–85). In contradistinction to biblical accounts, Adam's wife (unnamed in the Qur'an but named Hawwa' [Eve] in the exegetical literature) is not singled out for exclusive blame in these Qur'anic verses for having caused the "fall" of humankind; instead, it is noteworthy that the Qur'an either blames Adam exclusively for the fall or blames Adam and his wife equally for giving in to the blandishments of Satan. On balance, Adam in the Qur'an is the one who is morally culpable for failing to heed God's injunctions and succumbing to wrongdoing. He is however forgiven by God, and both he and his wife are given equal opportunity to redeem themselves by establishing a righteous and God-fearing community on earth. In its creation accounts, the Qur'an therefore does not assign any kind of ontological moral failing to the woman companion of Adam and thus by extension to womankind in general.[17]

Recuperation of the meaning of these Qur'anic verses concerning Adam and Eve is highly important for it provides a corrective to a very different story that emerges from the prolific exegetical literature (*tafsir*) concerning them. Commentaries from after the third/ninth century reveal that the Qur'anic assignment of blame primarily to Adam in the creation accounts proved unpalatable to a number of later Muslim male exegetes and they deliberately imported the biblical creation story into their interpretations to reassign the blame to his wife, whom they now call Eve. In addition to Eve's culpability, the creation story found in Genesis also refers to the story of her creation from the rib of Adam which allows one to conclude that the female is secondary to the male as a human being. Through the medium of hadith and the general importation of the Isra'iliyyat (literarily, "Israelite tales")[18] into the *tafsir* literature, the story of Eve's creation from Adam's rib took deep root in Muslim exegeses by al-Tabari's time, especially since its overall implications nicely accorded with the growing patriarchization of society in the third/ninth century.

Such exegetical construals are markedly in contrast to what the Qur'an actually states concerning the creation of humankind. Qur'an 4:1, cited above, specifically mentions the simultaneous creation of the first human—who is not gendered—and the mate who is similarly not gendered from a single soul (*nafs wahida*) and from whom subsequent generations of male and female ensue. Simultaneous creation from the *nafs wahida*, as described in this verse, negates the possibility of the male being granted an ontologically superior status by virtue of having been created first, from whose body is then derived the woman's. The Qur'an thus clearly undermines the notion of a hierarchical relationship between man and woman and grants them instead total ontological equality.

Another important point stressed by Muslim feminists and modernists is that woman's moral and legal agency in the Qur'an was, to a large extent, attenuated by a majority of the classical Muslim jurists. Culturally derived attitudes that progressively undermined women's equal status in society in the formative period of Islam continue to stand in tension with several passages in the Qur'an that affirm women's moral agency as equal to that of men. For example, Qur'an 9:71 (cited above) is a highly critical verse that establishes equal and complementary moral agency for men and women. The obvious intent of the verse is to establish complete parity between men and women as partners in the common venture to promote the good, righteous society on earth and in the fulfillment of their individual and communal obligations toward God. As obvious as this meaning may seem to us, male interpreters from the pre-modern period have largely understood this verse in ways that were subversive of its egalitarian thrust.[19]

Furthermore, a fuller sense of the equal, complementary roles that men and women are expected to assume within an Islamic marriage emerges when other Qur'anic verses that are relevant to this discussion are brought in. Prominent among them is Qur'an 2:187 which reads, "wives are your garments and you [husbands] are their garments," where "garments" serve as a metaphor for mutual comfort and joy and the equal rights shared by wives and husbands vis-à-vis one another in the marital relationship. Another equally relevant verse is Qur'an 30:21 (cited above) which describes a loving, harmonious relationship between the spouses as the ideal state within an Islamic marriage, in which wives and husbands have reciprocal rights and duties. Read alongside Qur'an 9:71, believing women and men are understood to be the equal partners or allies of one another.

When we import into our discussion this Qur'anic assertion of men and women enjoying equal rights vis-à-vis one another and their complementary roles as partners in establishing a good, just society, the patriarchal conceptions of marriage and family, which spilled over into the socioeconomic sphere, are logically rendered untenable within the Islamic milieu. This did not, of course, prevent most male Muslim scholars, particularly jurists, from promoting the patriarchal model of familial and marital relations as worthy of adoption, no doubt because it was in conformity with the prevailing cultural notions and sensibilities of their day. Historicizing juridical and exegetical discourses as specific products of their time and milieu that often subverted the fundamental Qur'anic ethos of justice and equality with respect to gender continues to propel Muslim feminist and modernist hermeneutics.[20]

Such historicization becomes essential when we consider legal rulings on two complicated issues within Islamic law that ostensibly appear unequal and skewed in favor of the male: the division of inheritance shares between men and women and the practice of polygamy in Muslim-majority societies. Invoking considerations of justice and equity in the discussion of these two topics allows for deeper and more nuanced perspectives to emerge.[21]

With regard to inheritance, if we were to adopt a purely bean-counting approach, then the division of inheritance shares as described in Qur'an 4:11–12 would strike us as unfair, since the male is generally given two shares compared to the female, except in the case of parents who receive equal shares. This last exception—often given scant attention in discussions of inheritance—compels us to think of the rationale behind the apportionment of inheritance shares, ostensibly on the basis of gender. The Qur'an in its own milieu underscores the responsibility of men as the sole breadwinners to support their families; in other words, their economic dependents—traditionally wives and children—have a claim on whatever wealth they inherit. Women have no such economic obligations mandated for them; as is well-known, married Muslim women hold on to their property in their own names and are not required to spend any part of it to support their families. The extra share apportioned for men can then be understood to take into consideration their additional economic responsibilities toward their families. This *ratio legis* (legal rationale) for the disparity in inheritance shares would then not apply in the case of parents who need to be equally supported, especially in their old age.

Similar considerations of justice arise in regard to polygyny, where men, once again, as the principal breadwinner in the pre-modern period, had the economic responsibility to look after especially widows and their orphaned children. This is indicated by the larger context of Qur'an 4:3, which states:

> If you fear that you will not be able to deal justly with the orphans, marry women of your choice, two, three, or four. But if you fear that you will not be able to deal justly, then only one or those that your right hand possesses; that is more proper so that you do not incline to injustice.

In the same chapter, however, the Qur'an goes on to warn: "You will never be able to treat each of your wives with absolute equity" (Qur'an 4:129). When read together, it is clear that the monogamous marriage is the ideal one, since men are unable to treat multiple wives "with absolute equity," as is the requirement. In times of social and economic malaise and unrest, especially during wars when male lives are disproportionately lost leaving behind vulnerable widows and orphans, legal but restricted polygyny allowed a man to financially support up to four wives. This would have been an act of compassion particularly in the pre-modern period when women were not capable of earning an independent living. Whether such a proviso is necessary in the modern period when women's access to economic opportunities has changed drastically is a matter being revisited by feminist and modernist Muslim scholars.

JUSTICE BETWEEN RELIGIOUS COMMUNITIES AND NATIONS

The Qur'an strongly advocates for peaceful intercommunal relationships between Muslims and non-Muslims, especially in regard to the adherents of the two other Abrahamic faith communities. Specific verses in the Qur'an also mention the great importance of maintaining harmonious relations among all communities of people, regardless of their religious affiliation and of promoting peacemaking with a variety of means when conflict erupts. Peace (*al-salam* and its derivatives) is idealized as the state that governs the life of the faithful and defines their relationship with the Creator and His creation. The very revelation of the Qur'an is associated with the concept of peace (Qur'an 97). Embracement of Islam is equated with entering into a peaceful state; Qur'an 2:108 addresses the believers thus: "O you who believe, enter into peace (*al-silm*) wholeheartedly!" Entering into Islam further means entering into the "abode of peace" (*Dar as-salam*); the Quran (10:25) states: "God summons to the Abode of Peace; He guides whom he pleases to a way that is straight." Muslims may invoke peace even on those who harass them for their beliefs and cause them mental anguish. Qur'an 25:63 praises "the servants of the All-Merciful who walk humbly on earth; and when the foolish jeer at them, they reply, 'Peace!'" Within the Qur'anic worldview, peace is the ultimate desideratum, the achievement of which is the most noble objective of human striving and existence on earth.

Peace in the Qur'an is, however, not just the absence of violence and conflict, which has been called by some a "negative peace." It is rather a holistic concept that is based on two key factors: (1) the recognition of the equal dignity of every human being as God's creation and (2) the guarantee of justice for all on earth. These two key factors allow for peace to be conceptualized as resting on a fundamental restructuring of socioeconomic relations and interpersonal relations that are conducive to establishing and nurturing a just and egalitarian society. Such a society can achieve what many call today "positive peace" – that is to say, a lasting and enduring peace because it addresses the root causes of violence and conflict—inequality and injustice—and seeks to transform society by uprooting them.[22] With regard to the first of the two key factors of positive peace, the Qur'an (17:70) declares, "Indeed, we have honored every human being," and that every human being has been shaped "in the best of molds" (Qur'an 95: 4), thereby establishing the intrinsic dignity and equal worth of all human beings—regardless of gender, ethnicity, race, and social status – by virtue of being human.

With regard to the second factor, a number of Qur'anic verses establish the necessity of justice as a characteristic of the ideal human community. This is, for example, evident in Qur'an 57:25 which states: "We sent before Our messengers with clear signs and sent down with them the Book and the Balance (of right and wrong), so that humans may stand forth in justice." And, as previously mentioned, Qur'an 4:135 and Qur'an 5:8 affirm that justice, according to the Qur'an, is an essential and indispensable component of peace that allows for human flourishing on earth.

The hadith literature similarly emphasizes the concepts of non-violence, peace, and cordiality in relation to the daily life of the pious Muslim. In the best-known collection of hadith, known as *Sahih al-Bukhari*—generally revered by Sunnis as the most authoritative source after the Qur'an—the prophet is quoted as uttering the golden rule, as related by the Companion Anas b. Malik, "No one among you is a believer until they love for others what they love for themselves."[23] The compiler of this collection, al-Bukhari (d. 256/870), lists another significant hadith narrated by the Companion al-Bara' b. 'Azib who related that the prophet had commanded Muslims to habitually visit the sick, attend funerals, quench the thirst of people, come to the aid of the weak, help the oppressed, and spread peace among people.[24] Another Companion 'Abd Allah b. 'Umar narrated, "A man asked the Prophet, peace and blessings be upon him: 'Which Islam is best?'" Muhammad replied, "The offering of food [to the hungry] and giving greetings of peace to those you know and those you do not know."[25]

A number of hadiths stress the importance of justice as a corollary to peace and social stability. In a hadith narrated by Abu Hurayra, the prophet is quoted as saying, "Whoever deals justly with people has carried out an act of charity."[26] In a *hadith qudsi* (sacred statement), God Himself speaks and declares: "I have made tyranny and oppression (*zulm*) unlawful for Myself and I have done the same for you. Do not oppress one another!"[27]

The concept of peace raises questions about how to establish and nurture it when human nature tends to incline toward conflict and strife. Does the Qur'an establish any kind of protocol for effecting enduring, just peace among people of good will, especially with members of the two other Abrahamic faith communities?

Possibly, the most important Qur'anic verse in this context is Qur'an 29:46 which scholars have long understood to advocate a certain protocol of dialogue for Muslims, particularly with adherents of the Abrahamic religions. The verse states:

> Do not dispute with the People of the Book save with what is better; except for those who do wrong among them, and say [to them]: "We believe in that which was revealed to us and revealed to you, and our God and your God is one, and we submit to Him."

The early exegete from the Umayyad period Mujahid b. Jabr (d. 104/720) understands the first part of the verse as counseling Muslims to speak only what is good (*khayran*) when some among the People of the Book utter what is wrong (*sharran*). Citing Sa'id b. Jubayr (d. 95/714) as his authority, Mujahid glosses "those who do wrong among them" as those among the People of the Book who have not signed a treaty with the Muslims and consequently engage in hostilities against them.[28]

The famous exegete Muhammad b. Jarir al-Tabari (d. 310/923) from the Abbasid period comments that the critical phrase in the verse "save with what is better" (*illa bi-llati hiya ahsan*) means "except for what is good or fine speech" (*illa bi-'l-jamil min al-qawl*). "Good speech" consists of inviting to God by means of His verses/signs (*bi-ayatihi*), and drawing attention to His proofs (*hujajihi*). As for those who do wrong among the People of the Book, they are understood by al-Tabari to be those who erroneously ascribe partners to God as well as those who refuse to submit to Muslim authority.[29]

Some of the later post-Tabari exegetes, however, offer more nuanced and less confessional interpretations of this verse. For example, al-Zamakhshari (d. 538/1144) states that examples of doing "what is better" might consist of offering a gentle response to those who engage in rough behavior; of preserving one's equanimity in the face of another's anger; and of displaying forbearance in the face of aggressive behavior. He similarly offers a non-confessional understanding of "those who do wrong among the People of the Book," commenting that they are those who are "excessively hostile and obstinate, refusing to accept good counsel, and with whom gentleness and compassion are of no avail." According to al-Zamakhshari, those who do wrong among the scriptuaries are so considered not on account of theological error on their part, but on account of their bad manners and hostile attitude.

In the late sixth/twelfth century, Fakhr al-Din al-Razi (d. 606/1210) is of the opinion that this verse counsels Muslims in general to deal gently with the People of the Book because of the religious tenets they have in common. Jews and Christians after all also have faith in the one God and believe in the revelation of books, in the sending of messengers, and in the final resurrection. Each of these articles of belief is designated a *husn* ("a goodness") by al-Razi. He maintains that despite their failure to acknowledge the mission of the Prophet Muhammad even though their scriptures contain references to him, Muslims can acknowledge the aggregate goodness (*ihsanihim*) of the People of the Book, on account of which they should debate with them with what is better/best. Al-Razi leaves undefined here the precise nature of "what is better/best." But since he proceeds to say next that Muslims should not treat the opinions of Jews and Christians lightly nor ascribe error to their ancestors, as they might in the case of polytheists, then we may assume that "what is better/best" is a reference to the adoption of such conciliatory and respectful modes of conversation across confessional lines.[30]

Given this Qur'anic emphasis on civil discourse with the People of the Book and non-Muslims in general (see Qur'an 6:107–108),[31] one may well contrast this depiction with the image of Muslims in the Western media as intolerant and violent who are required to incessantly wage the military jihad. Many Western orientalists, pundits, and the global media polemically equate jihad with "holy war," an equation that conveys the impression that it is a no-holds barred, scorched-earth military campaign that aims to obliterate everything in its path until the targeted enemy—non-Muslims in general—convert or at least succumb to Muslim rule. Such views have become endemic in the public sphere so much so that one may be compelled to ask how the Qur'an's invitation to engage in gentle, civil discourse with non-Muslims can be reconciled with this assumed imperative within Islam to wage the military jihad incessantly against them.

The simple and quick response is that the Qur'an contains no such imperative. On the topic of armed combat, it emphasizes instead that just cause must exist for Muslims to resort to defensive fighting against an intractable enemy and that during battle, Muslim soldiers must comport themselves humanely. Fighting – and the taking of human life—is not to be taken lightly and the Qur'an, along with hadith, lays down a specific protocol for waging justified and limited warfare. During the twelve-year Meccan period when the prophet began receiving revelations that later became part of the written Qur'an,

Muslims faced grievous persecution for proclaiming their monotheistic faith in pagan Arab society. Despite this persecution, Muslims were not allowed to physically retaliate and were counseled to practice patient forbearance and forgive their assailants (Qur'an 3:200; 42:43). After the famous emigration known as the *hijra* to Medina from his birthplace Mecca, the prophet received divine permission to fight in self-defense, as mentioned in Qur'an 22:39–40, lifting the earlier prohibition against fighting. Muslims after all had been physically and verbally attacked for publicly practicing their religion and driven out of their homes unjustly. These revelations allowed them to fight back but only to the extent that they had been harmed. The two verses in Qur'an 22:39–40 state:

> Permission is given to those against whom fighting has been initiated because they have been wronged/oppressed, and God is able to help them. These are they who have been wrongfully expelled from their homes merely for saying 'God is our Lord.' If God had not restrained some people by means of others, monasteries, churches, synagogues, and mosques in which God's name is mentioned frequently would have been destroyed. Indeed God comes to the aid of those who come to His aid; verily He is powerful and mighty.

Recourse to defensive fighting was established in these verses for Muslims not for the sake of propagating their religion but for the protection of their lives and property, as well as potentially those of non-Muslim monotheists who faced similar persecution, since Christian and Jewish houses of worship are clearly mentioned in Qur'an 22:39–40 as being worthy of protection.

Another critical verse Qur'an 2:190 unambiguously forbids Muslims from attacking the enemy first. The verse states, "Fight in the way of God those who fight you and do not commit aggression." Accordingly, a number of exegetes insisted that Muslims could only fight back after they had been attacked—no ifs, ands, or buts – and that the counter-attack had to be proportional to the original attack. This is the documented position of the early exegetes Mujahid b. Jabr (d. 104/722) and Muqatil b. Sulayman (d. 150/767) who wrote their Qur'an commentaries during the late Umayyad period and early Abbasid period, respectively.[32] These early positions continued to be maintained by later exegetes, such as the late twelfth-century exegete Fakhr al-Din al-Razi (d. 606/1210).

Similar reasons which legitimate an armed response to the adversary are contained in another important group of verses – Qur'an 9:12–13—which state:

> If they break their pacts after having concluded them and revile your religion, then fight the leaders of unbelief. Will you not fight a people who violated their

oaths and had intended to expel the Messenger and commenced [hostilities] against you the first time?

The overwhelming majority of exegetes stress that the violation of pacts by the polytheists, their denigration of Islam, their hostile intent to harm Muhammad, and their initial act of aggression toward Muslims had made defensive fighting necessary against them. In his commentary on Qur'an 9:12, the late third-/ninth-century exegete al-Tabari (d. 310/923) says that it is a critique of those from among the tribe of Quraysh who violated the terms of their pact with the prophet according to which they had agreed not to fight the Muslims nor provide aid to their enemies.[33]

Another verse Qur'an 4:75 exhorts Muslims to defend militarily those who are among "the feeble among men, women and children who cry out, 'Our Lord! Deliver us from this town in which the people are oppressors!'" In the understanding of some pre-modern jurists, this verse establishes humanitarian reasons for military intervention to aid those who are defenseless against their oppressors and who specifically call upon Muslims to provide them with help against injustice and oppression.[34]

In addition to stating who can be fought against and for what reasons, the Qur'an also unambiguously refers to those who cannot be fought against. Thus, in several verses, the Qur'an states that Muslims cannot fight non-Muslims who are peaceful and show no hostile intent toward them. One verse (Qur'an 4:90) states: "If they hold themselves aloof from you and do not wage war against you and offer you peace, then God does not permit you any way against them."

Two significant verses (Qur'an 60:8–9) mandate kind and just interactions with those who are peaceful, regardless of their religious beliefs, in contrast to those who willfully commit aggression; these verses state:

> God does not forbid you from being kind and equitable to those who have neither made war on you on account of your religion nor driven you from your homes; indeed God loves those who are equitable. God forbids you however from making common cause with those who fight you on account of your religion and evict you from your homes and who support [others] in driving you out.

Another important verse, Qur'an 8:61, warns that should the adversary refrain from fighting and incline toward peace, Muslims had to reciprocate. Qur'an 8:61 is therefore the quintessential verse concerning peacemaking; it states: "And if they should incline to peace, then incline to it [yourself] and place your trust in God; for He is all-hearing and all-knowing."

Against this overall thrust of the Qur'an, we start to detect a strong exegetical tendency on the part of certain Muslim scholars to infer a general mandate from the Qur'an to fight offensive or expansionist wars roughly by the fourth/tenth century when the legal schools (*madhahib*) began to crystallize. Two Medinan verses are often cited by a number of jurists as setting up a religious obligation to fight non-Muslims until they convert to Islam or at least capitulate to Muslim rule. The first is Qur'an 9:5 which states:

> When the sacred months have lapsed, then slay the polytheists (*al-mushrikin*) wherever you may encounter them. Seize them and encircle them and lie in wait for them. But if they repent and perform the prayer and give the *zakat*, then let them go on their way, for God is forgiving and merciful.

The second is Qur'an 9:29, which states:

> Fight those who do not believe in God nor in the Last Day and do not forbid what God and His messenger have forbidden and do not follow the religion of truth from among those who were given the Book until they proffer the *jizya* humbly with [their] hands.

In order to make their case, a number of these scholars wielded the hermeneutic tool of *naskh* (abrogation) according to which chronologically later verses in the Qur'an may be understood to have abrogated or nullified earlier verses. Thus, they privileged Qur'an 9:5 and 9:29 which occur in a late Medinan chapter over more numerous conciliatory and peaceful verses that were part of earlier revelations. This view patently contradicts the views of earlier exegetes who understood these verses to refer to specific factions hostile to Muslims in the seventh century and not to non-Muslims en masse. For example, the second-/eighth-century exegete Muqatil ibn Sulayman understands the *mushrikin* mentioned in Qur'an 9:5 to be a reference only to those polytheists during the time of the prophet with whom there was no pact (*'ahd*) and who constituted a hostile faction who had aggressed against Muslims; Muslims could therefore legitimately defend themselves against their attacks.[35] Similarly, al-Tabari understands the verse to refer only to the hostile polytheists during the time of the prophet and to have no further applicability beyond that time and place.[36]

Likewise, in contrast to some of the later scholars, early scholars understood Qur'an 9:29 as a reference to specific hostile Christians who posed a military threat to Muslims in the first century of Islam. Therefore, the early second-/eighth-century exegete Mujahid b. Jabr understood this verse to have been revealed as a specific reference to the battle of Tabuk,[37] thereby implying that the scriptuaries referenced in this verse are specifically the hostile Byzantine Christians.[38] Al-Tabari also acknowledges that the historical context for the revelation of this verse was war with Byzantium, although he himself understood this verse to have a broader application.[39]

Disregarding the historical contextualization of these verses allowed pro-abrogation scholars to wield them as proof-texts to buttress their worldview predicated on an expansionist conceptualization of the Islamic empire.[40]

QUR'ANIC ETHICS OF REFRAINING FROM FIGHTING AND PEACEMAKING

It should be noted that the hermeneutic stratagem of abrogation was vigorously opposed by other scholars. After all, a holistic reading of the Qur'an establishes that in addition to being defensive, fighting in the Qur'an is clearly limited in nature. The Qur'anic ethics of desisting from fighting and making peace are just as important as the rules it sets down for conducting a justified war. Qur'an 60:7–9 referenced above is a highly important cluster of verses that explicitly states that peaceful non-Muslims cannot ever be fought; their religious commitments are not a factor in this consideration. These verses instead make very clear that Muslims may fight only those who have clearly aggressed against them and persecuted them for their faith. Non-Muslims of good will who peacefully coexist with them are to be treated kindly and equitably, regardless of what they choose to believe. A majority of the exegetes that I surveyed in an earlier study affirm that the three verses in Qur'an 60:7–9 remain unabrogated and their injunctions to treat peaceful non-Muslims justly and kindly remain valid for all times.[41] This position is powerfully expressed by al-Tabari who affirms that the most appropriate exegesis of Qur'an 60:7–9 is as follows: God has not forbidden Muslims from acting kindly and fairly with all those from any and every religion and creed who do not fight them and do not expel them from their homes. Al-Tabari summarily dismisses the suggestion that this verse is abrogated, for the verse clearly permits the faithful to be kind to "the people of war" (*ahl al-ḥarb*), whether blood-relatives or not, who bear no ill-will toward Muslims and as long as such relationships do not compromise the security of Muslims. For God loves those who are equitable (*al-munsifīn*), who give people their due rights, are personally just to them, and do good to those who are good to them, he asserts. As for Qur'an 60:9, it forbade believers from helping and befriending those from among the unbelievers in Mecca who fought them over religion and evicted them from their homes. To do otherwise would have constituted wrongdoing and a violation of the command of God.[42]

With regard to the peacemaking verse Qur'an 8:61 as cited above, al-Tabari says that God in this verse addresses the prophet and counsels him that if he should fear treachery and perfidy on the part of a group of [unspecified] people (*qawm*), then he should withdraw from them and fight them. But "if they should incline to making peace with you and abandon warfare," either through entry into Islam, or payment of the *jizya*, or through the establishment of friendly relations (*muwada'a*), then you should do the same for the sake of peace and peacemaking.⁴³ Al-Tabari states trenchantly that the view of those who say that this verse had been abrogated by Qur'an 9:5 cannot be supported either on the basis of the Qur'an, the *sunna*, or reason. Qur'an 9:5 has to do *only* with Arab polytheist idolaters from whom *jizya* cannot be taken. Neither verse invalidates the injunction contained in the other and both remain unabrogated (*muḥkam*) concerning its specific content.⁴⁴ Al-Ṭabari's unequivocal defense of the unabrogated status of Qur'an 8:61 and the reasons he advances for rejecting Qur'an 9:5 as an abrogating verse in this case are particularly noteworthy.

Al-Tabari's views were repeated by a number of exegetes after him: for example, ar-Razi in the late sixth/twelfth century said that after the preceding verse (Qur'an 8:60) exhorted Muslims to assemble their forces against the enemy, should the same enemy incline to peace, then Muslims are commanded to accept their offer of peace. Furthermore, this injunction to make peace with the enemy is a broad and general one, not restricted to the generation of the first Muslims.⁴⁵

One may therefore conclude that these verses taken together—Qur'an 60:7–9 and 8:61—clearly establish that the military *jihad* in the Qur'an is most categorically not holy war that is fought to impose a religion; it is a defensive war undertaken to protect the rights, including the religious freedom, of those who have already been attacked by hostile forces. The desire for religious or ideological supremacy fuels holy war; the quest for justice is at the root of the military jihad in the Quran.⁴⁶

CONCLUSION

Justice in all its forms and varieties is a non-negotiable, cardinal virtue for Muslims in every aspect of their lives. The Qur'an's insistence on this point—and amplified in the hadith literature—leaves its imprint in virtually every area of religious reflection and scholarly production. In my survey of relevant literature above, it becomes abundantly clear that this was a topic that exercised the minds of Muslim scholars as they deliberated upon the parameters of this complex concept and pondered how best its mandate could be implemented in the circumstances of their time.

In our contemporary world in which increasingly the Global South demands increasing political enfranchisement and even reparations from the Global North for past and continuing political and economic exploitation, especially under the aegis of colonialism, justice has acquired a new urgency and valency. Islamic perspectives on justice are rarely discussed in the global arena, a lacuna which bears addressing since such perspectives would enrich current conversations on just and equitable sharing of world resources, on reconciliation and peacemaking, and the upholding of the dignity of every human being as stewards of this earth, among other critical topics. In Europe and North America, social and political malaise deepens as race relations worsen, religious bigotry directed particularly at Muslims continues to escalate, and environmental degradation spearheaded by the affluent Global North threatens to spiral out of control. What a mere two decades ago may have struck us as a hyperbolic doomsday scenario now seems increasingly realistic. Issues of social and political justice must be given paramount importance if the world is to pull back from the abyss of self-destruction. Our inability to account for our moral failures as a global community toward those who are less privileged and whose voices are effectively muzzled must be candidly acknowledged. Justice cannot be just a buzzword that we pepper our discourses with so that past and present injustices can be papered over and we can avoid accountability for them. As al-Tabari reminded his audience in the late third/ninth century, "Let your characters and dispositions be of the kind that makes you stand up for justice (*al-'adl*) with regard to your allies and your enemies." The Qur'an reminds us that the praxis of justice is more than a legal and sociological concept—it is a way of being in the world and leads to the inculcation of a moral and ethical trait that conditions us to call out injustice wherever we may encounter it and seek to undermine it.

NOTES

1. This is by no means an exhaustive list; my typology recognizes the most predominant forms of justice that I discern in the Qur'an. For more categories of justice, see Ramon Harvey 2018.
2. Muslim b. Hajjaj 1995, 3:1159, # 4493.
3. Both men and women served in this important role in the early history of Islam. 'Umar ibn al-Khattab, the second caliph, appointed a woman Shifa bt. 'Abd Allah as the market inspector during his time.
4. Al-Tabari, *1997*, 4:482.
5. Ibid., 4:483.
6. Ibid.
7. 'Ata' ibn Abi Rabah (d. 115/733) was a prominent Successor (*tabi'i*)—that is to say, from the second generation of Muslims who followed the first generation of Muslims, the contemporaries of the Prophet, known collectively as the Companions.
8. Al-Razi 1999, 4:320.
9. Ibid.
10. Rida, 1999, 6:228–29.
11. Ibid., 6:229.

12. Ibid.
13. Smith 1983, 36.
14. See the seminal works by Wadud 1999 and Barlas 2019.
15. A number of these historical changes, especially during the Abbasid period due to the increasing influence of Persian cultural and societal norms at this time, are documented in Ahmed 1992, as well as in Marlowe 1997 who additionally traces the impact of Byzantine notions of social hierarchy on Abbasid society.
16. See Afsaruddin 2015, 2023.
17. Hassan 1985; Stowasser 1996, 25–38.
18. This term refers to stories of biblical origin that were used by some Muslim exegetes to flesh out Qur'anic references to biblical figures.
19. See this discussion in Afsaruddin 2015, 88–89.
20. See in this context the writings of the Moroccan feminist Asma Lamrabet which expound upon the notion of *wilaya* or partnership adumbrated in Qur'an 9:71 and its potential for effecting long-term social reform with respect to gendered relationships in Muslim-majority societies; for example, Lamrabet 2015.
21. Afsaruddin 2023; wadud 1999, 80–85.
22. "Positive peace" is to be contrasted to "negative peace"; see this discussion in Galtung 1996.
23. al-Bukhari n.d., 1:69, #12.
24. Ibid., 7: 394, #1109.
25. Ibid., # 1110.
26. al-Bukhari n.d., 4:366, #911.
27. Muslim b. Hajjaj 1995, 4:1583, #2577.
28. Mujahid 2005, 205.
29. al-Tabari 1997, 10:149–50.
30. al-Razi 1999, 9:63–64.
31. These verses state:

> Had God willed, they would not be idolaters; but We have not appointed you [addressing the Prophet] a watcher over them, nor are you their guardian. Do not abuse to whom they pray apart from God, or they will abuse God in retaliation without knowledge.

32. Afsaruddin 2013, 43–58.
33. al-Tabari 1997, 6:330.
34. al-Sulami 1996, 610.
35. Muqatil 2002, 2:157.
36. Ibid.
37. This verse refers specifically to the Byzantines who are said to have amassed their forces on the Syrian border in preparation for an attack on Muslims in the year 630. Arabic sources refer to the event as the Battle of Tabuk, although no battle was eventually fought since the Byzantine forces failed to materialize.
38. Mujahid 2005, 99.
39. al-Tabari 1997, 6:349.
40. See Afsaruddin 2013b for this discussion.

41. Afsaruddin 2013a, 82–90.
42. al-Tabari 1997, 12:63.
43. al-Tabari, 1997, 6:278.
44. Ibid., 6:278–79.
45. al-Razi 1999, 5:500–01.
46. See further Afsaruddin 2022.

REFERENCES

Afsaruddin, Asma 2013a. *Striving in the Path of God: Jihad and Martyrdom in Islamic Thought*. Oxford: Oxford University Press.

Afsaruddin, Asma 2013b. "The *Siyar* Laws of Aggression: Juridical Re-interpretations of Qur'anic *Jihad* and Their Contemporary Implications for International Law." In *Islam and International Law: Engaging Self-Centrism from a Plurality of Perspectives*, edited by Marie-Luisa Frick and Andreas Th. Müller, 45–63. Leiden: Brill/Martinus Nijhoff.

Afsaruddin, Asma 2015. *Contemporary Issues in Islam*. Edinburgh: Edinburgh University Press.

Afsaruddin, Asma, 2020. "Jihad in the Qur'an." In *The Oxford Handbook on Qur'anic Studies*, edited by Mohammad Abdel Haleem and Mustafa Shah, 512–526. Oxford: Oxford University Press.

Afsaruddin, Asma 2022. *Jihad: What Everyone Needs to Know*. Oxford: Oxford University Press.

Afsaruddin, Asma 2023. "Modern Muslim Women's Gender-Egalitarian Readings of the Qur'ān." In *The Oxford Handbook of Islam and Women*, edited by Asma Afsaruddin, 80–118. Oxford: Oxford University Press.

Barlas, Asma 2019. *Believing Women in Islam: Unreading Patriarchal Interpretations of the Qur'ān*, Rev. ed. Austin: University of Texas Press.

Al-Bukhari, Muhammad b. Isma'il. n.d. *Sahih*. Ed. Qasim ash-Shamma'i ar-Rifa'i. Beirut: Dar al-qalam.

Galtung, Johan 1996. *Peace by Peaceful Means: Peace and Conflict, Development and Civilisation*. Oslo: PRIO.

Harvey, Ramon 2018. *The Qur'an and the Just Society*. Edinburgh: Edinburgh University Press.

Hassan, Rifaat 1985. "Made from Adam's Rib": the Woman's Creation Question. *al-Mushir*, 124–155.

Lamrabet, Asma. "An Egalitarian Reading of the Concepts of *Khilafah*, *Wilayah* and *Qiwama*." In *Men in Charge? Rethinking Authority in Muslim Legal Tradition*, edited by Ziba Mir-Hosseini, Mulki al-Sharmani, and Jana Rumminger, 65–87. Oxford: Oneworld Publications, 2015.

Marlowe, Louise 1997. *Hierarchy and Egalitarianism in Islamic Thought*. Cambridge, UK: Cambridge University Press.

Mujahid b. Jabr 2005. *Tafsir Mujahid,* edited by Abu Muhammad al-Asyuti. Beirut: Dar al-kutub al-'ilmiyya.

Muqatil b. Sulayman 2002. *Tafsir*. edited by 'Abd Allah Mahmud Shiḥata. Beirut: Mu'assasat al-ta'rikh al-'arabi, 2002

Muslim b. Hajjaj, *Sahih Muslim*. Beirut, Dar Ibn Hazm, 1995

al-Razi, Fakhr al-Din 1999. *al-Tafsir al-kabir*. Beirut: Dar iḥya' al-turath al-'arabi.

Rida, Rashid 1999. *Tafsir al-manar*. Beirut: Dar al-kutub al-'ilmiyya.

Smith, Dorothy E. 1983. "Women, Class and Family." *The Socialist Register*, 1–44.

Stowasser, Barbara 1996. *Women in the Qur'an, Traditions and Interpretation*. Oxford: Oxford University Press.

al-Sulami, Abu 'Abd al-Rahman 1995. *The Minor Qur'an Commentary of al-Sulami (Ziyadat haqa'iq al-tafsir)*. Ed. Gerhard Böwering. Beirut: Dar el-Machreq.

al-Tabari, Muhammad b. Jarir 1997. *Jami' al-bayan fi tafsir al-qur'an*. Beirut: Dar al-kutub al-'arabi.

Wadud, Amina 1999. *Qur'ān and Woman: Rereading the Sacred Text from a Woman's Perspective* New York: Oxford University Press.

Chapter 3

Sensory Aesthetics of Belief and Unbelief in the Qur'an and Its Impact on Interreligious and Intersocietal Relations

Abdulkader Tayob

Interreligious tensions and conflicts threaten societies in an increasingly globalized world. Conceptions of the Other generated by religious, nationalist, and ethnic preconceptions are often transformed into conflict, violence, and even death. Mutual relations of acceptance and tolerance are easily forgotten as social media exaggerate insider–outsider representations. Like others, Muslims are both victims and perpetrators of such representations. When Islamic symbols become the subject of offensive public representations, they are challenged by deeply held values and practices toward the religious other. In many conflict zones, the following verse is often cited to advise Muslims to tolerate those who insult Islam, the Qur'an, or the Prophet:

> Abuse not those whom they worship, apart from God, or they will abuse God in revenge without knowledge. *So We have decked out fair to every nation their deeds* (emphasis added); then to their Lord they shall return, and He will tell them what they have been doing. (Qur'an 6:108)[1]

While the first part of the verse advises believers not to insult the gods of the Other, the second part points to the sensory perception of disbelief. In this essay, I argue that an ethic toward the Other is advocated through this recognition of the sensory mediation of belief.

In the well-known understanding of Qur'anic aesthetics, truthful belief may be apprehended through revelation, nature, and history. This aesthetic is driven by signs and manifestations (*āyāt*) that point to the distinction between good and evil and between belief and disbelief. This aesthetic of clarity (*bayān*) is familiar to readers of the Qur'an in particular and to scholars of monotheism in general. This essay points to a more complex aesthetic that occupies a place alongside it. It argues that this aesthetic is exemplified in verses that make a connection between beauty and disbelief and between beauty and belief.

I offer an analysis of this ethic in a close reading of the root word z-y-n in the Qur'an. The words *zīna* (beauty, adornment), *zayyana*, and *izzayyana* (beautifying and adorning) intimate that belief and disbelief are mediated by beauty until the end of time. While most verses point to beauty obscuring belief, there are some that suggest that beauty is part of everyday experiences, including belief and truth. I show that this aesthetic mediation of belief and disbelief is a universal condition, one that generates an ethical empathy toward the belief of others. After presenting the semantic map of z-y-n in the Qur'an, I examine this complex aesthetic and its ethical implications in the intellectual history of Islam among theologians (*mutakallims*) and exegetes (*mufassirīn*).

AISTHESIS AND THE LITERARY MIRACLE OF THE QUR'AN

The aesthetic style of the Quran is inseparable from its self-identification as a *muʿjiza* (miracle, implying inimitability). Historically, the literary nature of the Qur'an has been elaborated for its unique and sublime literary tropes and styles.[2] Some contemporary Muslim scholars, starting in the Indian subcontinent and continuing in Egypt, have revisited this question by positing the Qur'an as a cohesive literary work. Their work has created space for appreciating a sensory experience (*aesthesis*) referred to in the z-y-n verses in the Qur'an.

Mustansir Mir traced a trend in South Asian exegesis in the nineteenth and twentieth centuries on the thematic unity (*naẓm*) of the Qur'an. For Hamiduddin Farahi (1863–1930) and Amin Ahsan Islahi (1904–1997), rhetoric and meaning converge in the Qur'an.[3] Later in Egypt, Amīn al-Khūlī (1895–1966) approached the Qur'an as "the greatest Arabic book" (*Kitāb al-ʿarabiyya al-akbar*).[4] His students closely examined the form of the Qur'an, arguing that there was no fundamental contradiction between its miraculous nature and its literary, aesthetic qualities. Among them was ʿĀʾisha ʿAbd al-Raḥmān (Bint al-Shāṭiʾ) who elaborated a systematic intertextual method of reading the Qur'an. She proposed that its miracle was rooted in both its form and meaning (*al-iʿjāz al-bayānī*).[5] Nasr Ḥāmid Abū Zayd (d. 2010) took this approach one step further by arguing for a deep historicist approach to the Qur'an as literature. From this vantage point, he argued for a "special linguistic dynamics through which the Qur'anic language influenced Arabic . . . [and] transformed . . . linguistic signs, vocabulary, into semiotic signs."[6]

In this chapter, I want to turn attention to the Qur'an's generation and self-awareness of *aisthesis* defined as "a total sensorial experience of the world and to . . . (a) sensuous knowledge of it."[7] Scholars in the study of religion, materiality, and aesthetics have revived this Aristotelian term to reflect on the role played by the senses in the experience of religion. Turning away from a predominant cognitive apprehension of religion in the social sciences, they point to sensory experiences pervasive in religious practices.[8] Religion comes alive through touch, sight, smell, and feeling. In the case of the Qur'an, multiple sensorial experiences may be identified in Muslims listening, reading, reciting, writing, and also sometimes ingesting its parts.

Going one step further, I want to turn attention to the self-referential nature of the *aisthesis* in the Qur'an.[9] At one level, the Qur'an refers to sensory experiences generated by its verses. Readers or listeners of the Qur'an are prompted to reflect on their sensory experiences through the choice of words used. For example, the following verse captures the sensory experience of hell: "*Lā yadhūqūna fīhā bardan wa la sharāban* (neither coolness shall they taste nor any [thirst-quenching] drink)" (Qur'an 24). In another verse, those destined to hell:

> have hearts which they fail to grasp the truth, and eyes with which they fail to see, and ears with which they fail to hear (*lahum qulūb la yafqahaūn bihā wa lahum a'yun lā yubṣirūn bihā wa lahum ādhān la yasma'ūn bihā*). (Qur'an 7:179)

But there is more to this aesthetic when taking a closer look at z-y-n verses. I will show that the latter points to an aesthetic self-awareness, including an ethical relation and disposition to the religious Other and the self. But first, I turn to a brief reflection on current studies on belief and disbelief in the Qur'an.

STUDIES ON BELIEF AND DISBELIEF IN THE QUR'AN

Since the 1960s, three approaches may be identified in the study of belief and disbelief in the Qur'an. Toshihiko Izutsu and Marilyn Waldman represent, respectively, semantic and historical approaches, while Muslim reformist scholars combine these with a semiotic approach that privileges readers and interpreters in the understanding of key concepts in the Qur'an. A brief review of this literature prepares the ground for my proposal that an aesthetic sensitivity may add a new dimension to the study of belief and disbelief.

Toshihiko Izutsu proposed a worldview (*Weltanschauung*) in the Qur'an through key terms that show how "(b)eing is structured, . . . the major constituents of the world, and how they are related to each other."[10] Among these terms, belief and disbelief occupy a significant binary pair in the worldview of the Qur'an. According to Izutzu, *Kufr* unifies a conceptual universe of terms such as *fisq, shirk, ḍalāl, 'isyān, ẓulm, takdhīb, nifāq*, and *istikbār* (respectively malevolence, polytheism, waywardness, oppression, rejection, hypocrisy, and pride). *Kufr* (disbelief) is more than the sum of these terms. The word and its related terms are, however, clearly differentiated from *īmān* (security, fidelity), which connotes terms such as *shukr, taṣdīq, and islām* (gratitude, acceptance, and submission). Izutsu shows how the meaning of belief and disbelief emerged through these interlocking and interrelated terms.[11]

In contrast to Izutsu's semantic analysis, Marilyn Waldman offers a historical analysis of *kufr* in the Qur'an that points to its "accumulation of meanings" over time. Following a Nöldeke-Schwally dating of the Qur'an, she identifies *kufr* in the preaching of the Prophet Muhammad over three periods in Mecca. In the first period, *kufr* is associated with rejection (*takdhīb*) which reflects the opposition faced by the Prophet. This is followed by an emphasis on ingratitude associated with disbelief in the second period. *Kufr* in the third Meccan period pointed to God's "control of the *kāfir's* perception and understanding."[12] According to Waldman, the will of God at this third stage adds a challenging dimension to *kufr*.

> This complex combination of man's failure to choose God and God's refusal to guide such a man is the broadest meaning of *kufr* to be derived from the Qur'an . . . [and] it is also the most difficult for a human being to assess.[13]

Waldman shows nuanced changes in the meaning of *kufr* over time, ending with the familiar theological enigma of belief between the absolute Will of God and human agency and responsibility. This issue became a significant point of contention in later theological debates in the intellectual history of Islam.[14] In her analysis of the third Meccan stage, however Waldman comes close to recognizing an aesthetic in the intervention of God and the devil between disbelief and belief. She describes the third stage as one where "God has chosen to *obscure* the faculties of perception" or has taken "control of the *kāfir's perception* and understanding" [my emphasis].[15] Waldman seems to recognize an aesthetic perception that confronts the unbeliever but does not pursue this dimension any further.

If Izutsu and Waldman represent semantic and historicist approaches to the study of belief and disbelief, some Muslim intellectuals and reformers have articulated an inclusive interpretation of the Qur'an through semiotic strategies.[16] By semiotics, I mean an interpretation that recognizes and privileges the reader over the text in the hermeneutical exercise. In this conception, every reading is regarded as a novel production of meaning.[17] Focusing on the productive role of the interpreter and reader, semiotics finds closure and openness in a religious text:

> The "canon" itself is both product of interpretation and definer of the parameters of interpretation. Subsequent interpretations either are conservative, i.e., stay within the bounds of the received tradition, or innovative, i.e., claim to find "the real" meaning in the canon, a meaning which departs from the received interpretations.

Using a semiotic strategy in reading a text like the Qur'an means that traditional interpretations may give way to new readings. A few examples from contemporary scholarship show this semiotic play in the reading of belief and disbelief.

Asma Afsaruddin's analysis of the "exemplary nation" (*ummatan wasaṭan*) represents a good example of a historical and semiotic analyses woven together. She approaches the term for its signification of salvation in this world and the next. In a close study of the exegetical record, she shows that some of the earliest commentators favored an inclusive interpretation of the term. For them, salvation was not guaranteed exclusively for Muslims. Later commentators read the Qur'an in a more exclusivist manner whereby Muslims were regarded as the only exemplary nation. According to Afsaruddin, most contemporary Muslims followed this later development in interpreting the "exemplary nation." Afsaruddin concludes that the verses in the Qur'an invite modern Muslims to produce a new, more inclusive meaning of salvation for contemporary society. As a key concept in the Qur'an, the idea of an exemplary nation "can be deployed as a universal socio-ethical organizational principle in pursuit of the common good of humanity."[18]

Mun'im Sirry examined a similarly inclusivist approach through contemporary interpreters of the following verse of the Qur'an:

> For each one of you We have appointed a law (*shir'a*) and a way (*minhāj*). If God had so willed, He would have made you a single people (*umma wāḥida*), but [His plan is] to test you in what He has given you: so compete with one another in good works (*khayrāt*). The goal of you all is to God. It is He that will show you the truth of the matters in which you dispute. (Qur'an 5:48)

Sirry discusses the interpretation of this verse by prominent public intellectuals in the United States (Abdulaziz Sachedina), Indonesia (Nurcholis Majid), and India (Asghar Ali Engineer). According to Sirry, Sachedina argues for a pluralism in the Qur'an that was suppressed by a later hegemonic caliphal state. In the absence of religious hegemony in modern states and societies, the true meaning of this verse may be recovered. More generally, Sachedina has argued that a primary moral and ethical responsibility in the Qur'an offers a foundation for religious pluralism.[19] According to Nurcholish Majid in Indonesia, Muslims should distinguish between an absolute truth of inclusivity and human subjective understandings. The place for the Other may be found in the former.[20] The Indian public intellectual Asghar Engineer emphasized the unity of religions which may only be differentiated by the good that believers of various religious faiths do. Sirry concludes that there was no fixed meaning to the verse studied by the intellectuals and that new meanings were by them in contemporary times.[21]

Such inclusive meanings are not universally accepted by contemporary Muslim scholars, as is shown in a book on salvation in Islam edited by Mohammad Hassan Khalil.[22] The book includes reflections on disbelief in the Qur'an by Yasir Qadhi, Reza Shah-Kazemi, and Sajjad Rizvi. Qadhi disagrees with the inclusive interpretation in modern readings of Qur'an, arguing that these have distorted its exclusive message of salvation for Muslims.[23] Shah-Kazemi agrees with Qadhi but suggests that such exoteric readings obscure an esoteric reading of inclusivity.[24] Rizvi's study of Shabestari and Soroush echoes the view of Nurcholish Majid mentioned above. According to Rizvi, these two prominent reformists in Iran offer an interpretation of the Qur'an that stresses the subjectivity of its readers.[25] The articles in the edited volume demonstrate that disbelief and salvation were subject to divergent views among contemporary scholars, ranging between exclusive, literal meanings and mediated meanings through reader subjectivities. They show how some contemporary readers are extending the reading of inclusive salvation in the Qur'an against strong resistance.

Studies on the Qur'an have employed historical, literary, and semiotic approaches that point to a complex meaning of belief and disbelief. Some see a clear binary relation between belief and disbelief (Izutsu, Qadhi), while others show a historically grounded meaning of disbelief that unfolds over time (Waldman and Afsaruddin). In response to global challenges of the late twentieth and twenty-first centuries, reformist Muslim scholarship has pointed to nuances that challenge a binary reading of belief and disbelief. Using historical and literary analysis, they have justified an inclusive message in the Qur'an for late modernity. However, these approaches used to study belief and disbelief hardly pay any attention to the aesthetics of belief and disbelief.

This chapter contributes to this discussion on the religious Other by focusing on the *aisthesis* (a sensory experience) of the Qur'an through z-y-n verses and their implication for belief and disbelief. The aesthetic condition of belief and disbelief points to a middle way between inclusivist and exclusivist readings of the Qur'an. It intimates the fragility of judgment, which in turn opens a space for an empathetic reading of disbelief and a self-reflexive reading of belief.

AISTHESIS AND DISBELIEF

A sensory experience of disbelief is exemplified in the verse cited at the beginning of this essay: "So We have decked (*zayyannā*) out fair to every nation their deeds" (Q 6:108). Most z-y-n verses imply that a sensory perception of beauty leads to the rejection of the truth of revelation. This awareness invites an ethical relation toward the Other, namely, not to insult the gods that are thus beautified for all who hold them to be true. Moreover, there are some very powerful indicators in the Qur'an and in the exegetical archive that belief is also aesthetically mediated. In the following pages, an analysis of z-y-n verses in the Qur'an shows how adornment, belief, and disbelief are connected, and how this ethic toward the religious Other and to one's own belief may be revisited.

The triliteral root z-y-n words (*zayyana, zīna, izzayyanat*) appear forty-four times in the Qur'an. These verses may be divided into two broad groups. The first includes verses where *zayyana* (beautification) and *zīna* (beauty) refer to beauty in a generally amoral sense. The second larger group includes an explicit cognitive and moral dimension. This group may be further divided: twenty verses point to the negative implication of beautification for human belief and moral action, nine verses refer to beauty as a test for moral action, and one is unconditionally positive about the beauty of belief. I have included, in the latter, two other verses that point to the universality of aesthetic perception. I now offer an analysis of these groups (see table 3.1).

Thirteen verses refer to the beauty of creation and human life and do not directly imply belief or morality. Here are two examples that refer to the beauty of creation:

> We have set up in the heavens great constellations and endowed them with beauty (*zayyannāhā*) for all to behold. (Qur'an 15:16)

> We have adorned (*zayyannā*) the lower heaven with the adornment of the stars and to preserve against every rebel Satan. (Qur'an 37:6)

Beautification in these verses is directed to the contemplation of the natural world. They are examples of clear signs of revelation shown in creation.

Table 3.1 Analysis of z-y-n Verses in the Qur'an

Thematic	Neutral		Related to Morality or Belief		
	Creation	Mundane	Clearly Negative Human Zayyana	Negative: Test or Fleeting zīna	Positive and Universal Human
Count	6	6	20	9	1 plus 2
Verses in the Qur'an	15:16; 16:8; 37:6; 41:12; 67:5; 50:6	7:31,32; 20:59, 20: 87; 24:31, 24: 60;	2:212 (zuyyina); 3:14 (zuyyina); 6:43 (zayyan -S), 6:122 (zuyyina), 6: 137 (zayyana); 8:48 (zayyana -S); 9:37 (zuyyina); 10:12 (zuyyina), 10:88 (zīna); 13:33 (zuyyina); 15:39 (uzayyina Iblis); 16:63 (zayyana S); 27:4 (zayyannā G), 27: 24 (zayyana Amb); 29:38 (zayyan- S); 35:8 (zuyyina – G); 40:37 (zuyyina); 41:25 (zayyanū); 47:14 (zuyyina); 48:12 (zuyyina);	10:24; 11:15; 18:7, 18: 18:46; 28:60, 28:79; 33:28; 57:20;	49:7 6:108; 17:7

Eight verses of z-y-n refer to beauty in a mundane sense (clothing, festivals, and animals). The following demonstrates the breadth of beauty in social life:

> "Your tryst shall be upon the Feast Day [lit day of *zīna*]", said Moses. "Let the people be mustered at the high noon." (Qur'an 20:59)

> Such women as are past child-bearing and have no hope of marriage—there is no fault in them that they put off their clothes, so be it that they flaunt no ornament (*zīna*); but to abstain is better for them; and God is All-hearing, All-knowing. (Qur'an 24:60)

The following verse goes one step further by stating that beauty is part of God's creation to be enjoyed:

> Say: "Who has forbidden the ornament (*zīna*) of God which He brought forth for His servants, and the good things of His providing?" (Qur'an 7:32)

Together, these thirteen verses suggest that beauty is part of nature or the social world. There is no explicit allusion to the *aisthesis* of belief in these verses.

Going further, the next major group of verses (thirty-two) connects beautification with belief and moral action, mainly with a negative connotation. The negative effect of beautification is mainly attributed to the devil (*shaytān*) but occasionally to God. Sometimes, the passive form (*zuyyina*) is used, and the beautifying subject is assumed. An example from each is presented here:

> [I]f only, when Our might came upon them, they had been humble! But their hearts were hard, and Satan decked out fair (*zayyana*) to them what they were doing. (Qur'an 6:43)

The following is an example where God is the beautifying subject:

> Those who do not believe in the hereafter, we have beautified for them their deeds so they are blind. (Qu'ran 27: 4)

In the overwhelming number of verses (ten of twenty), the beautifying subject is implied with a passive voice:

> The world appears beautiful (*zuyyina*) to the unbelievers and they mock the believers. (Qur'an 2:212)

Beautified by the devil, God, or some other condition, these twenty verses indicate that beauty obscured belief and moral action.

These verses are supported by a further nine verses where beauty (*zīna*) is a probable moral or cognitive impediment. In these verses, the sensory perception of beauty is not unconditionally negative. Thus, beauty is trial in the following:

> We have appointed all that is on the earth for an adornment (*zīnatan*) for it, and that We may try which of them is fairest in works; and We shall surely make all that is on it barren dust. (Qur'an 18:7)

Sometimes, a more negative connotation may be inferred when the ephemerality of *zīna* is stressed:

> Wealth and children are an adornment (*zīna*) of this world's life; but good deeds, the fruit whereof endures forever, are of far greater merit in thy Sustainer's sight, and a far better source of hope. (Qur'an 18: 46)

Beauty is transient in comparison with that which is with God. Beauty may thus be a temptation that distracts one from belief and moral deeds. Taken together, these twenty-nine verses connote the impression that beautification affects belief and moral action negatively. Sensory perception does not lead to clarity and truth but reaffirms and consolidates disbelief and immoral action. Beauty acts as a veil to the truth.

However, a key Qur'anic verse gives a completely different impression of beautification as part of a commitment to belief. And then, there are two verses that imply that beautification is a universal human experience that cannot be avoided. These three verses tip the scale against a wholly negative connotation of the *aisthesis* in the Qur'an. In the following, beauty and beautification are central to virtue and belief:

> And know that the Messenger of God is among you. If he obeyed you in much of the affair, you would suffer; but God has endeared to you belief, making it beautiful (*zayyanahu*) in your hearts, and He has made detestable to you disbelief, ungodliness and disobedience. Those—they are the right-minded. (Qur'an 49:7)

The verse refers to the community of Muslims formed around the Prophet Muhammad. Belief (*īmān*) and obedience to the Prophet were made beautiful and agreeable to those with Muhammad. Beautification is here central to a virtuous self and community. *Aisthesis* in the life of the first Muslims was central to their belief and moral action.

In addition, two verses declare that beauty, belief, and moral action are a universal human experience. The verse with which I started this essay makes beautification part of every moral judgment: "So We have decked out fair (*zayyannā*) to *every* nation their deeds" (emphasis mine). The fragment suggests that aesthetics is an inescapable part of human judgment. The following verse makes a similar universal statement: "We have appointed all that is on the earth an adornment, so that We may try which of them is fairest in works" (Qur'an 18:7). These two verses indicate that sensory experience cannot be dissociated in experiencing the world and thus are involved in all forms of beliefs and moral actions.

The signification of z-y-n in the Qur'an indicates that beautification is primarily a negative and threatening condition of human belief and moral life. Beauty may sometimes be neutral concerning morality or belief, but it is overwhelmingly deleterious toward correct belief and moral action. But the positive connotation of beauty in the Prophet's community weighs against the generally negative *aisthesis* for belief and good deeds. Moreover, verses 6:108 and 18:7 indicate that beatification is a universal condition of moral life that cannot be avoided. Belief and disbelief are always mediated through sensory experience (*aisthesis*).

With this analysis of *z-y-n* verses, I return to the verse with which I opened the essay to consider the ethical implication of beautification for the religious other:

Abuse not those whom they worship, apart from God, or they will abuse God in revenge without knowledge. *So We have decked out fair to every nation their deeds*; then to their Lord they shall return, and He will tell them what they have been doing. (Qur'an 6:108)

The universal *aisthesis* in the phrase comes immediately after a moral action about the other is commanded. One may read the phrase as a justification or an explanation for not abusing or insulting those who hold beliefs that are not true (as far as the Qur'an is concerned). Readers of the Qu'ran are given a reason for the moral action expected of believers. From this point of departure, one may read the other occurrences of z-y-n in the Qur'an as a further elaboration of the beatification of disbelief and immoral action. Believers might always remember that the beliefs and actions of disbelievers are made beautiful for them. Moreover, the presence of this aesthetic mediation in the community of the Prophet confirms that beautification and beauty are also present in the experience of truth. Aisthesis cannot be dissociated from any moral or cognitive judgment and in turn points to a particular moral action. The ethical command suggests empathy for those who experience the world differently.

The *aisthesis* of the z-y-n (beauty) in human judgment does not advocate pluralism or universality of belief. The overwhelming aesthetic experience of belief supports a commitment to the truth revealed and disclosed to the other. But the general human condition of aesthetics in belief and disbelief opens the door to empathy for the other in their persistent rejection of the truth. The awareness of *aisthesis* prepares the ground for appreciation and not an outright condemnation of the other. I turn now to some exegesis of the Qur'an that has appreciated this challenging condition.

MORAL IMPLICATION OF BEAUTY AND BEAUTIFICATION IN ISLAMIC DISCOURSE

The intellectual history of Islam has addressed the aesthetics of belief and disbelief in various ways. The question of beatification challenged the Muʿtazili view of ultimate human responsibility. More widely, the question of beauty and belief has also been discussed in the exegesis of the Qur'an (*tafsīr*). I begin with two Mu'tazili deliberations on z-y-n in the Qur'an and then turn to the exegesis of two of the verses examined in the previous section. I show that while aesthetics has been seen as a challenge to moral action, it has generally been embraced for individual ethical development. A full appreciation of the aesthetics of disbelief may be added to this tradition.

Among theologians in the history of Islam, the Muʿtazila have argued that humans are entirely responsible for their moral decisions. While Ashʿari opponents attribute ultimate moral rectitude and salvation to the will of God, the Muʾtazila emphasize the human perception of values and responsibility.[26] I begin with the Zaydī Imam Yaḥyā b. al-Ḥusayn b. al-Qāsim (245/859–297/910) who are known to have held Muʿtazili leanings in general (Madelung 2002). He discussed tazyīn and human responsibility in a treatise entitled "Kitāb al-Radd wa 'l-iḥtijāj ʿalā al-Ḥasan b. Muḥammad al-Ḥanafiyyah."[27] In Qur'an 6:108 ("So We have decked (zayyannā) out fair to every nation their deeds"), he highlighted its historical meaning, arguing that the verse was revealed for Abū Jahl (the inveterate opponent of the Prophet Muhammad). In pointing to its specific (khāṣṣ) purpose, Imām Yaḥyā implied that the verse was not universally applicable (ʿāmm). Concerning the other verses of z-y-n, the Imam says that God had given disbelievers many opportunities to revert to the truth. God used beauty to delay what they justly deserved for their iniquity.

The question of beautification and belief was also discussed by Qāḍī ʿAbd al-Jabbār b. Aḥmad al-Hamadānī (d. 415H), one of the leading Muʿtazila thinkers whose work has been extensively studied in recent years. His interpretation is very similar to the Zaydi Zaydī Imam. In his *Mutashābih al-Qurʾān* (Allegories in the Qur'an), Qāḍī ʿAbd al-Jabbār also emphasizes human responsibility against the apparent meaning of the z-y-n verses. He recognizes that Qur'an 6:108 demands an interpretation and says that beautification is a form of recommendation for an act that does not take away human responsibility.[28] Concerning the verses that suggest that God or the devil beautifies moral action, he says that they should be read as forms of encouragement (targhīb) and discouragement (tarhīb). They do not limit human responsibility for moral action in any way.[29]

Privileging reason and human responsibility, al-Qāḍī ʿAbd al-Jabbār and Imam Yaḥyā downplayed any *aesthesis* in the perception of the world and scripture. For them, the aesthetics of z-y-n was merely a medium through which moral responsibility was made known. The Muʿtazili reflection on these verses shows that the aesthetics of belief challenged their view of moral action guided by reason alone. Despite the evident meaning of these verses, they insisted that humans can apprehend values and act upon them. They seem to avoid the full implication of the aesthetics of belief mentioned in these verses in the Qur'an.

In contrast to the theologians, the exegetical literature (*tafsīr*) did not avoid the implications of aesthetics of belief and disbelief. Various works of commentary show an engagement with the aesthetics of belief and disbelief. Selecting nine authors from al-Ṭabarī in the ninth century to Ibn ʿAjība in the late eighteenth century, I discuss the exegesis of two verses (6:108 and 3:14) on aesthetics, ethics, and human responsibility. My selection includes Sunni, Muʿtazili, Ashʿari, Shiʿi, and Sufi interpretations:

Jāmiʿ al-bayān fī tafsīr āyi al-qurʾān, by the great historian and exegete Muḥammad b. Jarīr al-Ṭabarī. (d. 923/310)

al-Kashshāf ʿan ḥaqāʾiq al-tanzīl wa ʿuyūn al-aqāwīl fī wujūh al-taʾwīl by the Muʿtazilite Muḥmūd b. ʿUmar al-Zamakhsharī. (d. 467/1075 to 538/1144)

al-Jāmiʿ li aḥkām al-Qurʾān wa ʾl-mubayyin limā taḍammana min al-sunna wa āyāt al-furqān, by the Cordoban-born Mālikī exegete ʿAbd Allah Muḥammad b Aḥmad al-Anṣārī al-Qurṭubī. (d. 671/1272)

al-Tibyān Jāmiʿ al-ʿulūm al-qurʾān, by the great Shi'i scholar Muḥammad b. Ḥasan u. (597/1201 to 672/1274)

Anwār al-tanzīl wa asrār al-taʾwīl, by ʿAbd Allah b. ʿUmar al-Bayḍāwi. (d. 6851286 or 692/1293 or 716/1316)

al-Ṣāfī fī tafsīr kalām allah al-wāfī, by the Shi'ī commentator of Ibn al-ʿArabī, ʿAbd al-Razzāq al-Kāshānī. (d. between 730–6/1329–35)

al-Baḥr al-Madīd fī tafsīr ʿan Qurʾān al-majīd, by the Darqāwī Sufi Aḥmad Ibn ʿAjība. (1747–1809)

The exegetical archive offers a rich palette of reflections on beauty and human responsibility in Qur'an 6: 108 ("So We have decked (*zayyannā*) out fair to every nation their deeds"). Zamakhshari and al-Ṭūsī follow the Muʿtazili position I have discussed above: only disbelief is beautified which does not take away human decision-making and responsibility. Against this position, al-Ṭabarī, al-Qurṭūbī, al-Bayḍāwi, al-Kāshānī, and Ibn ʿAjība say that both belief and disbelief are beautified.

Al-Qurṭūbī and al-Bayḍāwi stand out for drawing an ethical principle from the verse. They say that a good deed (insulting false gods in this example) may not be permitted when it would lead to a worse outcome (insulting the true God). Al-Qurṭūbī specifically recalls the juridical principle for this ethic (*sadd al-dharāʾiʿ* [closing the door to adverse outcomes]). The Sufi Ibn ʿAjība goes further than al-Qurṭūbī and al-Bayḍāwi by recognizing an ethical opportunity in *aisthesis* in this verse. The believer sees an allusion (*ishāra*) for ethical self-formation everywhere:

> [T]he real knower does not neglect any of the creation of God, and he does not belittle that which God has determined, but he grows his ethical self (*yataʾdddabu*) with everything, as he sees the creation (*ṣunʿat*) of God in

everything. And so the wise (*al-labīb*) seeker creates himself from the appearance of everything in his time, whether it is truthful or not.[30]

Belief and disbelief provide material for reflection and, more importantly, self-formation. Ibn ʿAjība's vision of good and evil is led by an expansive appreciation of the multiplicity and contradiction of appearances (aesthetic experience). He recognizes the value of the aesthesis of the world for moral refinement.

Qur'an 3:14 ("Decked out fair (*zuyyina*) for humans is the love of desires (*shahawāt*)") has attracted equally detailed elaboration. The exegesis has focused on the agents of beautification (God or the devil), the nature of desires, and how they might be overcome. The passive form of beautification in this verse (*zuyyina*) prompted exegetes to reflect on the agent of beautification. Most say that God is the ultimate beautifier, but some also mention the role of the devil (*shayṭān*) as a possibility (al-Qurṭūbī, al-Ṭūsī, Bayḍāwī). Zamakhsharī supports the argument that God is the one who beautifies desires but reports a statement from Ḥasan al-Baṣrī, the pious ascetic, that the devil is also a beautifier.[31] In contrast, al-Qurtubī believes that only God is the beautifier. But he too cites in full the statement attributed to Ḥasan al-Baṣrī that God and the devil beautify moral action in different ways:

وقالت فرقة: المزيّن هو الشيطان وهو ظاهر قول الحسن، فإنه قال: مَنْ زيّنَها؟ ما أحدٌ أشدّ لها ذَمّا من خالقها. فتزيين الله تعالى إنما هو بالإيجاد والتهيئة للانتفاع وإنشاء الجِلّة على الميل إلى هذه الأشياء. وتزيين الشيطان إنما هو بالوَسْوَسة والخديعة وتحسين أخْذِها من غير وجوهها .

> One group said that the one who beautifies is the devil, which is the evident statement of al-Ḥasan: "Who has beautified it? No one has blamed it more than its creator. The beautification (*tazyīn*) from God happens through the creation and facilitation of the useful, and by creating inclinations to these (good) things. In contrast, the devil beautifies by whispering, and treachery, and the misperception of its true realities."[32]

Ibn ʿAjība adds to this tradition by saying that the devil has agency from a juridical perspective (*sharīʿatan*). The Sharīʿa is a "cloth to wipe away the 'dirt of the impurities'."[33] In contrast to the Maʿtazili scholars, the exegetes do not see a contraction between the final agency of God and human responsibility. Many quote the statement of Ḥasan al-Baṣrī to support the agency of the devil in addition to God. But they re-affirm the general Ashʿari position that God is the ultimate agent.

Al-Qurṭubī's reference to the caliph ʿUmar's response to this verse shows more clearly the close connection between beauty and belief. The caliph is reported to have said: "Now, God, you have made this beautiful for us!"[34]

Al-Qurṭubī then connects this verse with Qur'an (18:7): "Verily, we have made all that is on the earth as an ornament (*zīna*) for it, that We may try them as to which of them is best in conduct". Al-Qurṭubī narrates the caliph's response to this verse as well: "God, we can only be happy with what you have beautified for us. We ask your help that we expend (*unfiqahu*) that which is due to it."[35] The caliph recognizes God's favor for beautifying belief and virtuous action and expresses gratitude for determining his belief and conviction. As narrated by al-Qurṭubī, the caliph's response reveals the fragility of the judgment on belief and disbelief due to its aesthetic mediation. His statements suggest that he could have experienced the beauty of evil or disbelief. Al-Qurṭubī connects a verse that may be read as a criticism of one deluded by beauty Qur'an (3:14) with one in which beauty is ubiquitous Qur'an (18:7). Linking the two verses through the words of the caliph, his exegesis confirms beautification as an inescapable part of the human experience of belief and disbelief. While al-Qurṭubī supports generally ʿAsharī position that God creates all, he also alludes to a general aesthetic condition of experience. With this statement, al-Qurṭūbī goes beyond those deluded by the beauty of the world and reminds readers of the Qur'an that a pious believer like the caliph is also vulnerable.

On Qur'an (3:14), exegetes also discuss the source and the nature of desires as enumerated in the verse: "women, progeny, gold and silver, horses, livestock and crop." The exegetical discussion of desires points to beauty, sometimes as obstruction and sometimes as value. The general drift is toward desires as unavoidable, with some seeing more value than others in them. Al-Ṭabarī limits his discussion on this verse to the specific occasion on which it was revealed, namely, in his view of the Jews who loved the world and leadership. The other exegetes offer a more general conception of desires and beauty. Al-Kāshānī discusses in detail the beauty of women as the greatest source of desires to the detriment of ethical development. Al-Kāshāni also says that desires are determined by God, but they are mirror images of desires in the afterlife.[36] Al-Qurṭubī agrees but concludes more positively that women and men were created to be desirable for each other.[37] Taking a more philosophical approach, Zamaksharī sees desires as essences (*aʿyān*) obscured by beautification.[38] On the contrary, al-Ṭūsī sees desires as necessities without which human life is impossible.[39] Ibn ʿAjība again associates desires to aesthetic experiences and ethical possibilities (*ishāra*): "everything that prevents the listener to witness, or break his journey to the worshipped king (*al-malik al-maʿbūd*), is a desire" and "everything that presents its sweetness, but does not lead to witnessing and the essence, it is in its nature a desire."[40]

In their exegesis of Qur'an (3:14), then, the aesthetic mediation of desires is highlighted. The exegetical tradition reveals an attempt to show the essential and valuable role played by desires toward an ethical life. Ibn ʿAjība reveals the full potential of beauty for a path that leads to the consciousness of God. But the other exegetes point to the obstruction of desires (whether in women, necessities or conjugal life) that turn men (and women too) away from God. The exegesis shows a keen apprehension of the aesthetic experience of the good through desires.

CONCLUSION

Sensory perception of belief and disbelief may be added to recent scholarly reflections on belief and disbelief in the Qur'an. Belief and disbelief were not only derived from a cognitive engagement with signs of God in scripture and the world. Sensory perception played a central role in the work done by the verses as signs (*āyāt*). Most of the verses in the Qur'an suggest that sensory perception was efficacious for truth and values. But some verses unsettled this promise of clarity that leads to belief and moral action. In particular, this essay shows that the verses of z-y-n pointed to an unavoidable aesthetic condition of the perception of belief and disbelief. Beautification mediated belief and disbelief. And that mediation was self-reflexive and encouraged an ethical stance toward the Other.

My analysis of z-y-n in the Qur'an revealed that, in most verses, the "aesthesis" of beatification was deleterious for belief and moral life. But then I showed that a universal human aesthetic condition implied that *aisthesis* could not be avoided. Its efficacy of beauty in the belief and moral rectitude of the companions of the Prophet was a counterpart to the negative connotations of beauty and beautification elsewhere. The implications of beauty and beatification were not lost in Qur'an exegesis. From al-Ṭabarī to ibn ʿAjība, exegesis addressed the consequences of beauty for belief and morality. Most of the exegesis grappled with accounting for human responsibility in the face of a divinely created aesthetic that obscured moral life. But then, the references to beauty and beautification led to the inescapable connection between the experience of beauty and belief and moral action.

The z-y-n verses suggest that the universal aesthetic condition of moral life cannot be ignored in the Qur'an. This universality makes fragile all human apprehension and expression. Qur'an 6:108 connects aesthetics with an ethic toward the other. The verse did not merely advocate a pragmatic approach to ethics that prevents greater evil. The latter was only the starting point to an opaque aesthetic of the Qur'an. The declaration that God has "decked out fair to every group their deeds" does not stop at assessing the consequences of actions. It suggests, as some of the exegesis has alluded, to truth and morality that can only be encountered through aesthetics. And that means that one appreciates the other, even if the other is opposed to one's beliefs and values, with a great deal of sympathy and some self-doubt.

NOTES

1. All translations are based on Arberry, Arthur J., *The Koran Interpreted* (London; New York: George Allen & Unwin Ltd.; The Macmillan Co, 1955).
2. Issa Boullata, "The Rhetorical Interpretation of the Qur'ān: I'jāz and Related Topics," in *Approaches to the History of the Interpretation of the Qur'an*, edited by Andrew Rippin (Oxford: Clarendon Press, 1988), pp. 139–57; also Angelika Neuwirth, "Rhetoric and the Qur'ān," in *Encyclopaedia of the Qur'ān*, edited by Jane Dammen McAuliffe, 4:461–476 (Leiden: Brill, 2001). Mustansir Mir, "Some Figures of Speech in the Qur'an," *Religion & Literature* (2008) 40 (3): 31–48.
3. Mustansir Mir, "Thematic and Structural Coherence in the Qur'an: A Study of Islahi's Concept of 'naẓm'," Diss. (University of Michigan, 1983); also Mustansir Mir, "The Sūra as a Unity: A Twentieth-Century Development in Qur'ān Exegesis," in *Approaches to the Qur'ān*, edited by G. R. Hawting and Abdul-Kader A. Shareef (London: Routledge, 1993), pp. 211–24.
4. Navid Kermani, *Offenbarung als Kommunikation: Das Conzept Waḥy in Naṣr Abū Zayds Mafhūm Al-Naṣṣ* (Frankfurt: Peter Lang, 1996); see also Setiawan, M Nur Kholis, "Liberal Thought in Qur'anic Studies: Tracing Humanistic Approach to Sacred Text in Islamic Scholarship." *Al-Jami'ah: Journal of Islamic Studies* (2007) 45 (1): 2–28; Shuruq Naguib, "Bint al-Shāṭl''s Approach to Tafsīr: An Egyptian Exegete's Journey from Hermeneutics to Humanity." *Journal of Qur'anic Studies* (2015) 17 (1): 45–84; and Mohammad Izdiyan Muttaqin, "Afkār Amīn al-Khulī fī ta'līm al-balāgha al-'arabiyyah." *Arabiyat : Jurnal Pendidikan Bahasa Arab dan Kebahasaaraban* (2017) 4 (1): 39–57.
5. 'Ā'isha 'Abd al-Raḥmān (Bint al-Shāṭi'), *Al-I'jāz al-Bayān li 'l-Qur'ān wa Masā'il Ibn Azraq: Dirāsa Qur'āinyya Lughawiyya Bayāniyya* (Cairo: Dār al-ma'ārif, 1984).
6. Nasr Abu Zayd, "The Qur'an: God and Man in Communication." Lecture published on line (2000): http://www.let.leidenuniv.nl/forum/01_1/onderzoek/lecture.pdf
7. Brigit Meyer and Jojada Verrips, "Aesthetics," in *Key Works in Religion, Media and Culture*, edited by David Morgan (Routledge, 2008), p. 21.
8. Brigit Meyer and Jojada Verrips, "Aesthetics," in *Key Works in Religion, Media and Culture*, edited by David Morgan (Routledge, 2008), pp. 20–30; see also Birgit Meyer, "Introduction: From Imagined Communities to Aesthetic Formations: Religious Mediations, Sensational Forms, and Styles of Binding," in *Aesthetic Formations: Media, Religion, and the Senses*, edited by Birgit Meyer, (New York: Palgrave, 2009), pp. 1–28; see also David Chidester, "Aesthetic Strategies in Western Religious Thought." *Journal of The American Academy of Religion* (1983) 51 (1):

55–66.; and David Morgan, "The Look of Sympathy: Religion, Visual Culture, and the Social Life of Feeling." *Material Religion* (2009) 5 (2): 132–54.

9. Stefan Wild (ed.), *Self-Referentiality in the Qurʾān* (Wiesbaden: Harrassowitz Verlag, 2006).

10. Toshihiko Izutsu, *God and Man in the Koran: Semantics of the Koranic Weltanschauung* (Tokyo: The Keio Institute of Cultural and Linguistic Studies, 1964), p. 3.

11. Toshihiko Izutsu, *The Concept of Belief in Islamic Theology: A Semantic Analysis of Īmān and Islām* (Tokyo: The Keio Institute of Cultural and Linguistic Studies, 1965); Izutsu, *God and Man in the Koran.*

12. Marilyn Robinson Waldman, "The Development of the Concept of Kufr in the Qur'Ān." *Journal of the American Oriental Society* (1968) 88 (3): 442–55, p. 449.

13. Ibid., p. 452.

14. Omar Farahat, *The Foundation of Norms in Islamic Jurisprudence and Theology* (Cambridge University Press, 2019). Feriel Bouhafa, "The Dialectics of Ethics: Moral Ontology and Epistemology in Islamic Philosophy," *Journal of Arabic and Islamic Studies* (2021): 21, Towards new perspectives on ethics in Islam: casuistry, contingency, and ambiguity, pp. 25–54.

15. Marilyn Robinson Waldman, "The Development of the Concept of *Kufr* in the Qur'Ān," *Journal of the American Oriental Society* (1968) 88 (3): 442–55.

16. Mohamed Arkoun, "Rethinking Islam Today," *Annals of the American Academy of Political and Social Science*, Islam: Enduring myths and changing realities (2003) 588: 18–39.

17. Richard C. Martin, "Clifford Geertz Observed: Understanding Islam as Cultural Symbolism," in *Anthropology and the Study of Religion*, edited by Robert L. Moore and Frank E. Reynolds (Chicago: Center for the Scientific Study of Religion, 1984), pp. 11–30; also Tim Murphy, "Elements of a Semiotic Theory of Religion," *Method & Theory in the Study of Religion* (2003) 15 (1): 48–67.

18. Asma Afsaruddin, "The Hermeneutics of Inter-Faith Relations: Retrieving Moderation and Pluralism as Universal Principles in Qur'anic Exegeses." *The Journal of Religious Ethics* (2009) 37 (2): 331–54, p. 352

19. Abdulaziz Sachedina, "Islamic Theology of Christian-Muslim Relations," *Islam and Christian–Muslim Relations* (1997) 8 (1): 27–38; also Abdulaziz Sachedina, "Advancing Religious Pluralism in Islam," *Religion Compass* (2010) 4 (4): 221–33.

20. Nurcholis Madjid, *The True Face of Islam: Essays on Islam and Modernity in Indonesia* (Jakarta: Voice Center Indonesia, 2003).

21. Mun'im Sirry, "'Compete With One Another in Good Works': Exegesis of Qur'an Verse 5.48 and Contemporary Muslim Discourses on Religious Pluralism," *Islam & Christian-Muslim Relations* (2009) 20 (4): 423–38.

22. Mohammad Hassan Khalil, ed., *Between Heaven and Hell: Islam, Salvation, and the Fate of Others* (Oxford University Press, 2013).

23. Yasir Qadhi, "The Path of Allah or the Paths of Allah? Revisiting Classical and Medieval Sunni Approaches to the Salvation of Others," in *Between Heaven and Hell: Islam, Salvation, and the Fate of Others*, edited by Hassan Khalil Mohammad (Oxford University Press, 2013).

24. Reza Shah-Kazemi, "Beyond Polemics and Pluralism: The Universal Message of the Qur'an," in *Between Heaven and Hell: Islam, Salvation, and the Fate of Others*, edited by Hassan Khalil Mohammad (New York, NY: Oxford University Press, 2013).

25. Sajjad H. Rizvi, "Oneself as the Saved Other? The Ethics and Soteriology of Difference in Two Muslim Thinkers," in *Islam and the Fate of Others: The Salvation Question*, edited by Mohammad Hassan Khalil (New York: Oxford University Press, 2012).

26. Omar Farahat, *The Foundation of Norms in Islamic Jurisprudence and Theology* (Cambridge University Press, 2019); and Kambiz Ghaneabassir, "The Epistemological Foundation of Conceptions of Justice in Classical "kalām": A Study of ʿAbd Al-Jabbār's "Al-Mughnī" and Ibn Al-Bāqillānī's "Al-Tamhīd"," *Journal of Islamic Studies* (2008) 19 (1): 71–96., 73)

27. "The Rebuttal and Response to al-Ḥasan b. Muḥammad b. al-Ḥanafiyya on Determinism, the confirmation of Truth and the contradiction of his statement.

28. Qāḍī ʿAbd al-Jabbār n.d, 257.

29. Qāḍī ʿAbd al-Jabbār n.d, pp. 257, 260-1.

30. Ibn ʿAjība, *al-Baḥr al-Madīd,* Accessed 14 March 2023, at https://www.altafsir.com/Tafasir.asp?tMadhNo=3&tTafsirNo=37&tSoraNo=6&tAyahNo=108&tDisplay=yes&UserProfile=0&LanguageId=1

31. al-Zamakhsharī, *al-Kashshāf*, accessed 14 March 2023, at https://www.altafsir.com/Tafasir.asp?tMadhNo=1&tTafsirNo=2&tSoraNo=3&tAyahNo=14&tDisplay=yes&UserProfile=0&LanguageId=1

32. al-Qurṭubī, *al-Jāmiʿ li aḥkām al-Qurʾān*, accessed 14 March 2023, at https://www.altafsir.com/Tafasir.asp?tMadhNo=1&tTafsirNo=5&tSoraNo=3&tAyahNo=14&tDisplay=yes&UserProfile=0&LanguageId=1

33. Ibn ʿAjība, *al-Baḥr al-Madīd,* Accessed 14 March 2023, at https://www.altafsir.com/Tafasir.asp?tMadhNo=3&tTafsirNo=37&tSoraNo=3&tAyahNo=14&tDisplay=yes&UserProfile=0&LanguageId=1

34. al-Qurṭubī, *al-Jāmiʿ li aḥkām al-Qurʾān*, accessed 14 March 2023, at https://www.altafsir.com/Tafasir.asp?tMadhNo=1&tTafsirNo=5&tSoraNo=3&tAyahNo=14&tDisplay=yes&UserProfile=0&LanguageId=1

35. al-Qurṭubī, *al-Jāmiʿ li aḥkām al-Qurʾān*, accessed 14 March 2023, at https://www.altafsir.com/Tafasir.asp?tMadhNo=1&tTafsirNo=5&tSoraNo=18&tAyahNo=7&tDisplay=yes&UserProfile=0&LanguageId=1

36. al-Kāshānī, *al-Ṣāfī fī tafsīr kalām allah al-wāfī*, accessed 14 March 2023, at https://www.altafsir.com/Tafasir.asp?tMadhNo=4&tTafsirNo=41&tSoraNo=3&tAyahNo=14&tDisplay=yes&Page=2&Size=1&LanguageId=1

37. al-Qurṭubī, *al-Jāmiʿ li aḥkām al-Qurʾān,* accessed 14 March 2023, at https://www.altafsir.com/Tafasir.asp?tMadhNo=1&tTafsirNo=5&tSoraNo=3&tAyahNo=14&tDisplay=yes&Page=2&Size=1&LanguageId=1

38. al-Zamakhsharī, *al-Kashshāf*, accessed 14 March 2023, at https://www.altafsir.com/Tafasir.asp?tMadhNo=1&tTafsirNo=2&tSoraNo=3&tAyahNo=14&tDisplay=yes&UserProfile=0&LanguageId=1

39. al-Ṭūsī, *al-Tibyān Jāmiʿ al-ʿulūm al-qurʾān*, accessed 14 March 2023 at https://www.altafsir.com/Tafasir.asp?tMadhNo=4&tTafsirNo=3&tSoraNo=3&tAyahNo=14&tDisplay=yes&UserProfile=0&LanguageId=1

40. Ibn ʿAjība, al-Baḥr al-Madīd, Accessed 14 March 2023, at https://www.altafsir.com/Tafasir.asp?tMadhNo=3&tTafsirNo=37&tSoraNo=3&tAyahNo=14&tDisplay=yes&Page=2&Size=1&LanguageId=1

REFERENCES

Abū al-Ḥusayn Yaḥyā b. al-Ḥusayn b. al-Qāsim b. Ibrāhim. 1988. "Kitāb al-Radd wa 'l-iḥtijāj ʿalā al-Ḥasan b. Muḥammad al-Ḥanafiyyah." In *Rasāʾil al-ʿadl wa 'l-tawḥīd*, edited by Muḥammad ʿImāra, 2:111–280. Cairo: Dār al-Shurūq.
Abu Zayd, Nasr. 2000. "The Qur'an: God and Man in Communication." http://www.let.leidenuniv.nl/forum/01_1/onderzoek/lecture.pdf,
Afsaruddin, Asma. 2009. "The Hermeneutics of Inter-Faith Relations: Retrieving Moderation and Pluralism as Universal Principles in Qur'anic Exegeses." *The Journal of Religious Ethics* 37 (2): 331–54.
ʿĀʾisha ʿAbd al-Raḥmān (Bint al-Shāṭiʾ). 1984. *Al-Iʿjāz al-Bayān li 'l-Qurʾān wa Masāʾil Ibn Azraq: Dirāsa Qurʾāinyya Lughawiyya Bayāniyya*. Cairo: Dār al-maʿārif.
Arberry, Arthur J. 1955. *The Koran Interpreted*. London; New York: George Allen & Unwin Ltd.; The Macmillan Co.
Arkoun, Mohamed. 2003. "Rethinking Islam Today." *Annals of the American Academy of Political and Social Science* 588, Islam: Enduring myths and changing realities, 18–39.
Bouhafa, Feriel. 2021. "The Dialectics of Ethics: Moral Ontology and Epistemology in Islamic Philosophy." *Journal of Arabic and Islamic Studies*, 21, Towards new perspectives on ethics in Islam: casuistry, contingency, and ambiguity, pp. 25–54.
Boullata, Issa. 1988. "The Rhetorical Interpretation of the Qur'ān: Iʿjāz and Related Topics." In *Approaches to the History of the Interpretation of the Qurʾan*, edited by Andrew Rippin, 139–57. Oxford: Clarendon Press.
Chidester, David. 1983. "Aesthetic Strategies in Western Religious Thought." *Journal of The American Academy of Religion* 51 (1): 55–66.
Farahat, Omar. 2019. *The Foundation of Norms in Islamic Jurisprudence and Theology*. Cambridge University Press.
Ghaneabassir, Kambiz. 2008. "The Epistemological Foundation of Conceptions of Justice in Classical "kalām": A Study of ʿAbd Al-Jabbār's "Al-Mughnī" and Ibn Al-Bāqillānī's "Al-Tamhīd"." *Journal of Islamic Studies* 19 (1): 71–96.
ʿImāra, Muḥammad, ed. 1988. *Rasāʾil al-ʿadl wa 'l-tawḥīd*. Cairo: Dār al-shurūq.
Izutsu, Toshihiko. 1964. *God and Man in the Koran: Semantics of the Koranic Weltanschauung*. Tokyo: The Keio Institute of Cultural and Linguistic Studies.
Izutsu, Toshihiko. 1965. *The Concept of Belief in Islamic Theology: A Semantic Analysis of Īmān and Islām*. Tokyo: The Keio Institute of Cultural and Linguistic Studies.
Kermani, Navid. 1996. *Offenbarung als Kommunikation: Das Conzept Waḥy in Naṣr Abū Zayds Mafhūm Al-Naṣṣ*. Frankfurt: Peter Lang.
Khalil, Mohammad Hassan, ed. 2013. *Between Heaven and Hell: Islam, Salvation, and the Fate of Others*. Oxford University Press.

Madelung, Wilfred. 2002. "Zaydiyya." In *Encyclopaedia of Islam*, edited by P. Bearman, Th. Bianquis, C.E. Bosworth, E. van Donzel, and W.P. Heinrichs, XI: 477–481. Leiden: Brill.

Madjid, Nurcholis. 2003. *The True Face of Islam: Essays on Islam and Modernity in Indonesia*. Jakarta: Voice Center Indonesia.

Martin, Richard C. 1984. "Clifford Geertz Observed: Understanding Islam as Cultural Symbolism." In *Anthropology and the Study of Religion*, edited by Robert L. Moore, and Frank E. Reynolds, 11–30. Chicago: Center for the Scientific Study of Religion.

Meyer, Birgit. 2009. "Introduction: From Imagined Communities to Aesthetic Formations: Religious Mediations, Sensational Forms, and Styles of Binding." In *Aesthetic Formations: Media, Religion, and the Senses*, edited by Birgit Meyer, 1–28. New York: Palgrave.

Meyer, Birgit, and Jojada Verrips. 2008. "Aesthetics." In *Key Works in Religion, Media and Culture*, edited by David Morgan, 20–30. Routledge.

Mir, Mustansir. 1983. "Thematic and Structural Coherence in the Qur'an: A Study of Islahi's Concept of '*naẓm*'." Diss., University of Michigan.

Mir, Mustansir. 1993. "The *Sūra* as a Unity: A Twentieth-Century Development in Qur'ān Exegesis." In *Approaches to the Qur'ān*, edited by G. R. Hawting, and Abdul-Kader A. Shareef, 211–24. London: Routledge.

Mir, Mustansir. 2008. "Some Figures of Speech in the Qur'an." *Religion & Literature* 40 (3): 31–48.

Morgan, David. 2009. "The Look of Sympathy: Religion, Visual Culture, and the Social Life of Feeling." *Material Religion* 5 (2): 132–54.

Murphy, Tim. 2003. "Elements of a Semiotic Theory of Religion." *Method & Theory in the Study of Religion* 15 (1): 48–67.

Muttaqin, Mohammad Izdiyan. 2017. "Afkār Amīn al-Khulī fī taʿlīm al-balāgha al-ʿarabiyyah." *Arabiyat : Jurnal Pendidikan Bahasa Arab dan Kebahasaaraban* 4 (1): 39–57.

Naguib, Shuruq. 2015. "Bint al-Shāṭī''s Approach to Tafsīr: An Egyptian Exegete's Journey from Hermeneutics to Humanity." *Journal of Qur'anic Studies* 17 (1): 45–84.

Nasr, Seyyed Hossein. 1990. *Islam, Art and Spirituality*. Delhi: Oxford University Press.

Neuwirth, Angelika. 2001. "Rhetoric and the Qur'ān." In *Encyclopaedia of the Qur'ān*, edited by Jane Dammen McAuliffe, 4:461–476. Leiden: Brill.

Qadhi, Yasir. 2013. "The Path of Allah or the Paths of Allah? Revisiting Classical and Medieval Sunni Approaches to the Salvation of Others." In *Between Heaven and Hell: Islam, Salvation, and the Fate of Others*, edited by Hassan Khalil Mohammad, 109–21. Oxford University Press.

Rizvi, Sajjad H. 2012. "Oneself as the Saved Other? The Ethics and Soteriology of Difference in Two Muslim Thinkers." In *Islam and the Fate of Others: The Salvation Question*, edited by Mohammad Hassan Khalil. New York, NY: Oxford University Press.

Sachedina, Abdulaziz. 1997. "Islamic Theology of Christian-Muslim Relations." *Islam and Christian–Muslim Relations* 8 (1): 27–38.

Sachedina, Abdulaziz. 2010. "Advancing Religious Pluralism in Islam." *Religion Compass* 4 (4): 221–233.
Schuon, Frithjof. 1975. *The Transcendent Unity of Religions*. New York: Harper & Row.
Setiawan, M Nur Kholis. 2007. "Liberal Thought in Qur'anic Studies: Tracing Humanistic Approach to Sacred Text in Islamic Scholarship." *Al-Jami'ah: Journal of Islamic Studies* 45 (1): 2–28.
Shah-Kazemi, Reza. 2013. "Beyond Polemics and Pluralism: The Universal Message of the Qur'an." In *Between Heaven and Hell: Islam, Salvation, and the Fate of Others*, edited by Hassan Khalil Mohammad, 87–105. Oxford University Press.
Sirry, Mun'im. 2009. "'Compete With One Another in Good Works': Exegesis of Qur'an Verse 5.48 and Contemporary Muslim Discourses on Religious Pluralism." *Islam & Christian-Muslim Relations* 20 (4): 423–38.
Waldman, Marilyn Robinson. 1968. "The Development of the Concept of *Kufr* in the Qur'ān." *Journal of the American Oriental Society* 88 (3): 442–55.
Wild, Stefan, ed. 2006. *Self-Referentiality in the Qur'ān*. Wiesbaden: Harrassowitz Verlag.

Chapter 4

The Islamic Inflection of Connective Justice

Between Cosmopolitan Civility, Institutional Relationality, and Intellectual Reflexivity

Armando Salvatore

Louay Safi has convincingly argued that the long trajectory of Islamic reform has played a role in the global process of idealistic rationalization of politics aiming to challenge the exploitation, oppression, and lack of justice resulting from the twin developments of the two systemic Molochs usually associated with modernity—namely the modern state and capitalism. Safi is keen on stressing the role of knowledge and thought in the form of "rational idealism" in the trajectory—a type of rationalism that cuts across civilizational boundaries and within which Islamic scholarly traditions acquired for long a historical primacy, prefiguring and affecting subsequent Western developments.[1] Likewise, in my previous work, I have argued that the intellectual vanguards of such thought in the modern West, exemplified by Habermas' theory of the public sphere, have built on premodern developments within Latin Christendom and, even more, on precolonial Islamic traditions—all while underplaying or denying their influence.[2]

However, I also felt the need to complement this type of cross-cultural intellectual history with a more sociological exploration of the cosmopolitan script of the civilizing process writ Islamic that enabled such developments.[3] In other words, even for "rational idealism" to arise and thrive, one needs a sustainable infrastructure of connective justice within society, able to form individual selves and inspire their collective ethos. This emerging type of sociology of Islam joins the history of thought to broader dimensions of political and civic culture—a step that is also resonant with Safi's approach.

In a further move, this line of analysis leads us to explore the distinctive institutional configuration that fed into a precolonial type of Islamic political modernity that resisted Western colonialism before succumbing to it. One still open question is whether this surrender to Western models (including the Westphalian state and its regulation of capitalism) was total and wholesale. In colonial and postcolonial times until today, several generations of Muslim reformers have tried to reinvent this Islamic heritage by combining it with non-oppressive, non-discriminatory, potentially emancipatory components of the hegemonic Western modernity. Of course, the effectiveness of such reform discourses is also contested.[4]

This chapter consists of three sections. The first section covers the civic and political culture inflected in terms that have been subsumed under "cosmopolitanism," whereby religion plays a meta-institutional role, that is, it provides the rationale, script, and ethos to institutional build-ups. This part includes a first assessment of the balance of merits and limits (long affected by cross-cultural myopia) of some fundamental concepts of Western sociology, most notably by Weber and Elias.

The second section delineates the rationality of the non-corporate institutional landscape that provided the flesh and bones to society within the broader Islamosphere, starting from a first reconstruction of some basic intuitions on the meta-institutional power of religion that we often associate with the sociology of Durkheim.

The third section briefly addresses how this legacy is still in the process of being reinvented through the turbulences of the colonial and postcolonial epochs, at the intersection of the rise of new social movements and continuous, if travailed, intellectual reflections on the postcolonial state–society relationship and particularly on the ever more visible gaps between fragile state sovereignty and the aspirations to autonomy within civic-public spaces. Like in the previous section, the fate of *waqf* (through the waves of its subjugation and revival) provides the primary foil to the analysis, which nonetheless cannot be brought to a conclusive dimension within the limited scope of this chapter.

THE COSMOPOLITAN ETHOS OF ISLAMIC CIVILITY

If our goal is to make sense of the original ethos of Islamic cosmopolitanism, the first step would be to question the nineteenth-century idea of a bifurcation between religion and civilization which was also adopted while making sense of Islam—an idea promulgated by European scholars of the age and still haunting most scholarship on Islam.[5] However, this questioning step, undertaken within the broader critique of Western Orientalism, would not be sufficient. While discarding the problematic concept of civilization, one needs to reflectively invest in how the notion of the institution was initially articulated from within the historical societies of the Islamosphere. I suggest exploring the extent to which the concept itself of the institution and its articulation in history, far from being a purely socio-political phenomenon, have a broadly cultural and specifically religio-intellectual foundation, which could match Safi's category of rational idealism. However, to perform this step, one must revisit the notion of civility, which, far from reproducing the rudimentary and biased idea of civilization, results from a complex, processual alchemy of knowledge and power within society and can provide the missing link between religion and institution.

In my book *Sociology of Islam*,[6] I undertook an analysis not so much of the Islamic discursive tradition and related practices as defined by Talal Asad's school, but rather of how some of their underlying ideas, which are religious at large, give form to social institutions. The main focus, from this sociological perspective, was on how institutions, broadly conceived, are formed at the intersection of religious ideas and demands for social regulation. To study the crucial intersection between religio-cultural ideas and social regulation, between knowledge and power, I critically focused on Norbert Elias' notion of the civilizing process. Far from reinstating the obsolete and biased notion of civilization in a new guise, in its crudest dimension enucleated by Elias a civilizing process could be seen as what we may nowadays define (after one global pandemic of massive proportions) as appropriate levels of social distancing among individuals, via restraint from undue bodily contacts—that is, the notion tends to be purely technical and does not retain any prejudiced view of civilized vs. uncivilized behavior. However, this fundamental dimension only represents the external level of regulation of social interaction finalized to minimizing the clash of bodies, that is, violence. An intermediate level is represented by codes of speech and non-verbal forms of etiquette, up to the level of social mannerisms and *bon ton*. Their inner kernel—and here I am going beyond Elias' understanding of the process—consists of instilling a sense of grace and even compassion among social interactants via the mores and customs that define a beautiful habitus and an ethical life form. It is not difficult to identify such a process, in Islamic contexts, as tied to the disciplines and genres of *adab*.

Indeed, while Elias used European examples, I preferred to employ Islamic ones. This is not just due to the main focus of my research but because the sociological approach of Elias tends to bundle together the various levels of the civilizing process into a reductionist pattern, by postulating their being strictly functional to instituting effective governance at the hands of a modern, centralized state. And yet, through more expansive sociological lenses, one could see state-building itself as imbricated in a broader (and deeper-going) type of socio-cultural transformations that are usually bracketed out by political theorists and political scientists but are intrinsic to the making itself of the social bond.

Elias' theory of the civilizing process represented an original inflection of Max Weber's search for the formulas of modern rationalization in capitalism and statehood. It provided a better integration of Weber's dichotomy between ideas and institutions. However, it was somewhat bent on describing how micro-processes of self-disciplining feed into macro-social processes of transformation, thus bracketing out solidarity and protest as engines of sociopolitical transformations at a meso-level. Therefore, Elias' approach could not fill the theoretical space previously taken by Weber's compelling yet perplexing notion of charisma—which continues to destabilize from within the paradigm that aspires to socio-culturally define specific modern forms of rationalization. No doubt, the idea of charisma at first evokes non-functional and non-evolutionary factors of social criticism and upheaval and often brings religion back into the picture, though frequently in non-conventional (non-institutional) guises. Weber's comparative sociology of religion in general and his ideas on charisma in particular have been often considered precursors of the more contemporary Axial Age theory that invests in the ethical revolution performed by prophets and sages of various regions around the middle of the first millennium BCE.[7]

Weber's opaque notion of charisma demarcates a particular type of practical knowledge that is powered up into a socioreligious and/or political movement under a gifted leadership able to acquire followers and build constituencies that subvert the balance of power in a given social context. While Elias' civilizing process works as a macro-engine of power-knowledge systematically disciplining the entire socio-political body through a trickle-down mechanism of manners and taste from the aristocracy through the bourgeoisie and, potentially, the entire population or citizenry, Weber's fuzzy notion of charisma reveals gaps and inconsistencies not only in the production and distribution of power in the social body but also in the knowledge-power chain of transmission—the process through which charismatic knowledge is turned into an effective movement leadership and, at a later stage, an institutional formation.

However, it is the fuzzy nature itself of the notion of charisma that accounts for unexpected, partly unexplainable outbursts of creativity and transgression of extant power balances through the shaping and propagation of original ideas of social and cosmic order. This is why the notion of charisma, despite Weber's efforts to turn it into a sociological concept, retains a distinctively mystical, unsociological side. It postulates an "originary," eruptive force producing cultural ideas, which, therefore, to the extent charismatic leaders and their movements succeed, are destined to be routinized into institutional forms that deplete the transformative elan of charisma's originary challenge.

This realization provides the doorway to conceptualizing the nature of an institution in terms that, as further explained below, highlight its religio-cultural foundations.

On the other hand, Weber's emphasis on charisma seems to fit his reluctance (in contrast to Durkheim) to preliminarily (or generally) define religion, given that according to the Heidelberg sociologist, a general understanding of religion should be the outcome of comparative analysis and theoretical work rather than being definitionally packaged at the outset of a research program.[8] In this sense, charisma is precisely what Weber preliminarily holds to be closest to religion as a force of ideas transcending a given social situation, especially to the extent he often identifies charismatic action and leadership with the tasks of magicians and prophets. This type of action represented for him the "other," as it were, of the spheres of social action determined by material factors and economic interests. In turn, Weber saw this immaterial force of history embodied through religious charisma as molding life conduct and ultimately providing the lifeline to what Elias would call the civilizing process. And yet, for Weber, the final outcome of the eruption and work of charisma in human communities is a process of routinization that leads to its institutionalization in the form of offices and statutes, which ultimately erode and destroy the pristine charisma. In the process, it is as if the forms of knowledge and conduct originating from charismatic (prophetic or otherwise) action impose limits and rules on how power is distributed and exercised not only at the top, among rulers and bureaucracies, but also in the citizenry. This is, in a nutshell, the process of formation of institutions in Weberian terms—from legislative assemblies down to free associational forms: a process that traps and codifies what used to be transformative charisma.

However, when Weber turned to the Islamosphere, he built a strategic contrast to what he saw as distinctively Western processes of rationalization. He turned the comparative study of differences into what looked very much like an inventory of deficits—aggravated by the fact that his references to Islam were mostly patchy and not sufficiently contextualized. The key institutions that only Europe possessed and the Islamosphere lacked were, accordingly, municipal autonomies. For Weber, the medieval European municipalities embodied autonomy (self-norming) in a chartered (legal and formulaic) fashion. This form guaranteed their autonomy from other institutions of the time, like the feudal lord and the rural monastery, up to the king, the pope, and the emperor. Of course, such autonomies rested on a legal fiction or, more precisely, on juridical constructions of ideas of charter, statute, and corporation provided by a singular combination of developments within the Roman law tradition, which we cannot cover here, given the limited scope of the chapter. It suffices to say that this tradition, in turn, was redirected by how Latin Christian theology invoked the idea of the body of Christ as a matrix to justify the collective juridical personality of institutions, both civil and ecclesiastical. Such institutions resulted from a long-drawn-out process of building reticulate, power-regulated hierarchies and networks, relying on highly hierarchical feudal ties of loyalty built on the ashes of the legal and institutional structure of the collapsed Western Roman Empire.[9]

A charter[10] thus provides the legitimacy suiting the specific legal parlance—and mytho-theological categories—of Latin Christendom. The fundamental mechanism here is the incorporation of individual subjects into a *corpus mysticum.* Both the body-politic and the capitalist corporations are built on the juridical presuppositions of corporate subjectivity, that is, the understanding of a corporation as a collective subject of rights. This process ultimately reflects a specific political theology, originating in the notion of the Church as the body of Christ. Modern civil law includes the law of incorporation as one of its most fundamental tenets. In this perspective, the Church as the body of Christ provides the model to any other collective association in becoming a corporate body thanks to a magico-sacramental uplifting of multitudes of subject positions into the collective body of an institution.

The often conceptually confused and/or biased dealing with (or outright neglect of) Islamic cases in Western comparative sociology, since after Weber, led to a lopsided narrative of Islam's decline within modernity strictly functional to establish sociological paradigms within Western academic discourse.[11] And yet, rather than finding comfort in denouncing the blatant orientalist prejudice of Western sociology, one should use the chance to critically build on its constructive side for enriching a historical sociology of Islam. This could be done by developing Weber's embryonic idea that an institution is defined and constructed differently within various traditions by drawing on specific religio-cultural ideas and ways of legal imagination. Given this variety in understanding and constructing institutions, in order to function, these do not need per se to be chartered and incorporated based on the theologico-political mythologies and juridical formatting that characterized the European trajectory of institution-building.

Combining Weber's intuitions and bias can also be used as a foil for determining what Western sociology neglects or obscures, even by contradicting its own premises and even why. However, this operation is not intended to reform or restore the missing integrity of Western sociology through an injection of critical, postcolonial sensibility. The Eurocentric faults of Western sociology's disciplinary development (and the legitimate question of "what went wrong with it," particularly in the study of Islam) will not be redeemed.[12] What I am attempting here is instead an inversion maneuver through which sociological concepts are built anew from within a perspective that attempts to restore the centrality of the Islamosphere[13] in the civilizational history of the "Old World," a centrality obscured and subverted by Western colonialism, imperialism, and Orientalism. Precisely given the affinity of the broader frameworks of "rational idealism" and even their deeper rooting within traditions, cultures, and sciences of the Islamosphere, I consider that what we may call the "sociological imagination" is not a monopoly of modern Western academia but is inherent in the reflections that accompany the process of building the social bond and the common good.

In this sense, by addressing the specific inflections of institutional flourishing and rationalization in the long-term unfolding of the civilizing process writ Islamic, one also provides a service to what is, by now, global sociology and social theory, helping their de-provincialization from their latently normative reliance on tendentially exclusivist Western concepts modeled on Westphalian patterns of state–society relationships. Global sociology and social theory need to account for what diverges from such patterns worldwide (even within the West itself), both in history and the present. The work to be done is to relocate some intuitions developed by Western social and political theorists but which were thwarted by their distorted lenses on Western exceptionalism and, often, superiority, by relocating them within themes and discussions belonging to the history of social relations in the Islamosphere, that is, as developed through the primary reflection of its actors and thinkers.

THE CIVIC RELATIONALITY OF RELIGION BETWEEN META-INSTITUTION AND INSTITUTION

One preparatory step in this direction would be to distinguish between religion as a source of civility and an institutional sphere, that is, between meta-institution and institution. In the sociology of Islam, the meta-institutional dimension is particularly relevant to the extent it originates from exemplary prophecy. However, the institutional dimension proper, even more if it concerns institutions generally considered as fundamentally religious, stands out for its non-sacramental, versatile, and civic character—in contrast to the wider West where even those macro-institutions claiming pristine secular credentials (like in contemporary "liberal-democratic" states) ultimately inherit the corporate mytho-theological icon of sovereignty embodied by Leviathan (like in the iconic shape of the *magnus homo* of Hobbes' *Leviathan*'s famous frontispiece) and rearticulate the legal discourse associated with it.

On the level of general conceptualization, the leading contemporary sociologist Johann P. Arnason[14] offers a first fundamental input in suggesting a distinction between meta-institutional (or "instituting") vs. institutional (or "instituted") dimensions of ordering the social world. Concurrently, he has endorsed the idea that religious knowledge can operate as a meta-institutional force, as distinguished from specific institutions. As far as the configuration of meta-institutional/instituting force vs. functional/instituted institutions is concerned, Marshall Hodgson provided us with initial inputs. While the Westphalian process of sacral incorporation (iconized by how the *magnus homo* of the Leviathan as a mega-person incorporates individual subjects as cells of his own body) became the medium of institutionalization of what Hodgson unabashedly called "Western corporativism," a combination of what he termed "contractualism" and "moralism" prevailed in the Islamosphere.[15]

Accordingly, Islamic contractualism empowered individuals to enter a variety of regulated, mutual relations within the purview of norms usually bundled together under the umbrella of what is known as *sharia* law. The process reflected the formation (and transformation) of a shared normative idiom rather than configuring a tool of institutional consecration of group agency via incorporation. As Hodgson explained, "ultimate legitimacy lay not in autonomous corporative offices but in egalitarian contractual responsibilities."[16] Against this contractualist background, there were no conditions in the Islamosphere for developing a theologico-political myth of incorporation comparable to the Leviathan. Nonetheless, it is undeniable that the Leviathan-like shape of the modern, Westphalian state was ambivalently globalized not only via European colonialism and world hegemony but also through the intense and tense interaction between the modern European powers and the Ottoman empire.[17] It remains, as Hodgson claimed, that the originality of Islamic contractualism, based on the rights and duties that *sharia* law attributes to all individuals, configured an altogether different model than Western corporativism, since it relied on a religious articulation of moralism pivoted on the absolute character of the individual's accountability to Allah,[18] which the Islamic schools of rational idealism conceived as supported by the notion of the individual as a moral agent endowed with a divine spark of consciousness. In other words, individuals exercise rights and observe duties in their mutual contractual relations precisely because they are empowered and made accountable by Allah to do so. Accordingly, the Islamic *umma* was understood as a community of individual Muslims and, as such, different from the Christian *ekklesia*, a consecrated gathering of the faithful built on the organic body of Christ, the Church. In contrast, the *umma* is ideally understood as a rather non-organic body, as it is fundamentally constituted by the free and horizontal aggregation of individually accountable Muslims entering mutual relations. Of course, we are here setting aside how hierarchies are constructed and legitimized in either case.

Hodgson's idea of an Islamic contractualism-*cum*-moralism needs revision. First, contractualism plays a crucial role in European political and legal theory, with the consequence that a rather unqualified use of the term in the Islamic case risks creating confusion. One should, at the very least, specify that early modern European contractualism, while resting on feudal ideas of rights and duties, was supported precisely by the formation of mega-corporate political entities overcoming the fragmentation of feudalism. Therefore, if we accept the idea of an Islamic contractualism as based on a reasoned rejection of corporativism, one should see it as a much more pristine type of contractualism embedded in meta-institutional habitualization and norms and therefore rather shunning the systematic formalism (the *-ism*) that denotes a political doctrine like Western contractualism. This is why I suggest defining the Islamic system as radically relational-interactional rather than contractualist. This step may help eliminate the ambiguity related to the fact that historically prevailing forms of contractualism in Europe needed to rely on corporativism as reflected both by the state form and the conceptual apparatus of civil law. Alongside, what Hodgson calls the moralism matching Islamic contractualism should better be identified with articulations of civility both within and outside the purview of *shari'a* law and encompassing the trans-legal, indissolubly aesthetic and ethical discourse of *adab*.[19]

While we may locate *sharia* and *adab* on the instituting side of the process, the main converter of the instituting power into the instituted landscape is what we may term the mother or matrix of all Islamic institutions, namely the *waqf*, variously translated as charitable trust or philanthropic foundation: an endowment of personal wealth made by any member of the community who can afford it, with the intent of pleasing Allah and through it "doing good to other." The endowing act reflects a crucial dimension of compassion that is at the core of religious ethics, and yet it is also deeply ingrained in civility as a code for dealing with multiple others. It is the very incarnation of the idea of giving, or of the gift, which is fundamental both to the anthropology of religion and the dynamics of community building. Neither inherently private nor public, and both localized and providing global interconnections, the *waqf* put into operation the imperative of creating connectedness between self and others, particularly by targeting the needs of specific groups whose welfare was of strategic importance for the endowers (starting from the support of their own enlarged families), or by feeding into the urban spatial organization of general interest (which we would call "public spaces"), or of particularly disfavored members of the community.

Not surprisingly, the modalities of endowment and administration and the targeting of beneficiaries could vary sharply (both creatively and adaptively) in various regions and periods.[20] This is why the *waqf* became the source of funding for a variety of services, goods, and enterprises, like schools, libraries, Sufi lodges, fountains, hospitals, burial societies, soup kitchens, as well as urban spaces like squares, inns, caravanserais, mobile equipment of coffee houses and baths, and other services for travelers and traders, among several others (which also included rural estates). In this sense, *waqf* secured functions that in medieval European cities were increasingly taken over by municipalities. However, it did so in conformity with the relational and civic ethos of Islamic norms, that is, in a rather de-centered way, even when (and this was often the case) among the wealthy endowers of *waqf* there were rulers, their families, and the bureaucratic elites, and, more generally, notables and their families.

Most remarkably, and differently from the radically local rooting of European municipalities, *waqf*s, though endowed locally, often provided the infrastructure for long-distance connectedness for the benefit of not only traders but also scholars, Sufis, and travelers in general. Louay Safi has observed how the famous journeys of Ibn Battuta across the Islamosphere would have been nearly impossible without the support of various *waqf* infrastructures and revenues.[21] Likewise, the *waqf* greatly enriched (also architecturally and aesthetically) famous Silk Road hubs such as Samarkand and Bukhara. Therefore, while we can consider the *waqf*'s intent pious (to please God) and charitable (to benefit various categories of others than the endowing self), its effect was more broadly relational and civic. It became the backbone of the Islamosphere's cosmopolitan civility and precapitalist exchange economy.

Through such multiple functionalities, the *waqf* provided the most potent institutionalization to the normative principle of *maslaha* or the idea of a "shared good or benefit," which, far from being an abstract concept imposed on the community from the top down, relied on continuous, de-centered interpretations by those involved in specific interactions. Jurists were needed both as *waqf* administrators and for weighing and adjudicating varieties of— sometimes conflicting—legitimate interests at stake within a given context initially determined by the endower's intentions. The legal discourse guiding the application of the *maslaha* principle was therefore ipso facto a practical manifestation of collective reflexivity based on notions of fairness and equity. *Maslaha* could not just fulfill elites' interests but required taking into account the needs (and the voices) of commoners, not just as beneficiaries but also— at least intermittently—as actors able to manifest consensus or dissent in the use or misuse of endowments. The process articulated a dimension of collective responsibility in the civic supervision of the use of *waqf* transcending a strictly legalistic scrutiny of accountability.

Unsurprisingly, Weber indicted the lack of incorporation in the Islamic system centered on the *waqf* for amounting to the absence of municipalities. This was one of the arguments he used to construct an Islamic "case" as contrastive to the exceptional trajectory of what he called the Occident.[22] Within this lopsided reasoning, a neo-orientalist discourse throve, making the *waqf* the centerpiece of an alleged bundle of deficits to be ascribed to society in the Islamosphere. The *waqf* became the main culprit in the alleged failure to develop civic autonomies like those of European cities and in curbing the rise of intermediate associations situated between the individual and the rulers. Ultimately, the *waqf* was seen as the enemy of capitalist enterprise for discouraging the use of private wealth as investment capital. In a nutshell, it became the symbol of a fundamental Islamic institutional deficit consisting of the absence of incorporation.[23] Such views make sense of the specific institutional culture of the Islamosphere (and, indirectly, of its meta-institutional, i.e., religious ethos) only through the prism of a distorting comparison with emerging standards spurned by a European global hegemony notoriously supported by colonial exploitation and imperial oppression, rather than by examining its underlying, and rather powerful, social imaginary articulated by its religion as meta-institution. This quintessentially orientalist interpretative syndrome lies less in discrete bias than in a twisted methodology, which works to effectively de-sociologize and de-civilize the cosmopolitan relational-civic-reflexive patterns of institutionalization found in the Islamosphere.

Rather than erasing (or, alternately, redeeming) the legacy of Western social theory, an honest, decolonized sociological view should rather focus on the sophisticated relational-civic-reflexive patterning of shared goods or benefits through which the *waqf*, while shunning the corporative sacralization of juridical personalities, allowed individuals of several social classes to participate in its deliberations.[24] One should also recognize that the *waqf* facilitated long-distance trade in ways that promoted hemisphere-wide capital accumulation even in a proto-global, still largely precapitalist economy. Clearly, the fact that the conditions for a specific type of hyper-calculative, individualistic, highly exploitative (toward both workers and the environment) European capitalist system did not develop within the Islamosphere cannot be counted as a deficit, but as a token of foresight, itself rooted in the underlying relational-civic-reflexive mode. This strength is even more evident if one considers that long-distance trade was integrated into flows and exchanges of spiritual, artistic, and scientific ideas across various borders, including those we conventionally associate with distinct religious traditions.

On the other hand, one could even discuss the extent to which the specific European form of capitalist enterprise and exploitation benefited, in the long term, from imposing their highly destructive system on the long-term flourishing of the infrastructural apparatus of the Islamosphere and its civic patterns providing connectedness to the entire Afro-Eurasian "Old World." The only major "achievement" of Western colonialism and imperialism in building a globally connected system may well boil down to the largely genocidal settlement of the Americas and the opening of an Atlantic trade with the "New World" where the rising capitalist greed for precious metals, raw matters, and colonial crops rose in parallel to new combinations of private and public forms of violence. This was also evident through the rise of new forms of piracy, alongside its repression and manipulation in the context of heightened imperial rivalry among European colonial powers. The entire development displaced the Islam-centered exchange economy of the Afro-Eurasian, Eastern hemisphere and turned many of its merits into deficits.

It is also remarkable that, while the *waqf* is orientalistically considered the enemy of incorporation, *sharia* law in general was indicted for obstructing the rise of civil law. And yet, what is ignored through this reasoning is that the *waqf* was both legitimized and regulated by what has been called quite appropriately the "civil law" of *waqf*. Given that there is no necessary correlation between the civil and the corporate (or that the opposite may be more plausible, as argued in this chapter), it is not surprising that this law did not contemplate the Western idea of incorporation. However, as a normative framework, while benefiting from the *maslaha* principle in the everyday management of discrete endowments, the civil law of *waqf* was not derived from any purportedly original Islamic legal doctrine. It was the outcome of the continuous, contingent, and pragmatic unfolding of Islam's development and expansion over vast civilizational areas also outside the core Nile-to-Oxus region, including the overland and maritime Silk Roads.[25] In other words, it is not just that the *waqf*, along with its legal framework, facilitated a proto-globalization of the Eastern hemisphere but also the other way around, namely that the variety of non-elite and also non-Islamic interests and practices found in the deep expanses of the Islamosphere and across its somewhat porous borders affected the way *waqf* operated as an institutional matrix.

Indeed, given the exorbitant costs of investing in the hubs of long-distance trade, no private capital, but only a quasi-global power (situated midway between meta-institution and institutions) like the *waqf*, could facilitate the creation of the necessary infrastructure of long-distance exchange and contribute to the socio-cultural attractiveness of such nodes on the Silk Road (particularly striking in their architectural aesthetics) like Samarkand and Bukhara. This rather flexible model provides a historical alternative to the prevalence, in late medieval Europe, of autonomous offices and statutes, like those acquired by municipalities and kingdoms, as they gradually emancipated themselves from feudal structures of authority distribution and transmission. The Islamic patterns of civility distinguished themselves for warranting a high degree of immunization against consecrating any institution as a corporation. They implied a refusal of such entrenched institutional demarcations as those represented in other regions by caste, estate, municipality, and corporate guild. It has also been suggested that the distorted approach to the *waqf* originating in Weberian bias conceals the way the *waqf* may have configured patterns of participatory citizenship based on action (and, we would add, interaction) rather than status.[26]

To sum up, construing a negative Islamic exceptionalism as the contrast to a positive Western exceptionalism in how institutions are built—given a purported deficit in institutionalizing autonomous collective bodies—is a dubious sociological operation, a truly neo-orientalist one, because of its turning specifically Islamic patterns of relational-civic institution-building into a civilizational deficit. Indeed, following Hodgson, one should recognize that the cosmopolitan vocations of Muslim cities were particularly encouraged by the absence of municipal autonomies. Internally, the city was socially fragmented; yet social groups in one city became closely tied to their counterparts in other cities. As a result, they came to depend on the standard norms of urban life throughout Islamdom, which were a combination of *shari'a* norms and *adab* codes. The ratio of mutual influence between these two habitual, normative, and instituting components of Islamic civility often depended on whether a city was more mercantile-oriented or rather tied to the ruling courts and their economies. In other words, relationality and cosmopolitanism could only thrive together because flexible urban powers needed no statutory incorporation of civility into municipal autonomies or other encompassing charters.

To wit, while decolonizing and de-orientalizing the sociological study of the Islamosphere, one would also need to simultaneously deflate static, Western-centric concepts like "religion" and "institution" (without any pretension to provincialize or ban them altogether) and focus instead on the actual civilizing-*cum*-institutionalizing processes by avoiding externally imposed, "etic" conceptual binaries as much as possible and instead relying as much as possible on "emic" ones like *sharia* and *adab*. On the other hand, exploring a new sociological understanding of religion as a meta-institution (i.e., as a cultural reservoir equipping social actors to provide institutional coherence to their practices and connectedness) through the lenses of an Islamic, rather than a Western-centered, perspective could even find some resonances within Western, particularly Durkheimian sociology. This step will both contribute to recalibrating the extant critique of Eurocentric notions of religion and institution and specify the broader cultural background of what the anthropology of Islam calls "instituted practices" while taking for granted the culturally specific processes through which practices are institutionalized.[27]

COLONIAL BREAKDOWNS AND INTELLECTUAL REINVENTIONS OF A POSTCOLONIAL CIVIC-PUBLIC SPHERE

Now, we move tentatively to explore the challenges faced by Muslim thinkers and activists in front of the erosion, starting in the colonial era, of the habitual and institutional matrices and networks on which the societies of the Islamosphere relied for their thriving and cohesion. In this process, the autonomy of the *waqf* as the cardinal hinge between the meta-institutional power of religion and the articulation of a rich institutional landscape was severely crippled. This erosion occurred even in regions not subjected to direct colonial occupation but more generally exposed to European pressures to conform with Westphalian institutional models through legal reform and the adoption of European-style civil codes.

The *waqf* paradigm, engaging the Muslim self in "doing good to other," started to be emptied as *waqf* services increasingly became a mere function in the broader equations of the reform of governance tools by state administrators, intended to maximize the future welfare of populations through increasing bureaucratic control of quantifiable metrics providing mere abstractions, rather than a participatory patterning, of shared goods/benefits, now made to fit notions of public utility and public order, which measured the effects of *waqf* via the ubiquitous notion of "charity."[28] Escalating the centralized steering of *waqf*, which became now legally redefined to fit the European (and Christian) notion of the corporation, fit into new disciplining dichotomies associated with Westphalian notions of governance, like the distinction by state authorities between good and bad poor. This conceptualization was bent on instituting mechanisms of surveillance and repression of what was now tagged as "deviance" among the urban poor and as "risky" components of the population, to be policed into becoming docile subjects.[29]

Such transformations occurred within a deeper metamorphosis of the civilizing process that was achieved not by suppressing but in large part via reformulating (both legally and in policy terms) traditional notions and practices linked to *waqf*, which were now strongly controlled by the centralizing governments. In the process, *waqf* was made to fit the notion of a corporation as a component of the so-called "third sector" or as a non-profit association.[30] In the final analysis, the *waqf*, once the matrix of a vibrant and sustainable (in the long term and over long distances) dimension of civility, was domesticated into being a vector of a regime for disciplining the weakest members of society inspired by a distinctly British notion ("charity") which had been in the making during the nineteenth century, both in the metropoles and in colonized regions. Charity in this context, regardless of its nominal origin in the Christian virtue of *caritas*, is a much more specific concept than "doing good to other," as it reflects a dichotomizing discourse of rewarding the well-behaving ("civilized") poor from the recalcitrant and fraudulent, ultimately uncivilized ones. While the process did not necessarily weaken the *waqf* financially, it made it subservient to the strategic goal, which was inherent in the turn to European forms of civil law, of replacing the reliability and reputation associated with the endowing (and, often, also benefiting) families with formal notions of accountability directly managed by the state and what was now clearly its (rather than the broader society's) law.

This development was matched by what occurred in Egypt in the context of a transition from the Ottoman administration to a direct subjection to colonialism via the institution of a British protectorate in the late nineteenth century. The management of the urban poor in Egypt happened to reflect even more directly utilitarian notions like those of a "social reformer" like Jeremy Bentham, whose name is strictly associated with the invention of a surveillance tool like the Panopticon. Intrusive interventions in the life of the poor were now legitimized in the name of abstract notions of "benevolence" that curbed the previously autonomous and relational inflection of "doing good to other."[31] Given this quite inexorable process of transformation, incorporation, and centralization of *waqf* in the macro-institutional Westphalian armature of colonial and postcolonial Muslim-majority societies and states, the relational-civic-reflexive principle originally built around *maslaha*-oriented practices imploded into an abstract idea around which one needed to reinvent Islamic normativity. This often occurred under the banner of a newly conceived, rather totalizing *shari'a*, which became the almost exclusive signet of a previously much more complex and versatile process of habitualization and institutionalization of an Islamic ethos of building and managing the social bond.

Particularly devastating was the collapse of the relation between the instituting and instituted dimensions of this ethos, which engendered, by way of reaction, a hyperdiscourse on Islam and the beginnings of an essentialization and weaponization of an idea of *sharia* divested from its time-honored plural narratives and institutional articulations.[32] An emerging array of Muslim thinkers unbound to the traditional class of religious scholars were now facing the task to recalibrate the balance of continuity and discontinuity between the early modern, precolonial patters of Islamic socio-political modernity and the adoption of Westphalian, nation-state frameworks during the colonial and postcolonial periods. This broader challenge encapsulated the crucial, though more specific, one concerning whether and how it was possible to restore a balance between the meta-institutional and the institutional dimensions of the cosmopolitan Islamic ethos. The emergent Muslim intellectuals needed to lay seeds of alternate arrangements of instituting powers and instituted structures.[33]

The paramount task can be summarized as designing civic-public spaces of socio-political autonomy where issues of justice are contentiously debated even if (or even more if) the mimetically Westphalian postcolonial state formations prove resistant to democratization—while authoritarianism was tolerated, when not actively supported, by the Western globally hegemonic forces. In this context, the relational-civic-reflexive patterning of such spaces provides the dimension of tradition to be reinvented after the traumas and discontinuities provoked by colonial domination or influence. Attempts to revive the ethos, if not the power, of *waqf* by freeing it from its subjection to the governmentality of postcolonial, mimetically Westphalian statehood have met mixed results.[34] Nonetheless, such attempts offer the foil through which one can deflate and critique the purported universality of standard Western theorizations of the state–society dyad and the expected mediating role of the public sphere. At stake here is the interrogation of the possibility of a neat alignment between civil society and liberal-democratic forms of Westphalian statehood as achieved within the core instances of Euro-American modernity. As articulated by Louay Safi in his criticism of the prevalence of authoritarian forms of postcolonial rule in the Muslim majority, and particularly Arab postcolony,

> [t]he reliance on coercion to effect social change is counterproductive, and overcoming centuries of conflict and mistrust requires more creative solutions. It requires more fundamental engagement in dialogues that aim at generating a common understanding of the relevance of Islam to the public-private dichotomy and the development of channels for such interaction away from political collaborations with authoritarian regimes. The goal should not be one of forcing one religious interpretation or another but to arrive at the rules of participation of all ideological groups in public space, regardless of whether the groups are secular or religious. The goal should also be one of ensuring that the critical interaction is fair and civilized.[35]

One could also observe that such notions of the public sphere have a deeper genealogy and broader articulation within the larger West than it might appear when only looking at the modern trajectories of those few European models that provided Jürgen Habermas[36] with the paradigmatic cases of both pragmatic and intellectual types of such public spheres. One should be ready to explore potential dimensions of postcolonial reconstructions of civic-public spaces transcending merely modern Western trajectories like those examined by Habermas and rearticulating those found within premodern Latin Christian and precolonial Muslim traditions of thought and practice.[37]

CONCLUSION

While I argued that the Habermasian notion itself of a public sphere relies on a rigid private–public dichotomy that is far from universal and should be revised by placing the intellectual reflection in a much broader and more complex framework than normally utilized by Western sociologists and philosophers, it is still possible to engage in a critical reading of Habermas' seminal work. Though no less Eurocentric than Weber's or Elias' approaches, one could submit Habermas' theory to the same treatment of the work of the two earlier German scholars and try to reconcile his seminal idea of communicative action, expressing the autonomy of individual participants in civic-public spaces, with the relationality and connectedness of Islamic forms of civic cosmopolitanism. Indeed, for example, the somewhat protean notion of the "common good" Habermas often invokes, which in itself has the advantage of circumventing the private–public dichotomy, can be much better substantiated with regard to the Islamic legal concept of *maslaha* than with the more convoluted dialectics of power and knowledge that characterized post-Kantian Western liberal thought.[38]

To pinpoint modern yet postsecular civic-public articulations of the social bond, the consideration of the common good, as elaborated upon within religious traditions, contributes to rendering it more inclusive and less subaltern to the anonymous metrics of populations' future welfare. This operation is ideally performed by merging an everyday habitus in shaping and maintaining human relationships which is oriented to common sense and a more disciplined orientation to, or even passion for, justice, which can be mediated and expressed via modern forms of collective mobilization, like in fighting authoritarian oppressions or foreign occupation—or any other form of direct and indirect exploitation inscribed in the current neoliberal order.

Even if we look at the collective mobilizations associated with the revolts of the "Arab Spring," the abstraction and the reductionism of Habermasian or any other comparable Western approaches to the "common good" or the "public sphere" become evident. These effects result from how the relational-civic-public dimension of collectively seeking justice against oppression and exploitation through largely postsecular idioms cuts through the conventional Western distinction between secular and religious ideologies[39] ingrained into the dominant forms of statehood. Future research is called to conceptualize the much more variegated and open-ended set of trajectories reviving semi-autonomous practices via the reshaping of civic-public space—often circumventing and infiltrating, rather than overtly subverting, a postcolonial statehood affected by a chronic deficit of popular legitimation. Such research has the potential to challenge the post-orientalist discourse that identifies popular challenges of authoritarian states (like in the "Arab Spring") through the sole lenses of the democratization of copycats of absolutist Leviathans.

NOTES

1. Louay Safi, *Islam and the Trajectory of Globalization: Rational Idealism and the Structure of World History* (New York and London: Routledge, 2022).

2. Armando Salvatore, *The Public Sphere: Liberal Modernity, Catholicism, and Islam* (New York: Palgrave Macmillan, 2007).

3. Armando Salvatore, *The Sociology of Islam: Knowledge, Power and Civility* (Oxford: Wiley Blackwell, 2016).

4. Muhammad Khalid Masud and Salvatore Armando. "Tradition and Modernity within Islamic Civilisation and the West." In *Islam and Modernity: Key Issues and Debates*, ed. Muhammad Khalid Masud, Armando Salvatore, and Martin van Bruinessen (Edinburgh: Edinburgh University Press, 2009), pp. 3–35.

5. Shahab Ahmed. *What is Islam? The Importance of Being Islamic* (Princeton, NJ: Princeton University Press, 2016).

6. Salvatore, *The Sociology of Islam*.

7. Johann P. Arnason. "Theorizing the History of Religions: The Weberian Agenda and its Unresolved Issues," Social Imaginaries, (2017) 3 (2): 109–143. Axial Age theory is also referenced in Safi, *Islam and the Trajectory of Globalization*, pp. 4–7, 70–75.

8. Johann Arnason, "Theorizing the History of Religion," pp. 117–123.

9. Salvatore, "East of Westphalia: Shaping the Body-Politic Via Institutional Charisma." In *Political Theologies and Development in Asia: Transcendence, Sacrifice and Aspiration*, ed. Giuseppe Bolotta, Michael Feener, and Philip Fountain (Manchester: Manchester University Press., 2020), pp. 18–39, 27.

10. "A charter is here the legal instrument that determines rights and duties, spaces of (in principle) intangible freedoms and of (in principle) sovereign offices (within the chartered chain of command that enshrines legitimate power)."

11. Armando Salvatore and Kieko Obuse, "What Went Wrong? Western Sociology and the Fiction of the Middle East." In *The Oxford Handbook of the Sociology of the Middle East*, ed. Armando Salvatore, Sari Hanafi, and Kieko Obuse (Oxford and New York: Oxford University Press, 2022), pp. 3–25.

12. Salvatore and Obuse, "What Went Wrong?".

13. Michael Cook. "The Centrality of Islamic Civilization." In *The Cambridge World History*, Vol. 5, *Expanding Webs of Exchange and Conflict, 500ce–1500ce*, ed. Benjamin Z. Kedar and Merry E. Wiesner-Hanks (Cambridge: Cambridge University Press, 2015), pp. 385–413.

14. Johann P. Arnason, *Civilisations in Dispute: Historical Questions and Theoretical Traditions*. (Leiden: Brill, 2003), p. 214.

15. Marshall G.S. Hodgson . *Rethinking World History: Essays on Europe, Islam and World History*, ed., with Introduction and Conclusion, Edmund Burke III (Cambridge: Cambridge University Press, 1993), pp. 126–170, 149–158.

16. Hodgson *Rethinking World History*, p. 146.

17. Almut Höfert, "The Order of Things and the Discourse of the Turkish Threat: The Conceptualisation of Islam in the Rise of Occidental Anthropology in the Fifteenth and Sixteenth Centuries." In *Between Europe and Islam: Shaping Modernity in a Transcultural Space*, ed. Almut Höfert and Armando Salvatore (Brussel: P.I.E-Peter Lang, 2000), pp. 39–69.

18. Salvatore, *The Sociology of Islam*, p. 281.

19. Armando Salvatore, "Secularity through a 'Soft Distinction' in the Islamic Ecumene? *Adab* as a Counterpoint to *sharia*." *Historical Social Research*, (2019) 44 (3): 35–51.

20. Pascale Ghazaleh. "Introduction: Pious Foundations: From Here to Eternity?" In *Held in Trust: Waqf in the Islamic World*, ed. Pascale Ghazaleh (Cairo: American University in Cairo Press, 2011), pp. 1–22; see also Mohammed A Bamyeh, *Lifeworlds of Islam: The Pragmatics of a Religion* (New York: Oxford University Press. 2019), pp. 146–147, and Safi, *Islam and the Trajectory of Globalization*, pp. 147–150.

21. Ibid., p. 149.

22. Max Weber , *Wirtschaft und Gesellschaft: Grundriß der verstehenden Soziologie*, ed. Johannes Winckelmann, 5th ed. (Tübingen: J.C.B. Mohr/Paul Siebeck, [1921–1922] 1980), p. 437.

23. Timur Kuran, "The Provision of Public Goods under Islamic Law: Origins, Impact, and Limitations of the Waqf System." *Law and Society Review*, (2001) 35 (4): 841–897; see also Timur Kuran, *The Long Divergence: How Islamic Law Held Back the Middle East* (Princeton: NJ: Princeton University Press, 2011).

24. Haim Gerber, *State, Society and Law in Islam: Ottoman Law in Comparative Perspective* (Albany, NY: SUNY Press, 1994); see also Haim Gerber, "The Public Sphere and Civil Society in the Ottoman Empire." In *The Public Sphere in Muslim Societies*, ed. Miriam Hoexter, Shmuel N. Eisenstadt and Nehemia Levtzion (Albany, NY: SUNY Press, 2002), pp. 65–82.

25. Said Amir Arjomand, "The Law, Agency and Policy in Medieval Islamic Society: Development of the Institutions of Learning from the Tenth to the Fifteenth Century." *Comparative Studies in Society and History*, (1999) 41 (2): 263–293.

26. Engin F. Isin. "Ottoman Waqfs as Acts of Citizenship." In *Held in Trust: Waqf in the Islamic World*, ed. Pascale Ghazaleh (Cairo: American University in Cairo Press, 2011), pp. 253–279.

27. A sustained discussion of such questions on the basis of historical examples exceeds the limits of this chapter; it should wait for a book-length study, still in progress, provisionally titled *Rereading Islam's Venture: The Interplay of Religion, Institutions, and Sovereignty*.

28. Nada Moumtaz. 2021. *God's Property: Islam, Charity, and the Modern State* (Oakland, CA: University of California Press).

29. Mine Ener, *Managing Egypt's Poor and the Politics of Benevolence, 1800–1952* (Princeton, NJ: Princeton University Press, 2003); see also Salvatore, *The Sociology of Islam*, 213–223.

30. Eman Assi. "Islamic Waqf and Management of Cultural Heritage in Palestine." *International Journal of Heritage Studies*, (2008) 14 (4): 380–385.

31. Armando Salvatore "New Media, the 'Arab Spring,' and the Metamorphosis of the Public Sphere: Beyond Western Assumptions on Collective Agency and Democratic Politics," *Constellations. An International Journal of Critical and Democratic Theory*, (2013) 20 (2): 214–215.

32. Armando Salvatore, "After the State: Islamic Reform and the 'Implosion' of Sharia," *Yearbook of the Sociology of Islam* (Vol. 3, *Muslim Traditions and Modern Techniques of Power*, 2001): 125–142.

33. See Mohammed A. Bamyeh and Armando Salvatore, "The Role of Intellectuals within Late-Colonial and Postcolonial Public Spheres," in *The Wiley Blackwell*

History of Islam, ed. Armando Salvatore, Roberto Tottoli, and Babak Rahimi (Oxford: Wiley Blackwell, 2018), pp. 561–583.

34. Daniela Pioppi, *From Religious Charity to the Welfare State and Back: The Case of Islamic Endowments* (waqfs) *Revival in Egypt* (Florence: European University Institute, RSC Working paper 34, 2004); andMoumtaz, *God's Property.*

35. Safi, *The Trajectory of Globalization*, p. 200.

36. Jürgen Habermas , *The Structural Transformation of the Public Sphere*, trans. Thomas Burger (Cambridge: Polity Press [1962] 1989).

37. Salvatore, "New Media"; see also Safi, *The Trajectory of Globalization*, pp. 291–296.

38. Reinhart Koselleck, *Critique and Crisis, Enlightenment and the Pathogenesis of Modern Society* (Oxford: Berg, [1959] 1988).

39. Hussein Ali Agrama, "Reflections on Secularism, Democracy, and Politics in Egypt." *American Ethnologist*, (2012) 39 (1): 26–31.

REFERENCES

Agrama, Hussein Ali. 2012. "Reflections on Secularism, Democracy, and Politics in Egypt." *American Ethnologist*, 39 (1): 26–31.

Ahmed, Shahab. 2016. *What is Islam? The Importance of Being Islamic*. Princeton, NJ: Princeton University Press.

Arjomand, Said Amir. 1999. "The Law, Agency and Policy in Medieval Islamic Society: Development of the Institutions of Learning from the Tenth to the Fifteenth Century." *Comparative Studies in Society and History*, 41 (2): 263–293.

Arnason, Johann P. 2003. *Civilisations in Dispute: Historical Questions and Theoretical Traditions*. Leiden: Brill.

Arnason. Johann P. 2017. "Theorizing the History of Religions: The Weberian Agenda and its Unresolved Issues," *Social Imaginaries*, 3 (2): 109–143.

Assi, Eman. 2008. "Islamic Waqf and Management of Cultural Heritage in Palestine." *International Journal of Heritage Studies*, 14 (4): 380–385.

Bamyeh, Mohammed A. 2019. *Lifeworlds of Islam. The Pragmatics of a Religion*. New York: Oxford. University Press.

Bamyeh, Mohammed A., and Armando Salvatore 2018. "The Role of Intellectuals within Late-Colonial and Postcolonial Public Spheres." In *The Wiley Blackwell History of Islam*, ed. Armando Salvatore, Roberto Tottoli and Babak Rahimi, 561–583. Oxford: Wiley Blackwell.

Cook, Michael. 2015. "The Centrality of Islamic Civilization." In *The Cambridge World History*. Vol. 5, *Expanding Webs of Exchange and Conflict, 500ce–1500ce*, ed. Benjamin Z. Kedar and Merry E. Wiesner-Hanks, 385–413. Cambridge: Cambridge University Press.

Ener, Mine. 2003. *Managing Egypt's Poor and the Politics of Benevolence, 1800–1952*. Princeton, NJ: Princeton University Press.

Gerber, Haim. 1994. *State, Society and Law in Islam: Ottoman Law in Comparative Perspective*. Albany, NY: SUNY Press.

Gerber, Haim. 2002. "The Public Sphere and Civil Society in the Ottoman Empire." In *The Public Sphere in Muslim Societies*, ed. Miriam Hoexter, Shmuel N. Eisenstadt, and Nehemia Levtzion, 65–82. Albany, NY: SUNY Press.

Ghazaleh, Pascale. 2011. "Introduction: Pious Foundations: From Here to Eternity?" In *Held in Trust: Waqf in the Islamic World*, ed. Pascale Ghazaleh, 1–22. Cairo: American University in Cairo Press.

Habermas, Jürgen. 1989 [1962]. *The Structural Transformation of the Public Sphere*, trans. Thomas Burger, Cambridge: Polity Press.

Hodgson, Marshall G.S. 1993. *Rethinking World History: Essays on Europe, Islam and World History*, ed., with Introduction and Conclusion, Edmund Burke III. Cambridge: Cambridge University Press.

Höfert, Almut. 2000. "The Order of Things and the Discourse of the Turkish Threat: The Conceptualisation of Islam in the Rise of Occidental Anthropology in the Fifteenth and Sixteenth Centuries." In *Between Europe and Islam. Shaping Modernity in a Transcultural Space*, ed. Almut Höfert and Armando Salvatore, 39–69. Brussel: P.I.E-Peter Lang.

Isin, Engin F. 2011. "Ottoman Waqfs as Acts of Citizenship." In *Held in Trust: Waqf in the Islamic World*, ed. Pascale Ghazaleh. 253–279. Cairo: American University in Cairo Press.

Koselleck, Reinhart. (1988 [1959]). *Critique and Crisis, Enlightenment and the Pathogenesis of Modern Society*. Oxford: Berg.

Kuran, Timur. 2001. "The Provision of Public Goods under Islamic Law: Origins, Impact, and Limitations of the Waqf System." *Law and Society Review*, 35 (4): 841–897.

Kuran, Timur. 2011. *The Long Divergence: How Islamic Law Held Back the Middle East*. Princeton, NJ: Princeton University Press.

Masud, Muhammad Khalid, and Armando Salvatore. 2009. "Tradition and Modernity within Islamic Civilisation and the West." In *Islam and Modernity: Key Issues and Debates*, ed. Muhammad Khalid Masud, Armando Salvatore and Martin van Bruinessen, 3–35. Edinburgh: Edinburgh University Press.

Moumtaz, Nada. 2021. *God's Property: Islam, Charity, and the Modern State*. Oakland, CA: University of California Press.

Pioppi, Daniela. 2004. *From Religious Charity to the Welfare State and Back. The Case of Islamic Endowments* (waqfs) *Revival in Egypt*. Florence: European University Institute; RSC Working paper 2004/34.

Safi, Louay M. 2022. *Islam and the Trajectory of Globalization: Rational Idealism and the Structure of World History*. London and New York: Routledge.

Salvatore, Armando. 2001. "After the State: Islamic Reform and the 'Implosion' of Shari'a," *Yearbook of the Sociology of Islam* (Vol. 3 *Muslim Traditions and Modern Techniques of Power*): 125–142.

Salvatore, Armando. 2007. *The Public Sphere: Liberal Modernity, Catholicism, and Islam*. New York: Palgrave Macmillan.

Salvatore, Armando. 2013. "New Media, the 'Arab Spring,' and the Metamorphosis of the Public Sphere. Beyond Western Assumptions on Collective Agency and Democratic Politics," *Constellations. An International Journal of Critical and Democratic Theory*, 20 (2): 217–228.

Salvatore, Armando. 2016. *The Sociology of Islam: Knowledge, Power and Civility*. Oxford: Wiley Blackwell.

Salvatore, Armando. 2019. "Secularity through a 'Soft Distinction' in the Islamic Ecumene? *Adab* as a Counterpoint to *Shariʿa*." *Historical Social Research*, 44 (3): 35–51.

Salvatore, Armando. 2020. "East of Westphalia: Shaping the Body-Politic Via Institutional Charisma." In *Political Theologies and Development in Asia: Transcendence, Sacrifice and Aspiration*, ed. Giuseppe Bolotta, Michael Feener, and Philip Fountain, 18–39. Manchester: Manchester University Press.

Salvatore, Armando and Kieko Obuse. 2022. "What Went Wrong? Western Sociology and the Fiction of the Middle East." In *The Oxford Handbook of the Sociology of the Middle East*, ed. Armando Salvatore, Sari Hanafi, and Kieko Obuse, 3–25. Oxford and New York: Oxford University Press.

Weber, Max. 1980 [1921–1922]. *Wirtschaft und Gesellschaft: Grundriß der verstehenden Soziologie*, ed. Johannes Winckelmann, 5th ed. Tübingen: J.C.B. Mohr (Paul Siebeck).

Chapter 5

Sharia and Freedom

A Reassessment

Mustafa Akyol

In 2002, a twenty-six-year-old Pakistani woman named Zafran Bibi went to the police station near her remote village in a tribal area to report that she had been raped. Her husband had been in jail for a long time, and the terrible man who abused her was none other than her brother-in-law, Jamal Khan. The "honor"-obsessed family had first tried a cover-up, but the young woman was finally seeking justice.

Yet what she found was not justice. The police took her to a local court, which soon made an outrageous decision: the woman did not have the necessary "four male eyewitnesses" against the man she was accusing. This, the court reasoned, cleared the man of the charges. But the very fact that she got pregnant without access to her husband was enough proof in itself that she somehow had committed the crime of "adultery." That is why, the court reasoned, Zafran Bibi deserved the grim penalty of death by stoning.

Soon, the poor woman was arrested and jailed, with her newborn in her arms, only to await her brutal execution. Luckily, after public outrage raised by human rights groups and an intervention by the then president Pervez Musharraf, a higher court overturned the verdict and released Zafran Bibi from prison. Yet her life was already ruined, and she would continue to face stigma from her family and community.[1]

All that tragedy was caused by patriarchy and misogyny, problems one may find in virtually any society. But there was also a specific problem in Pakistan's "Islamic laws," which were introduced in 1979 by the general-turned-president Muhammad Zia ul-Haqq. These laws criminalized rape, but not as something separate—and much more serious—than *zina*, the Islamic term for adultery (extramarital sex), traditionally extended to fornication (premarital sex) as well. Instead, rape was defined only as *zina bil-jabr* (adultery/fornication by force). That "force" factor saved the victims of rape from prosecution but did not bring any additional retribution to the rapists, as they were still only guilty of *zina*. In other words, no conceptual difference existed between a rapist who brutalized a female victim and another man who just had consensual sex with his unmarried lover.[2]

Moreover, because of this confusion between adultery/fornication and rape, the evidence required for the former was also required for the latter: testimony of four male eye witnesses. This extremely high, if not impossible, bar of proof often exonerated the rapists. But their victims could not be exonerated when their "adultery" was proved by their pregnancy, as in the case of Zafran Bibi.

Far worse, Zafran Bibi's tragedy was not an isolated incident. In the decades following the "Islamization of laws" under Zia ul-Haqq, Pakistan has seen more than 2,000 cases of gross injustice against its women.[3] Muslim scholar Hashim Kamali sadly observed the following in 2019:

> Rich landlords abused peasant women and servants, and when the latter complained of rape to the authorities, they were themselves punished because they could not find four male eyewitnesses of good character to testify for them.[4]

Why were Pakistani authorities allowing this horror, despite the rightful outrage in the nation, and even beyond? And why were local Islamic courts so obsessed with finding "four male eyewitnesses" in all cases of sexual misconduct?

WHY FOUR WITNESSES?

For anyone familiar with Islamic sources, the answer to the second question will be clear: this requirement of four eyewitnesses for sexual crimes comes from none other than the Qur'an. However, when we look carefully into what the Qur'an really says, we see a very different context and a totally different intention.

This context and intention are in the early verses of An-Nur, the 24th *sura*, or chapter, which were revealed soon after the famous "Necklace Affair" of Aisha, the young wife of the Prophet Muhammad. As the story goes, Aisha joined the Prophet on one of his military expeditions, but on the way back, she was accidentally left behind while looking for a necklace she lost in the desert. Luckily, she returned the next day thanks to a young man who had found her and given her a ride. This led to a rumor in Medina that the two had had an affair, troubling the Prophet and devastating Aisha herself. Soon, however, a new revelation came, condemning "the lie" and those who "concocted" it. "And why did the accusers not bring four witnesses to it?" the verse also asked. "If they cannot produce such witnesses, they are the liars in God's eyes."[5] Another verse legally enacted this strict condition to rule out any future libels:

> As for those who accuse chaste women [with *zina*], and then fail to provide four witnesses, strike them eighty times, and reject their testimony ever afterwards: they are the lawbreakers, except for those who repent later and make amends- God is most forgiving and merciful.[6]

In other words, the Qur'an had required four eyewitnesses for any accusation of illicit sex in order to protect women from false accusations—not to protect their rapists! However, centuries later, in Pakistan, the same requirement was exploited precisely to protect rapists, as we have seen.

Exactly how did this horror take place in Pakistan or Nigeria, where similar cases have also been reported?[7]

One problem was the crudity of the modern-day campaigns of "Islamization of laws," which came out of more ideological zeal than legal prudence. They were carried out so sternly that the leniency factors taken into account by most classical jurists—such as excusing the accused when there is "doubt"—were often disregarded.[8]

Yet classical jurisprudence had big problems as well. First, most classical jurists saw rape as nothing but "*zina* by force," not as a separate and more serious crime.[9] Second, some jurists (of the Maliki school) also considered the pregnancy of an unmarried woman as conclusive evidence of her *zina*, unless she herself proved that she had been raped, which was "a virtually impossible burden for the victim to meet."[10] Third, many jurists "limited the four witnesses in a *zina* case to men"—although the Qur'an didn't specify their gender.[11] Therefore, in the classical age of Islam as well, "women and girls seeking justice against their violators" often faced the "virtually insurmountable challenge" of making their case.[12]

And all these sad facts present us with a broader lesson: the Sharia, the legal tradition of Islam, rises on the most noble intentions, such as the Qur'an's safeguarding of women against libels. But not all the interpretations and implementations of the Sharia have really served those intentions.

THE SHARIA OF THE QUR'AN

What, really, is the Sharia? The Arabic word literally means "the way." In the whole Qur'an, it occurs only once: "Now We have set you [Muhammad] on a *sharia*, so follow it."[13] The term also has a cognate, where God says to Jews, Christians, and Muslims: "We have assigned a *shir'atan* and a path to each of you."[14] So *sharia* isn't specific to Islam; it is the "way" of any Abrahamic religion.

In this sense, for any Muslim, including myself, the Sharia is God-given. Hence, it is sacred and perfect.

However, when Muslims talk today about "following" or "implementing" the Sharia, most of them go beyond this pristine sense of the term. What they rather refer to *is fiqh* (jurisprudence), which is the human interpretation of the Sharia. This interpretation relies on the divinely revealed Qur'an, but more so on three other sources that all have human imprints on them: first, the *Sunna* (tradition) of the Prophet, largely represented by the hadiths, or "sayings," attributed to him in books canonized almost two centuries after the fact. Then, there are *ijma* (consensus) and *qiyas* (analogy), which are methods used by medieval jurists to extract verdicts from the Qur'an and the hadiths.

This surely is a complicated matter. But, in the footsteps of Islamic modernist scholars, such as Muhammad Abduh, Fazlur Rahman, or Khaled Abou Fadl, I believe in making a clear distinction between the Qur'an and the post-Qur'anic sources. The reason is not only because the latter are more human and therefore less sacred but also because, in the words of Fazlur Rahman (d. 1988), important differences exist between the "Qur'anic worldview" and the dominant post-Qur'anic worldview.[15]

So if we make this distinction and look at the divinely revealed Sharia of the Qur'an, what do we see?

We see that the majority of the Qur'an's 6,236 verses are about God, monotheism, creation, ethics, piety, the afterlife, the struggle of the Prophet, and the stories of former prophets. Only about 100 verses are on legal matters, such as marriage, divorce, inheritance, or contracts. A few of those legal verses are also about what we today call "criminal law." They enact five punishments for five specific crimes:

- *Qisas* (law of retaliation) for murder and intentional bodily injury with an encouragement for forgiveness.[16]
- Amputation of a hand for theft.[17]
- Execution, hanging, amputation of a hand and foot, or expulsion for *hirabah* (banditry).[18] (The term recently has also been associated with terrorism.)
- A hundred lashes for *zina*.[19]
- Eighty lashes for false accusation of *zina*.[20]

These five punishments of the Qur'an (often added with a few verdicts from hadiths) have been enshrined in Islamic jurisprudence as the *hudud* (boundaries) of God, to be implemented without much questioning.[21] In the modern era, Islamist movements often made their enforcement a primary goal, if not an obsession.

However, those Islamist movements seem to be missing three important points.

First, the five Qur'anic punishments do not constitute a fully defined penal code and neither do they claim to. Rather, they reflect the decade-long experience of the small Muslim community in Medina, to which the Qur'an responded in real time (622–632). That is why the Qur'an also legislated concepts that have no place outside of that immediate context, such as "forbidden months," or *zihar*—Arab customs unknown to other societies.[22]

Second, all Qur'anic punishments have something in common. They are corporal: they cause pain or harm to the body. That has led many Muslims, throughout centuries, to think that, for some mysterious reason, God prefers such punishments to what has become the norm in the modern era: imprisonment. However, we may also think that the Qur'an issued only corporal punishments because, in its immediate context, it was the only way: early seventh-century Arabia had nomadic tribes and little towns with shanty houses, but no state authority to build and operate long-term prisons. No wonder pre-Islamic Arabs also amputated hands for theft.[23]

Third, and the most important point, is that the five Qur'anic punishments target "crimes" in the common sense of that term—they have victims. This is quite clear in the case of murder, theft, violent robbery, and false accusation of *zina*. As for *zina* itself, it isn't often considered a crime today, but if it refers only to extramarital sex—as a few scholars have argued—then it does have a victim, which is the betrayed spouse.[24] Moreover, *zina* can also be condemned for confusing lineage, which was probably the main concern all along, evidenced by the fact that Muslim jurists defined it strictly as genital intercourse, the only kind of sex that leads to reproduction.[25]

SINS VERSUS CRIMES

Now, here is the crucial point that relates to our discussion on liberty: besides the five crimes listed earlier, the Qur'an religiously banned many other acts, but it did not legally penalize them. Examples are drinking wine, consuming pork, gambling, lying, gossiping, practicing sorcery, taking usury, looking at someone's private parts, or not fully covering your own private parts.[26] Against all such sins, the Qur'an warned Muslims of God's discontentment and even wrath in the afterlife, but it did not decree any punishment in this world. Similarly, the Quran decreed no earthly punishment for Muslims who do not pray or fast or for those who are regarded as apostates or blasphemers.[27]

In other words, we can theorize that the Qur'an made *a distinction between crime and sin*. Crimes were public offenses, such as theft that victimizes people and needs to be punished by people. Sins, on the other hand, were moral offenses that would be left to God. (All crimes were also sins, but not all sins were crimes.)

However, in a few centuries after the Qur'an, this distinction between crime and sin largely disappeared. Scholars who interpreted the Sharia—through *usul al fiqh,* or jurisprudence—criminalized virtually all sins. Accordingly, drinkers were to be flogged and their wine had to be poured out. Those who did not perform their daily prayers were to be beaten with sticks.[28] Apostates were to be executed unless they recanted in three days. Blasphemers would also be executed, according to some jurists, even if they repented.[29]

It is this traditionalist jurisprudence that gave us the coercive interpretation of the Sharia, whose champions find the Qur'anic maxim, "There is no compulsion in religion," troubling. No, they insist, in fact "There *is* compulsion in religion."[30] The same jurisprudence also gave more attention to the literal wordings of Qur'anic commandments than the intentions behind them. That is how the requirement of four eyewitnesses for proving *zina* could be passed on to proving rape, regardless of the disastrous consequences.

THE TRADITIONALIST (POST-QUR'AN) JURISPRUDENCE

How did this traditionalist jurisprudence develop? The question requires a longer answer that I offer in another work, but here is the story in a nutshell.[31]

Because of Islam's emphasis on both religious practice and its early fusion with state power, lawmaking proved to be a crucial matter in the formative centuries of Islam. To this end, some jurists first turned to the Qur'an, but it had very limited legal content, as we have seen. They also respected Sunna, the tradition of the Prophet, but understood it only as "a set of practices and beliefs of the Muslim community as passed on from the companions," in addition to the small number of massively transmitted *(mutawatir)* reports. Then, both to interpret the meaning of the Qur'an and Sunna and to judge rationally even without scripture, they emphasized the authority of human reason. Some were known as *Ahl al-Ray* (people of reason); others were known as *Ahl al-Ka/am* (people of theology).[32]

Yet other jurists, mostly from more parochial areas, found these rationalist jurists too "whimsical." Instead of human reason, they prioritized hadiths, accepting a much bigger pool of them, despite the fact that generations had passed since the Prophet, and oral reports (and a limited number of texts) about his words and deeds had been mixed with countless hearsays and forgeries. They were called *Ahl al-Hadith* (people of hadith).

It is the hadith collections of the *Ahl al-Hadith,* who ultimately prevailed thanks to political reasons, that established the basis of most of the coercive rules in Islamic jurisprudence. The grim verdict on apostasy, for example, comes from a questionable hadith: "Whomever changes his religion, kill him."[33] The same is true for the killing of blasphemers, the stoning of adulterers, the flogging of wine drinkers, the banning of images, or the belittling of women as "lacking in reason and religion."[34] Since the nineteenth century, some prominent Islamic scholars have challenged the authenticity of such hadiths—and others that seem "vulgar, absurd, theologically objectionable, or morally repugnant"—arguing that they may be later inventions projected back to the Prophet.[35] I agree with those critics, and their forerunners in the formative centuries of Islam, that the hadith literature is an indispensable source of historical knowledge; however, it needs caution in light of the Qur'an, reason, and moral intuition.

But why would the High Middle-Age Muslim jurists be so fond of establishing coercive rules—through either hadiths or jurisprudential tools? The answer is that coercion was normal in their time and milieu. The empires that the early Muslims faced—the Christian Byzantines and the Zoroastrian Sassanids— imposed their official religion, with laws that criminalized apostasy, often with the death penalty.[36] Until the Enlightenment, in fact, many Christians believed in the coercive doctrine of *compelle intrare* (compel to enter), which was inferred from a single commandment in the Gospel of Luke: "Compel them to come in, that my house may be full."[37] Even after the end of outright religious coercion, "moral coercion" survived in Western societies. It was only a century ago that the temperance movement, rooted in Protestant churches, succeeded in criminalizing the production and sale of alcohol in the United States—only to find out that this prohibition did not help anyone other than those involved in organized crime. And it was only half a century ago that British laws stopped criminalizing homosexuality, hesitantly accepting that "there is a realm of private morality which lies outside the law."[38]

All these mean that we can't judge medieval Islamic jurisprudence by today's standards, which would be a mistake. The problem, however, is that some Muslims still see the standards of that medieval Islamic jurisprudence, which reflect the culture of those times, as the divinely mandated Sharia that is valid for all times and all peoples.

A TEST OF SLAVERY

To those strictly conservative Muslims, one needs to ask a simple question: What is the verdict of the classical Islamic jurisprudence on slavery?

Unless they represent an extreme fringe, they may affirm, "Islam is against slavery." But if they are a bit informed, they will probably be aware that slavery was justified by virtually all Muslim jurists until the nineteenth century—when it was abolished, luckily, thanks to both Western pressures from outside and reformists' efforts from within.[39]

Of course, one may argue it was the original intention of Islam to abolish slavery—as seen in the Qur'an's praise for the act of "freeing a slave"—but social conditions matured only in the modern era.[40] This argument—often offered by mainstream Muslim authorities who may be too conservative on other issues—is indeed a good one. But it only opens a wider discussion: If we are acknowledging that it was right to reinterpret the Sharia on slavery, why don't we do the same on other matters? Why don't we, more specifically, also reinterpret all the violent, coercive, patriarchal, or discriminatory elements in traditional jurisprudence?

That is the basis of the much-discussed "reform" needed in Islam today—a reform in jurisprudence, the interpretation of the Sharia, toward less coercion and more liberty. And it will not be a betrayal of the Sharia but a revival of its spirit in the new context of the modern world.

But wait . . . A "revival" of the Sharia? Why would we need that? Why can't we just move on with secular laws and principles?

Some people may ask these questions, especially if they are among the "secularists" of the Muslim world. The reason is that although they may see what is wrong with all the implementations of the Sharia, they may not see anything right about it that deserves any attention. Consequently, they may not see anything wrong with the secular experiments that the Muslim world has seen in the past century—Kemalism in Turkey, Baathism in the Arab world, or the Shah's regime in Iran.

Yet the truth is more nuanced. For besides all its troubling interpretations, the Sharia was also the gatekeeper of a crucial value in the classical Muslim world, whose disappearance had grim consequences in the modern era. So to this other side of the coin, we will now turn.

SHARIA AS RULE OF LAW

In his masterwork *Seyahatname* (Book of Travels), the famous Ottoman chronicler Evliya Çelebi (d. 1682) narrates an interesting story about Sultan Mehmed II, also known as *Fatih* (the Conqueror), for his conquest of Constantinople in 1453. As Çelebi tells us, soon after capturing the magnificent city, the triumphant sultan wanted a similarly magnificent mosque built in his name. For the difficult job, he employed a Greek architect named Atik Sinan, who successfully raised the early version of what is still known as Istanbul's Fatih Mosque. It was an impressive building, but the sultan was disappointed that its dome was lower than that of Hagia Sophia. He took this as an insult, lost his temper, and punished the architect by cutting off both his hands.

The story, so far, seems like a lesson about the misery of the medieval world, where people's precarious lives were at the arbitrary hands of capricious rulers. But there is more to it, as Evliya Çelebi keeps narrating, which adds a silver lining.

The day after he lost his hands, the poor architect went to a *qadi* (Islamic judge) to sue the sultan. The judge heard the case and immediately called on the sultan to give his testimony. "The order is from the Sharia of the Prophet," said the sultan, who wore his robes, picked up his mace, came to the court, and sat down. "Don't sit down, my sir," the judge warned him, though. "Stand up together with your challenger."

Then the judge listened to both sides. At the end, he found the sultan guilty. First, he told him that his obsession with the height of the dome was absurd:

> Vanity is only a disaster, and a low ceiling is not an obstacle to worship. Your stone, even if it is a diamond, is only a stone, but a man, more blessed than an angel, is raised up only in forty years. By cutting his hands, you have acted unwisely out of rage He has many children, whose maintenance is now on you.[41]

Then, the judge announced the punishment for the sultan: according to the Sharia, he deserved *qisas* (retaliation), which means that he had to suffer the same pain that he had inflicted on the innocent architect. Both his hands, in other words, were to be amputated.

The convicted sultan asked for a way out: instead of facing retaliation, he could compensate the architect and his family. "An amount that would be enough," he offered, "and to be paid from the *bayt-ul mal* [public treasury]."

"No," the judge replied sternly:

> I will not put this burden on the *bayt-ul mal*. This deed has happened without the permission of the Sharia, and the fault is yours. From your own salary *[ulufe]*, you need to pay ten silver coins a day.

The sultan said he would even pay twenty coins, as he only craved to be forgiven by the architect, in the sight of God. The architect accepted the offer and the sultan was dismissed. At the end of the story, Evliya Çelebi adds that the sultan told the judge, "If you had favored me over the architect because I am the sultan, I would have finished you with this mace." In return, the judge proved only more defiant: "Oh my sir, if you did not abide by what I have decreed according to the Sharia, I would have destroyed you with the dragon under my prayer rug."

That dragon, obviously, was only metaphorical. Yet apparently, it was more powerful than the sultan's mace.

What is this story's lesson?

Reading it almost four centuries later, it is hard to know how much of it is historical truth versus pious fiction. But in any case, the story gives us a glimpse of what the Sharia meant in Ottoman society: a law above each and every one, including even the mighty sultan.

A LAW ABOVE EVERYONE

All these bring us to the fundamental character of the Sharia that is obvious but too often missed: it was a law that derived not from the rulers but from a much higher authority—God. Moreover, the people who articulated this law via jurisprudence and guarded it with judicial power—the *ulama* (religious scholars)—were not fully subservient to the rulers. For sure, throughout the complex history of the Islamic civilization, rulers co-opted some of these scholars or encroached on their independence. (And the surge in that encroachment, according to contemporary scholar Ahmet Kuru, was the doom of the Islamic civilization.[42]) Nevertheless, the moral authority of the Sharia never disappeared and it preserved a check on arbitrary power. Noah Feldman, professor of law at Harvard University, explains why:

The scholars' commitment to the law derived from their understanding of it as God's law, greater certainly than the ruler, but also greater than themselves. The ruler's promise to back up the legal decisions of the scholars with force recognized the formal elevation of law over the arbitrary whims of any one individual. This constitutional arrangement made the law supreme. It established, we might even say, the rule of law.[43]

This rule of law was symbolized in the Ottoman Empire in the office of *Sheikh-ul Islam,* the top jurist, with whom the sultans had to consult—a system that checked some of their excesses. One example was when Sultan Selim, the Grim (r. 1512–1520) wanted to forcibly convert all Christians under his rule into Islam, "to unify the empire within"—only to be stopped by Sheikh-ul Islam Zembilli Ali Efendi, who asserted the Christians' right to preserve their faith.[44] The same jurist also prevented the same sultan from executing a large group of his civil servants, out of mere wrath, reminding him that such punishments could not be given without a proper court decision.[45]

Another story comes from Muslim-ruled India, where the ruthless sultan Alauddin Khalji (r. 1296–1316) wanted to mutilate some officers who annoyed him and also claimed the public treasury to be his personal wealth—only to be challenged by the top scholar Qadi Mughisuddin. Neither the ruler nor his children have any right to the treasury, Mughisuddin said to the face of the angry sultan. "Whether you send me to prison, or whether you order me to be cut to two," he bravely added, "all this is unlawful."[46]

The point, again, was that the Sharia was above everyone, even the sultan.

Yet not all legal systems had the same spirit. A strong contrast was the tradition of *lex regia* (royal law), codified by the Eastern Roman Emperor Justinian in the sixth century. "What has pleased the prince has the force of law," it read, also clarifying: "The prince is not bound by the laws."[47] The same idea was reflected in the medieval English principle, "The monarch can do no wrong," which itself led to the notion of "sovereign immunity"—a judicial doctrine that prevents the government and its agencies from being sued without their consent.[48] (The United States has a version called "qualified immunity," which gives an "unlawful shield" to law enforcement, as libertarians have rightly criticized.[49])

In the Sharia, however, the notion of legal immunity has been "totally absent,"[50] because no sovereign or official was ever above the Sharia. Just like the Ottoman sultan mentioned earlier, they had to stand up in court in case they broke the law.

That is why, as Ernest Gellner, prominent philosopher and anthropologist of the past century, had realized, "a certain kind of separation of powers was built into Muslim society from the very start." That is why, as Gellner added, the Muslim idea of rule of law "did not need to wait for some Enlightenment doctrine."[51]

But let's stop here and think for a second. It is nice to recall the legendary stories of medieval Muslim rulers. But today, can you imagine the powerful leader of any Muslim-majority country, such as Turkey, Egypt, Syria, Iran, or Saudi Arabia, facing justice in a court while he is still holding power?

Personally, I can't. At least, I have never seen that in my lifetime. (Conversely, I have seen Muslim leaders facing prosecution, sometimes extremely unjustly, *after* they lose power—but that is the other side of the same coin.) However, I have seen sitting presidents and prime ministers in liberal democracies in non-Muslim-majority nations—such as the United States, Canada, Italy, and South Korea—being investigated by independent prosecutors or by legislative assemblies that have the power of impeachment.[52] While I was writing these lines, I even saw the Norwegian prime minister being fined by the police for breaking "social distancing" rules, which was hard to imagine in any Muslim society that I know of.[53]

> Why do you think this may be the case? Why do Muslim rulers seem to be above the law now, whereas the law seems above the rulers elsewhere?

WHAT WENT WRONG IN ISLAM

The short answer is that, in the past few centuries, rule of law dramatically declined in the Muslim world, whereas it admirably ascended in liberal democracies of the West and elsewhere.[54]

A bit longer answer requires a historical overview, which I can offer through the modern history of my country, Turkey. It began in the early nineteenth century, when some Ottoman statesmen and intellectuals began to realize that their system, which took the Sharia as sacrosanct, was becoming inadequate to meet the *icabat-z zamaniye* (requirements of the age). In other words, they realized the need for legal reform. But in most cases, the existing interpretations of the Sharia were too untouchable, and its guardians, the *ulama*, were often "empty of any knowledge of the outside world."[55]

So these reformists found the solution in bypassing the Sharia by expanding the state's authority to issue *kanun* (secular law). Traditionally, it was assumed that the latter could not override the Sharia, but that balance began to shift.[56] When the Ottomans faced the need to accept more religious freedom, for example, they did not touch the Sharia's assumed verdict on apostasy—the death penalty—but in the 1850s, they initiated "a state policy to look the other way."[57] In 1856, they also issued an imperial edict declaring, "No one shall be compelled to change their religion," implying that apostates from Islam would not be forced to recant.[58] By rendering the mainstream interpretation of the Sharia ineffective, one could say that they revived the Qur'anic principle of "No compulsion in religion."

> Those Ottoman reforms occurred during the era of *Tanzimat* (Reorganization), which took its name from the historic imperial edict announced in 1839 by Sultan Abdulmejid II. Novelties included new limitations on the sultan's powers, affirmation of due process in trials, protections on private property, new commercial or criminal laws modeled after those of France, and legal equality for non-Muslims. The latter, especially, was an epoch-changing step, as put later by Halide Edip Adıvar, a prominent Turkish intellectual of the early twentieth century. "Down to Tanzimat, the Ottoman Turks had believed that only Muslims could be politically equal," as she wrote. "With Tanzimat they believed that all men could and ought to be politically equal."[59]

> This trajectory reached its pinnacle in December 1876, when the Ottoman Empire declared a remarkably liberal constitution. "Every Ottoman enjoys personal liberty on condition of non-interfering with the liberty of others," it read, "without distinction whatever faith they profess."[60] The constitution also established a political system based on the essential condition of the rule of law: "separation of powers," which means the separation of the executive, legislative, and judicial branches.[61]

All these mid-nineteenth-century Ottoman reforms marked one of the brightest chapters in the history of the Islamic civilization. However, this bright chapter was also cut too short. The constitutional regime announced in December 1876 lasted for only 14 months, to go down in Turkish history as the "First Constitutional Period." In February 1878, the new sultan, Abdul Hamid II, used the disastrous war with Russia (1877–1878) as a pretext to suspend the constitution, disband the parliament, and rule despotically for the next three decades.

The Ottoman parliament convened again in 1909, initiating the "Second Constitutional Period," only to soon fall victim to the dictatorship of the nationalist Party of Union and Progress, and the turmoil of World War I. When Ottoman general Mustafa Kemal (Atatürk) founded modern Turkey in 1923 as its first president, his motto was "unity of powers"—powers that would be united in his hands.[62] And when I was writing these lines in 2020, after some intermittent progress, Turkey had collapsed into "unity of powers" again, this time under the Islamist president Recep Tayyip Erdoğan—an ideological answer to, but also a political imitation of, the secularist Atatürk.[63]

In short, the evolution of the premodern Ottoman Empire to a modern state did not work well, if we judge it by the criteria of rule of law and its basis, the separation of powers. That is why U.S. scholar Ruth Austin Miller describes this history as a road that went "from *fiqh* [Islamic jurisprudence] to fascism." The latter term implies the glorification of the state and the instrumentalization of the law for the interests of the state.[64]

A similar, even darker, pattern has taken place in the Arab world, especially in dictatorial republics, such as Iraq, Syria, Egypt, Libya, and Algeria. The Sharia was bypassed through "modernization," but the latter only helped concentrate all powers—executive, legislative, and judicial—in the hands of draconian parties and narcissist dictators. Their powers were so "arbitrary and pervasive" that "no Arab caliph or Turkish sultan of the past could ever have achieved."[65]

In the meantime, Islamist movements emerged across the Muslim world, calling for the reinstitution of the Sharia. What they meant were objectives such as forcing women to cover their heads, banning alcohol, flogging fornicators, and executing apostates—religious coercion, so to speak. Yet these Islamists had little interest in separation of powers, because just like the secular autocrats they aimed to replace, they wanted to dominate all powers of the state. In Iran, Ayatollah Khomeini elucidated this by a constitutional design, which gave the top jurist —first himself, then his successor Khamenei—absolute power. In this so-called Islamic Republic, "the judicial, legislative, and executive branches of government" were not separated, but rather united as "the instruments of the leader."[66]

At the end of all this authoritarian "modernization," the Muslim world arrived at a terrible point: it lost the main blessing of the Sharia, which is to safeguard rule of law, while it preserved the troubling aspects of the medieval interpretation of the Sharia, which is to impose religion by force.

And in the meantime, the opposite took place in the West, thanks to a better—that is, liberal—modernization.

WHAT WENT RIGHT IN THE WEST

At the onset of liberalism, much of Europe was a land of absolutism. Kings had "divine rights" to rule, and no Sharia existed to stand above them. "The king is above the law, as both author and giver of strength thereto," as James I of England (r. 1603–1625) put it. So "where he sees the law doubt some or rigorous, he may interpret or mitigate the same."[67]

That is why, in this absolutist Europe, the power of kings was less limited than their Muslim counterparts. This aspect is reflected in a fascinating letter of the French ambassador to the Ottoman Empire sent back to Paris a few years before the French Revolution. The ambassador was asked by his government why the Ottomans were too slow in responding to queries in political negotiations. He responded that the system in Istanbul is different. "Here," he wrote, "things are not as in France where the king is sole master and does as he pleases." "Here," he added, "the sultan has to consult."[68]

One of the critics of those French kings who acted "as he pleases" was Baron de Montesquieu (d. 1755), the philosopher who popularized the term "despotism," only with contempt for it. He found its remedy in *trias politica* (separation of powers), which he defined, systematized, and added to the world's political parlance. The three powers of the state must be separated, he explained, "so that none can abuse power . . . that power shall check power."[69] He deeply impressed the American Founders, particularly James Madison, and also inspired the principles of the United States Constitution.[70] The latter, as Americans are often rightly proud of, established a system of "checks and balances," where the executive, legislative, and judicial branches are separate, so they control and limit each other.

Montesquieu, like John Locke, was one of the founding fathers of liberalism. Both believed in a notion called "natural law." This meant that there are moral truths, discernible by human reason, to "which all men, including governors themselves, should conform."[71] It was their version of the Sharia, so to speak.[72]

Thanks to the advancement of liberalism in the past three centuries, arbitrary power in the Western world has been curbed to a great extent. (Terrible alternatives that emerged in the same West—fascism and communism—have fortunately been defeated, at great costs and with great sacrifices.) Meanwhile, the same West also got rid of its own medieval laws that imposed Christianity at the expense of other religions or "heresies." Unlike the Muslim world, in other words, the modern West embraced rule of law, while getting rid of coercion in religion.

That is why since the nineteenth century, some critical Muslim minds have realized that the virtues they expect to see in the Muslim world are now in the West. One of them, the Egyptian religious scholar Muhammad Abduh (d. 1905), put it poetically: "I went to Europe, and I saw Islam without Muslims," he said, as word has it. "I came back to Egypt, and I saw Muslims without Islam."[73]

In short, the modern-day Muslim world today needs to revive the Sharia's political function in the premodern Islamic civilization: a sense of law that is above all rulers, a law to which we can hold them accountable.

However, a literalist attachment to the Sharia, the dominant perspective today, will not offer any remedy. We even saw how it can be disastrous, as in the example of Pakistan's adultery laws that required four eyewitnesses for any sexual crime, which persecuted innocent women while protecting their rapists.

Yet that same example also showed us that the Sharia was built on the best *intentions.*

So it is those intentions that Muslims should perhaps reconsider.

Fortunately, a scholarly tradition in Islam has already studied those intentions—the *maqasid* (objectives) of the Sharia. We owe this tradition to a few classical Muslim jurists, the most prominent of whom was Abu Ishaq al-Shatibi (d. 1388), a scholar from Granada in Muslim Spain. Unlike most of his predecessors and contemporaries, who focused on the commandments of the Sharia, al-Shatibi also focused on the objectives behind those commandments. "Every legal ruling in Islam has a function which it performs," he argued, regardless of whether or not this function is explicitly stated in the ruling itself. He also tied all these functions to an overarching aim: "to realize benefit to human beings, or to ward off harm or corruption."[74]

For example, God had banned and penalized theft to achieve an objective: *hifz al-mal* (protection of property), which itself was essential for human welfare. With a systematic analysis of Sharia rulings, al-Shatibi mapped four more such objectives: the protection of religion *(deen),* life *(nafs),* lineage *(nasl),* and the intellect *('aql).* In the twentieth century, Tunisian scholar Ibn Ashur, who tried to revive the much-forgotten wisdom of al-Shatibi, added a sixth objective: freedom *(hurriyyat).*[75]

It is worth noting here that classical jurists, such as al-Shatibi, mapped the objectives of the Sharia mainly to defend the Sharia—rather than reinterpreting it—and taking the latter step requires a theological breakthrough that I addressed elsewhere.[76]

Yet still, even in its classical form, there is something remarkable about the objectives of the Sharia: they are all about protecting the rights of humans—their religion, life, property, lineage, intellect, and freedom. They are *not* about protecting the state, its security, authority, or perpetuity—notions that are easily put above human rights in many parts of the world today, especially in authoritarian regimes, quite a few of which rule over Muslims.

And therein lies the reason why we Muslims need to revive the Sharia—more precisely the spirit of the Sharia. That spirit tells us that the rights of humans—that we may establish either by divine law or by human reason—should be above all states, whose legitimacy, if any, derives only from their protection of those rights. And the law, the guardian of those rights, should rule above everyone, including the most powerful ruler.

NOTES

1. "Sentenced to Death, Rape Victim Is Freed by Pakistani Court," *New York Times,* June 8, 2002.

2. For a summary of Pakistan's history with rape laws, see Maliha Zia Lari, "Rape Laws in Pakistan: A History of Injustice," *The Dawn,* March 30, 2014.

3. For some of these cases, see Moeen H. Cheema, "Cases and Controversies: Pregnancy as Proof of Guilt under Pakistan's Hudood Laws," *Brooklyn Journal if International Law* 32, no. 1 (2006): 121–60. Mohammad Hashim Kamali notes that the number of unjustly jailed women in Pakistan was at some point more than 2,000. Kamali, *Crime and Punishment in Islamic Law: A Fresh Interpretation* (New York: Oxford University Press, 2019), p. 247.

4. Kamali, *Crime and Punishment in Islamic Law*, p. 247.

5. Qur'an, 24:10–13.

6. Qur'an, 24:4–5 (italics added).

7. Chineze J. Onyejekwe, "Nigeria: The Dominance of Rape," *Journal if International Women's Studies* 10, no. 1 (2008): 53. According to the author, "The way current Sharia laws [in Nigeria] are framed make it virtually impossible to prosecute rape," because of "the burden of proof that courts place on a victim."

8. See Intisar A. Rabb, *Doubt in Islamic Law: A History if Legal Maxims, Interpretation, and Islamic Criminal Law* (New York: Cambridge University Press, 2015), pp. 115–20. Hina Azam also agrees that a specific Maliki problem-taking pregnancy as conclusive evidence of *zina*-has unfortunately been adopted by most contemporary "Islamic" legal systems, which made things typically worse by conjoining "the most problematic and gender discriminatory aspects of the Hanafi and Maliki approaches." Azam, *Sexual Violation in Islamic Law: Substance, Evidence, and Procedure* (Cambridge: Cambridge University Press, 2017), pp. 243–44.

9. Azman Mohd Noor, "Problem of Crime Classification in Islamic Law," *Arab Law Quarterly* 24, no. 4 (2010): 427–33. As Noor mentions in this article, only a few

classical jurists considered rape as hirabah (violent robbery), which is a more serious crime than adultery, and this view has gained more popularity in the modern era.

10. Kamali, Crime and Punishment in Islamic Law, p. 68; and Rabb, Doubt in Islamic Law, p. 159.

11. Asifa Qyraishi, "Her Honor: An Islamic Critique of the Rape Laws of Pakistan from a Woman-Sensitive Perspective," *Michigan Journal if International Law* 18, no. 2 (1997): 305.

12. Azam, Sexual Violation in Islamic Law, p. 170. Azam makes this comment specifically for the Hanafi school, which considered rape a "violation against God," rather than "a dual violation against both God and a human victim." Intisar A. Rabb observes the same problem in the Maliki school, adding that, in general, "in Islamic law contexts rape was notoriously hard to prove." *Rabb, Doubt in Islamic Law*, p. 15.

13. Qur'an, 45:18.

14. Qur'an, 5:48.

15. See Fazlur Rahman, *Islam and Modernity: The Transformation of an Intellectual Tradition* (Chicago: University of Chicago Press, 1982), pp. 3–4. Here, Fazlur Rahman uses the term "Qur'anic weltanschauung," which I translated as "Qur'anic worldview." He contrasts this Qur'anic worldview mainly with "Ash'arism, the dominant Sunni theology throughout medieval Islam." For an extensive critique of Ash'arism, see Mustafa Akyol, Reopening Muslim Minds.

16. Qur'an, 2:178.

17. Qur'an, 5:38.

18. Qur'an, 5:33.

19. Qur'an, 24:2

20. Qur'an, 24:4.

21. Interestingly, qisas isn't always listed among the hudud, as it comes with an option of forgiveness. Meanwhile, non-Qur'anic hudud-such as execution for apostasy and flogging for drinking-have been extracted from the hadiths.

22. "Forbidden months" were four consecutive months in the Arab lunar calendar-Rajab, Dhu al-Qidah, Dhu al-Hijjah, and Muharram-during which war was banned so people could travel for pilgrimage. This preexisting Arab custom was honored by the Qur'an (in 2:217, 2:194, 5:2, 5:97, 9:5, and 9:36) but was largely forgotten by later Islamic jurisprudence that grew in a context where the notion was neither known nor functional. Zihar, another pre-Islamic Arab custom, was an act of instant and unilateral divorce by men-by saying to their wives, "You are like my mother"-which is disapproved by the Qur'an in 33:4 and 58:2–3.

23. The Qur'an contains a verse about detention in homes (4:15) and there are some narrations about short-term detainment of criminals or prisoners of war, but they do not refer to formal prisons, and these detainments "were not main punishments, but temporary measures such as arrest until the verdict." Ali Bardakoglu, *"Hapis," jslam Ansiklopedisi* (Istanbul: Tiirkiye Diyanet Vakf, 1997), vol. 16, p. 55. For more of this argument, see Mustafa Akyol, Reopening Muslim Minds, pp. 169–72.

24. The Qur'anic term for adultery, zina, is defined by neither the Qur'an itself nor the hadiths, whereas Islamic tradition took it to mean both premarital and extramarital

sex. However, a case can be made that it refers only to extramarital sex. A hadith reads that it is a grave sin to "commit zina with the wife of your neighbor," suggesting that zina is something done with a married woman. Sahib Muslim, "Kitab al-Iman," hadiths 156 and 157. According to such indicators, Islamic scholars Muhammad Abduh and Rashid Rida argued that "the punishment of zina is only applicable to offenders who were parties to a valid marriage at the time of committing the offence." Kamali, Crime and Punishment in Islamic Law, p. 76.

25. Islamic scholars have almost agreed that zina is the intercourse of male and female sex organs, in a way that they "meet like the kohl needle entering the kohl bottle." On the basis of this argument, Hanafi scholars excluded homosexuality from the definition of zina. Azam, *Sexual Violation in Islamic Law*, pp. 171–72. This does not mean that other forms of sexuality other than zina were religiously approved. Virtually all nonmarital sex has been defined as sinful, yet not necessarily as zina, which is defined as a criminal act.

26. Qur'an, 2:102, 2:278, 5:3, 5:90–91, 22:30, 24:30, 24:31, 49:12.

27. See Mustafa Akyol, "The Freedom to Sin," in *Islam without Extremes: A Muslim Case for Liberty* (New York: W.W. Norton, 2011), pp. 262–72.

28. For an example, see a classic manual of Hanafi law: Hasan Shurunbulali, Nur al-Idah, *The Light of Clarification*, trans. Wesam Charkawi (Damascus, 2007), p. 200:

> "The one who intentionally neglects prayer due to laziness or idleness, is to be beaten harshly until blood flows from his body and is then imprisoned during which he is subject to physical pain, until he performs his prayers or dies in confinement. This ruling also applies for one who does not fast [in] Ramadan due to laziness."

29. See Mustafa Akyol, "Freedom Matters III: Blasphemy," in *Reopening Muslim Minds*, p. 206.

30. A Turkish preacher, Ahmet Vanlioglu, put this in a sermon in Istanbul in 2017:

> "Now, let's say there is someone who does not do his [five-times-a-day] regular prayers. Some say, 'How can you force him, there is no compulsion in religion.' Well, yes, there is no compulsion to religion—but there is compulsion in religion. You cannot force a man who is not in the religion to accept it. But there is absolutely compulsion on a man who has entered the religion, who has accepted it."

31. See Mustafa Akyol, "How the Sharia Stagnated," in *Reopening Muslim Minds*, pp. 72–85.

32. Jonathan A. C. Brown, *Hadith: Muhammad's Legacy in the Medieval and Modern World* (London: Oneworld Publications, 2009), pp. 151–52. Ahl al-Ray is a reference mainly to early Hanafis, whereas Ah/ al-Ka/am is a reference to the Mu'tazila.

33. Sahih al-Bukhari, Book 88, Hadith 5. The same hadith, with slight variations, also exists in other major hadith collections, such as that of Sunan an-Nasa' i, Jami at-Tirmidhi, and Sunan ibn Majah. For an evaluation of their authenticity, see Mustafa Akyol, "Two Suspicious Hadiths," in *Reopening Muslim Minds*, pp. 197–99.

34. Hadiths relating to such verdicts can be found in various volumes of the canonical collections of the Sunni tradition. For killing of blasphemers, see Sunan

Abi Dawud, no. 4362; for stoning of adulterers, see Sahih al-Bukhari, no. 3635; for flogging of wine drinkers (and ultimately killing them), see Sunan Abi Dawud, no. 4482; for banning images, see Jami at-Tirmidhi, no. 1749; and for the defining of women as "lacking in reason and religion," see Sunan Abi Dawud, no. 4679. On the latter issue, also see Hidayet $efkatli Tuksal, "Misogynistic Reports in the Hadith Literature," in *Muslima Theology: The Voices of Muslim Women Theologians*, ed. Ed nan Asian, Marcia Hermansen, and Elif Medeni (Frankfurt: Peter Lang AG, 2013), pp. 133–54.

35. The quotation is a summary of the views of modern-day Muslim hadith critics. Daniel Brown, *Rethinking Tradition in Modern Islamic Thought* (Cambridge: Cambridge University Press, 1999), p. 95. Some of those scholars or public intellectuals are Syed Ahmad Khan, Muhammad Abduh, Rashid Rida, Mehmed Akif, MusaJarullah Bigiev, Ahmad Amin, Ghulam Ahmed Parvez, Muhammad Tawfiq Sidqi, Ismail Hakki Izmirli, Aksekili Ahmed Hamdi, Mahmud Abu Rayya, Mohammed al-Ghazali, Fazlur Rahman Malik, and Javed Ahmed Ghamidi.

36. See Paul]. Alexander, "Religious Persecution and Resistance in the Byzantine Empire of the Eighth and Ninth Centuries: Methods and Justifications," *Speculum* 52, no. 2 (1977): 238–64.

37. Luke, 14:23. This line was used for centuries by various Christian churches to justify coercion. It was challenged by Pierre Bayle, a French Protestant who contributed to the Enlightenment, in his influential 1686 book, A Philosophical Commentary on These Words of the Gospel, Luke 14.23, 'Compel Them to Come In, That My House May Be Full,' ed. John Kilcullen and Chandran Kukathas (Indianapolis: Liberty Fund Books, 2005). Also see Celine Rohmer, "'Compel Them to Come In!' (Luke 14:23): A Case of Holy Violence?," *Etudes Theologiques et Religieuses* 94, no. 1 (2019): 109–24.

38. In the United Kingdom, homosexuality was considered a crime until the Sexual Offences Act of 1967, which "permitted homosexual acts between two consenting adults over the age of twenty-one." For an evaluation of the discussions in the United Kingdom at the time, see Patrick Devlin, *The Enforcement of Morals* (Indianapolis: Liberty Fund Books, 2009), p. vi.

39. See Mustafa Akyol, "Lessons of Slavery and Abolition," in *Reopening Muslim Minds*, pp. 61–65.

40. The Qur'anic verse is 90:13. The argument that Islam's original intention to abolish slavery only took place gradually is common in mainstream contemporary Islamic sources.

41. This and all the preceding and following quotes from Evliya yelebi, with my translation from Turkish, are from Robert Dankoff, Seyit Ali Kahraman, and Yiicel Dagli, *Evliyd 9elebi Seyahatndmesi, Topkap1 Saray1 Kiitiiphanesi Bagdat 304 Numarah Yazmanm Transkripsiyonu* (Istanbul: Yap1 Kredi Yaymlan, 2006), vol. 1, 128–30.

42. See Ahmet Kuru, *Islam, Authoritarianism, and Underdevelopment: A Global and Historical Comparison* (New York: Cambridge University Press, 2019).

43. Noah Feldman, *The Fall and Rise of the Islamic State* (Princeton, NJ: Princeton University Press, 2008), p. 35.

44. Halide Adıp Adıvar, a towering Turkish female intellectual of the early 20th century, tells the story in *Turkiye'de $ark-Carp ve Amerikan Tesirleri* [East-West and American influences in Turkey] (Istanbul: Can Books, 2009, reprint of 1955 edition), p. 58.

45. Yusuf Kiis:iikdag, *"Zembilli Ali Efendi," jslam Ansiklopedisi* (Istanbul: Tiirkiye Diyanet Vakfi, 2013), vol. 44, 248.

46. The incident and the quotes are from Ishwari Prasad, *History of Medieval India* (Allahabad: Indian Press, 1927), pp. 242–43.

47. Brian Z. Tamanaha, *On the Rule of Law: History, Politics, Theory* (New York: Cambridge University Press, 2004), p. 13. On the same page, Tamanaha also says,

"There was no question that the emperor was above the law, for he made the law. Needless to say, this understanding is the very antithesis the rule of law ideal."

48. Guy I. Seidman, "The Origins of Accountability," *Saint Louis University Law Journal* 49, no. 2 (2004/5): 394–95.

49. See Cato Institute, Unlawful Shield website, http://www.unlawfulshield.com.

50. Under the Sharia, "immunities against prosecution . . . are totally absent,"and "no one can claim any immunity for his or her conduct merely on account of social and official status." John L. Esposito, ed., *The Oxford History of Islam* (New York: Oxford University Press, 1999), p. 149.

51. Ernest Gellner, *Postmodernism, Reason and Religion* (London: Routledge, 1992), p. 7

52. Three U.S. presidents have been impeached by the U.S. Congress: Andrew Johnson in 1868, Bill Clinton in 1998, and Donald Trump in 2019 and 2021. Richard Nixon resigned in 1974, facing near-certain impeachment. In 2019, Canadian prime minister Justin Trudeau was questioned by the ethics commissioner of the Parliament for an alleged political interference with the justice system. Italian prime minister Silvio Berlusconi faced various corruption charges while in office by independent prosecutors, such as Antonia Di Pietro. South Korean president Park Geun-hye was impeached in 2017 by the Constitutional Court, and later sentenced to imprisonment, for abuse of power and corruption.

53. "Norwegian PM Fined by Police over Coronavirus Rules Violation," Reuters, April 9, 2021.

54. See the World Justice Project Rule of Law Index, https://worldjusticeproject.org/rule-of-law-index/. As of 2019, the countries with the highest rule of law scores were Norway, Finland, and Denmark, whereas no Muslim-majority country made it into the top 25.

55. This comment is from Khayr al-Din al-Tunisi, to whom we will give more attention in the final chapter. The quote is from the translation of his book. Leon Carl Brown, *The Surest Path: The Political Treatise of a Nineteenth-Century Muslim Statesman* (Cambridge, MA: Harvard University Press, 1967), p. 72.

56. Noah Feldman persuasively makes this argument, adding that Ottoman reforms of the 19th century could have worked in establishing a liberal order but rather ended in "absolutism." Feldman, Fall and Rise of the Islamic State, pp. 59–79.

57. Selim Deringil, "There Is No Compulsion in Religion: On Conversion and Apostasy in the Late Ottoman Empire: 1839–1856," *Comparative Studies in Society and History* 42, no. 3 (2000): 551.

58. The edict in question is the Islahat Edict of 1856.

59. Halide Edip Adlvar, "Turkey Faces West," in *Modernist Islam, 1840–1940: A Sourcebook*, ed. Charles Kurzman (New York: Oxford University Press, 2002), p. 215.

60. Articles 8 and 9 of the first Ottoman Constitution, December 23, 1876, http://www.anayasa.gen.tr/1876constitution.htm.

61. In the Ottoman Constitution, the executive was held by the sultan and his Council of Ministers. Legislation was at the hands of a British-style parliament, with two chambers, one of which was freely elected. And the judiciary was left to independent tribunals.

62. For Atatiirk's devotion to "unity of powers," see Taha Akyol, *Ataturk'un jhtilal Hukuku* [Atatiirk's law of revolution] (Istanbul: Dogan Kitap, 2012).

63. For a critique of the "unity of powers" under Erdogan, see "Ergun Ozbudun: Kuvvetler aynlig1 gitti kuvvetler birligi geldi" [Separation of powers out, unity of powers in], interview by Taha Akyol, Karar, January 25, 2021.

64. See Ruth Austin Miller, "From Fikh to Fascism: The Turkish Republican Adoption of Mussolini's Criminal Code in the Context of Late Ottoman Legal Reform" (PhD diss., Princeton University, 2003). (Miller uses the Turkish term jikth, which I Anglicized asfiqh.)

65. Bernard Lewis, "Islam and Liberal Democracy," The Atlantic, February 1993. Lewis also adds that this authoritarian encroachment took place because "social and economic modernization enfeebled or abrogated the religious constraints and intermediate powers that had in various ways limited earlier autocracies."

66. Mohsen Kadivar, "Wilayat al-Faqih and Democracy" in *Islam, the State, and Authority: Medieval Issues and Modern Concerns*, ed. Asma Afsaruddin (New York: Palgrave Macmillan, 2011), p. 214.

67. James I, *The True Law of Free Monarchies and Basilikon Doron*, ed. Daniel Fishclin and Mark Fortier (Toronto: Centre for Reformation and Renaissance Studies, 1996), p. 72.

68. Bernard Lewis, *Faith and Power: Religion and Politics in the Middle East* (New York: Oxford University Press, 2010), p. 160. Lewis-who discovered the letter and has quoted it on various occasions-was also right to note that despotism is a somewhat "modern" problem in the Muslim world.

69. Montesquieu, Charles de Secondat de, "The Encyclopedia if Libertarianism, https://www.libertarianism.org/encyclopedia/ montesquieu-charles-de-secondat-de."

70. "Montesquieu."

71. J. W. Gough, *John Locke's Political Philosophy: Eight Studies* (Oxford: Oxford University Press, 1964 reprint), pp. 22–23.

72. Khayr al-Din al-Tunisi was wise enough to make this point in his The Surest Path: political power must be restrained, "either in the form of a heavenly Shari'a or a policy based on reason." Kurzman, Modernist Islam, p. 45.

73. The accuracy of this famous quote by Abduh is disputed, but it does reflect the spirit of Islamic modernists. See Jonathan A. C. Brown, *Hadith: Muhammad's Legacy in the Medieval and Modern World*, pp. 253–54.

74. This summary of al-Shatibi's approach is from Taha Jabir al-Alwani in Imam al-Shatibi's *Theory efthe Higher Objectives and Intents if Islamic Law*, trans. Ahmad al-Raysuni (Herndon, VA: International Institute of Islamic Thought, 2005), p. xi.

75. Muhammad al-Tahir Ibn Ashur, *Treatise on Maqasid al-Sharia*, trans. Mohamed El-Tahir El-Mesawi (Herndon, VA: International Institute of Islamic Thought, 2006), p. 155.

76. For a discussion of this "theological breakthrough," see Mustafa Akyol, "The Theory of Maqasid and Its Limits, A Non-Ash'arite Sharia," in *Reopening Muslim Minds*, pp. 79–85.

REFERENCES

Adıvar, Halide Edib, "Turkey Faces West," in *Modernist Islam, 1840-1940: A Sourcebook*, ed. Charles Kurzman (New York: Oxford University Press, 2002).

Adıvar, Halide Edib, *Türkiye'de Şark-Garp ve Amerikan Tesirleri II* [East-West and American influences in Turkey] (Istanbul: Can Books, 2009, reprint of 1955 edition).

Akyol, Mustafa, "The Freedom to Sin," in *Islam without Extremes: A Muslim Case for Liberty* (New York: W.W. Norton, 2011)

Akyol, Mustafa, *Reopening Muslim Minds: A Return to Reason, Freedom, and Tolerance* (Essentials, 2022).

Akyol, Taha, *Ataturk'un jhtilal Hukuku* [Atatiirk's law of revolution] (Istanbul: Dogan Kitap, 2012).

Al- Raysuni, Ahmad, *Imam al-Shatibi's Theory of the Higher Objectives and Intents of Islamic Law*, trans (Herndon, VA: International Institute of Islamic Thought, 2005).

Al-Tunisi, Khayr al-Din, *The Surest Path: The Political Treatise of a Nineteenth-Century Muslim Statesman*, Trans. Leon Carl Brown (Cambridge, MA: Harvard University Press, 1967).

Azam, Hina, *Sexual Violation in Islamic Law: Substance, Evidence, and Procedure* (Cambridge: Cambridge University Press, 2017), pp. 243–44.

Bardakoglu, Ali, "Hapis," jslam Ansiklopedisi (Istanbul: Tiirkiye Diyanet Vakf,, 1997).

Brown, Daniel, *Rethinking Tradition in Modern Islamic Thought* (Cambridge: Cambridge University Press, 1999).

Brown, Jonathan A. C., *Hadith: Muhammad's Legacy in the Medieval and Modern World* (London: Oneworld Publications, 2009).

Cheema, Moeen H., "Cases and Controversies: Pregnancy as Proof of Guilt under Pakistan's Hudood Laws," *Brooklyn Journal if International Law* 32, no. 1 (2006): 121–60.

Deringil, Selim, "There Is No Compulsion in Religion: On Conversion and Apostasy in the Late Ottoman Empire: 1839-1856," *Comparative Studies in Society and History* 42, no. 3 (2000): 551.

Devlin, Patrick, *The Enforcement of Morals* (Indianapolis: Liberty Fund Books, 2009).
Esposito, John L., ed., *The Oxford History of Islam* (New York: Oxford University Press, 1999).
Fazlur Rahman, *Islam and Modernity: The Transformation of an Intellectual Tradition* (Chicago: University of Chicago Press, 1982), pp. 3–4.
Feldman, Noah, *The Fall and Rise of the Islamic State* (Princeton, NJ: Princeton University Press, 2008).
Gellner, Ernest, *Postmodernism, Reason and Religion* (London: Routledge, 1992).
Gough, J. W. and John Locke, *Political Philosophy: Eight Studies* (Oxford: Oxford University Press, 1964 reprint).
Ibn Ashur, Muhammad al-Tahir, *Treatise on Maqasid al-Sharia,* trans. Mohamed El-Tahir El-Mesawi (Herndon, VA: International Institute of Islamic Thought, 2006).
James I, *The True Law of Free Monarchies and Basilikon Do*ron, ed. Daniel Fishclin and Mark Fortier (Toronto: Centre for Reformation and Renaissance Studies, 1996).
Kadivar, Mohsen, "Wilayat al-Faqih and Democracy" in *Islam, the State, and Authority: Medieval Issues and Modern Concerns*, ed. Asma Afsaruddin (New York: Palgrave Macmillan, 2011).
Kamali, Mohammad Hashim, *Crime and Punishment in Islamic Law: A Fresh Interpretation* (New York: Oxford University Press, 2019).
Kilcullen, John and Chandran Kukathas, *A Philosophical Commentary on These Words of the Gospel, Luke 14.23,* 'Compel Them to Come In, That My House May Be Full,' (Indianapolis: Liberty Fund Books, 2005).
Kucukdag, Yusuf, *"Zembilli Ali Efendi," jslam Ansiklopedisi* (Istanbul: Turkiye Diyanet Vakfi, 2013).
Kuru, Ahmet T., *Islam, Authoritarianism, and Underdevelopment: A Global and Historical Comparison* (New York: Cambridge University Press, 2019).
Lewis, Bernard, *Faith and Power: Religion and Politics in the Middle East* (New York: Oxford University Press, 2010).
Miller, Ruth Austin, "From Fikh to Fascism: The Turkish Republican Adoption of Mussolini's Criminal Code in the Context of Late Ottoman Legal Reform" (PhD diss., Princeton University, 2003).
Montesquieu, Charles de Secondat de," *The Encyclopedia if Libertarianism.*
Noor, Azman Mohd, "Problem of Crime Classification in Islamic Law," *Arab Law Quarterly* 24, no. 4 (2010): 427–33.
Nur al-Idah, *The Light of Clarification*, trans. Wesam Charkawi (Damascus, 2007).
Onyejekwe, Chineze J., "Nigeria: The Dominance of Rape," *Journal if International Women's Studies* 10, no. 1 (2008): 53.
Paul, Alexander, "Religious Persecution and Resistance in the Byzantine Empire of the Eighth and Ninth Centuries: Methods and Justifications," *Speculum* 52, no. 2 (1977): 238–64.
Prasad, Ishwari, *History of Medieval India* (Allahabad: Indian Press, 1927)
Qyraishi, Asifa, "Her Honor: An Islamic Critique of the Rape," *Laws of Pakistan from a Woman-Sensitive Perspective Michigan Journal of International Law* 18, no. 2 (1997): 305.

Rabb, Intisar A., *Doubt in Islamic Law: A History if Legal Maxims, Interpretation, and Islamic Criminal Law* (New York: Cambridge University Press, 2015).

Rohmer, Celine, "'Compel Them to Come In!' (Luke 14:23): A Case of Holy Violence?,"' *Etudes Theologiques et Religieuses* 94, no. 1 (2019): 109–24.

Seidman, Guy I., "The Origins of Accountability," *Saint Louis University Law Journal* 49, no. 2 (2004/5): 394–95.

Tamanaha, Brian Z., *On the Rule of Law: History, Politics, Theory* (New York: Cambridge University Press, 2004).

Tuksal, Hidayet Sefkatli, "Misogynistic Reports in the Hadith Literature," in *Muslima Theology: The Voices of Muslim Women Theologians*, ed. Ed nan Asian, Marcia Hermansen, and Elif Medeni (Frankfurt: Peter Lang AG, 2013). https://www.libertarianism.org/encyclopedia/ montesquieu-charles-de-secondat-de."

Chapter 6

Toward a Civilizational Ethos

From the Homo Moralis *to the* Homo Ethicus

Mohammed Hashas

This chapter[1] offers a new perspective on modernity, anchored in Islamic traditions, that explores its different manifestations, strengths, and limitations. The argument here is that Islam is not alone in encountering modern challenges, nor is it thus alone able to find solutions for them. There is now apparently one human civilization that shares the outputs of individual creativity and communal enginuity. High technology and digital world have *united* the world as never before but has not *elevated* it to the level of fair interaction and exchanges worthy of global justice. The Islamic moral and ethical paradigm can play an important role in contributing to overcoming some major misunderstandings of what human potentiality can do in relation to the individual, society, the natural world, and the universe at large. Such a state of global relations requires an elaboration of an inclusive normative framework and reexamining major concepts, like faith and religion, morality and ethics, sharia and law, spiritualism and spirituality, and idealism and realism. This essay argues that human beings need to embrace a set of ideas and ideals through a process of "spiritual self-criticism" that engages both the private and public spheres. Classical faith traditions as containers of moral and ethical energies will still have a major role to play in world affairs led by utilitarianism and realism alone. Political Islam as known today is nothing compared to the energies generated by Islamic philosophical understanding of the world and humanity. It is these energies that make the classical spirit of the Islamic civilization and its ethos still vibrant today and continues to be relevant for tomorrow.

INTRODUCING THE RAGING ETHICAL CRISES

World society is experiencing moral and ethical crises across religious, philosophical, and political boundaries. These crises seem to have accelerated since the 1990s with the domination of neoliberalism. Transnational neoliberal corporations and policies are led by international oligarchs who are willing to work with both authoritarian and democratic regimes in pursuit of economic opportunities. Heavy industrialization has deepened the gap between the North and the South in many parts of the world, and the economic pressure generated by the technologically advanced North is brought to bear on the postcolonial states of the South. The moral and ethical predicaments of postmodern humanity are inseparable from unfair competitions among industrial powers that dominate global markets. Wars over geopolitical interests and natural resources reflect this unsatiated appeal for dominance over the world. Narratives grounded in liberty, secularism, and democracy, however great they are and however promising they may be, are failing modern society. Rather than liberating humanity from religious, racial, ethnic, and ideological tutelages, they have become, in some parts of the modern world, shallow narratives as they are often used as excuses to invade other societies and lands to sustain the appeal of sovereignty and hegemony. The reemerging neocolonialism is, in many ways, the manifestation of double standards in interpreting liberal and progressive narratives that have attained universal following, since they do appeal to the principles of liberty, equality, and human dignity. They have the potential to bring humanity to embrace shared "civilizational ethos," to use the Moroccan philosopher Taha Abderrahmane's terms. Karl Jaspers's notion of the "Axial Age" may still be considered a potential idea for the shared civilizational ethos that various traditions can engage, including the Islamic tradition which can potentially make a significant contribution, as Louay Safi has shown in his recent work on Islam and globalization.[2]

The rise of digital technology has given a great advantage to societies that have mastery over it, leaving behind people who lack the capacity and resources to utilize it. Furthermore, the newly acquired capacity to harvest big data technology in monitoring habits of consumption has increased the capabilities of corporations that own it to influence choices of consumption and of thought. Crisis itself has become "liquid" and "blind," to borrow the concepts from Zygmunt Bauman; it permeates all spheres of physical and digital lives.[3] The private sphere of the individual which the family represents is being invaded with all sorts of market and ideological temptations through digital communications that are now part of the daily interaction of people. Individuals now can be distracted even in their utmost private spheres and most intimate moments through this device. Digital technology is gradually becoming the superego of the individual, and the means the state and the market can use to control the public.

Rational choices are often the result of balanced and reasonable options that are developed after a great deal of critical thinking and dialogue. They are so much linked to the human psyche and the innermost human values. They are originally spiritual choices, that is, spiritual in the sense of coming from the bottom of both the heart and mind. These spiritual choices are often individualistic and egoist, and they become communal and altruist only when they are measured through more sophisticated spiritual traditions that have passed the test of time. They take first the form of what I would refer to as "spiritualism" but may later be transformed to what I would call "spirituality." Spiritualism leads to shallow and egoistic humanism. Spirituality leads to genuine humanity and real altruism.[4]

This state of affairs has prompted Muslim scholars, like Taha Abderrahmane, to call for a new vision of the future of humanity anchored in ethical demands. He argues that rationalism has for long served the interest of the few, and it is about time that it should be guided by ethical concerns for the wider humanity. Human reason, he contends, is not only capable of promoting instrumental rationality (*al-'aqlāniyya al-ma'qula*) but can also pursue ethical ends (*al-akhlāqiyya*) and ethical humanity (*al-insāniyya al-akhlāqiyya*). He says, "human identity is essentially of an ethical nature."[5] The "unfinished project" of modernity, as Jurgen Habermas calls it,[6] has taken ethics from the reservoir of different faith traditions and philosophies. Modernity has so far been associated with unbridled capitalism and the use of advanced technology to promote overconsumption, armament, and hegemony. The other bright story of modernity is its normative discourses on human rights, equality of all before the law, accountability, and constitutional democracy. These ideals have the potential to unite humanity in its aspirations to create a more inclusive global justice. Islam and Muslims find themselves enmeshed in these global transformations and challenges; they are neither alone nor exceptional in facing them. Generalizing from a peculiarly European experience, modernity has pushed all faith traditions to the margin, preventing non-Western cultures from utilizing the spiritual and moral powers of their religious traditions.

Is there a way out? We will explore the relevance of Islamic ethical ideas and experiences to the current stage of human thought and its different manifestations, strengths, and limitations. The argument here is that Islam is not alone in encountering modern challenges, nor is it thus alone able to find solutions for them. There is now apparently one human civilization that shares whatever some individuals or communities produce or invent. High technology and the digital world have *united* the world as never before—but have not *elevated* it. The moral compass of Islam can play an important role

THE FUTURE OF FAITH

To envisage the future role that can be played by faith requires a deep understanding of the philosophy of religion and of faith traditions. That is, it requires a revision of not only the actions demanded by the faith but most importantly the imagery and the meaning it embodies. Faith principally calls people to position themselves in human history, by posing the most fundamental question: *why* I am here in this world and in this particular time and space? Out of this existential question comes the question of *how* one should act in the world in this particular time and space. Faith requires thinking for a balanced way of being, and a balanced way of being requires the mental and moral discipline at the core of any religion. The Quran, for example, is full of verses that remind the reader/believer of these two main tasks: to think, and to act accordingly, so as not to lose one's natural (*fiṭri*) disposition of humanness that is shared by all human beings, irrespective of their chosen traditions of belief or nonbelief. Muhammad Iqbal's *The Reconstruction of Religious Thought in Islam* (1930) tried in a concise and genuine manner to revive this spirit in Islam in modern times, through what he calls "higher Sufism," "higher religion," and "higher experience" of faith.[7] Iqbal's quest for religious revival is inspired, among others, by al-Ghazali's quest in his twelfth-century perennially influential work *The Revival of the Religious Sciences*. I will return to this point later in this chapter.

Since thinking is part of *becoming*, faith requires a framework of analysis along the triadic axis of "world-society-individual." This comprehensive framework can lead us to grasp the dynamics of faith according to three other lenses, namely time, space, and the "mindscape"[8] or discipline from which we look at faith. This makes the task of defining it a daunting one, since we live in definite time and space and have a limited rationality, while faith appears everlasting, super-dynamic, transtemporal, ahistorical, and multilinguistic. That is why whatever we say about a particular faith remains relative, limited to time, space, and our particular intellectual or political interests. It follows from this that whatever we say about faith cannot grasp the idea of God that it speaks of; this God, too, remains beyond time and space, and beyond our cognitive grasp. It is for this very reason that faith is a value that can only be spoken about and never be grasped fully, like the values of love, justice, mercy, and beauty. That is why comprehensive faiths build traditions, and traditions are plural and dynamic, even when they appear to belong to a singular faith tradition. And if a tradition is summarized in one book like the Bible or the Quran, it still cannot be grasped, since these books have influenced times and spaces and minds over the centuries. The Quran by implication then is not God/Allah, nor is Islam. The Quran speaks of God, as the Word of God for Muslims, and Islam is the religion of recognizing God. The Quran leads to Islam, and Islam leads to God. They are pathways to God, the Ultimate Reality, or the Real (*al-ḥaq*), the only One (*al-aḥad*).

Faith will become more important in future human societies, but it will not be orthodox faith. It will be needed for, clung to, one major reason: for being a source of moral being and of ethicist critique and revival. Human beings have always adhered to religion for this reason, to find meaning in life, and meaning requires freedom. The current crises and future endeavors to overcome them will make faith essential for human life for the reasons started with above: human freedom is now profoundly being encroached upon and must be reclaimed. Neither faith nor reason alone can reclaim it. Only human beings that combine spirituality and rationality can. This tendency can be seen, for instance, in the work of two American scholars. Khaled Abu El Fadl calls for a "universal overlapping consensus" to combat world atrocities and promote social justice as he echoes the demand made earlier by John Rawls.[9]

But what is faith, and how should it be conceptualized? Like love, faith can be felt, expressed, and manifested but can never be fully comprehended, as Wilfred Cantwell Smith (d. 2000), the renowned Canadian scholar of religion and of Islam, says in his classic *The Meaning and End of Religion* (1962).[10] Islam, too, is a faith, a love story for its believers; they live it, feel it, and express it, but they know that whatever they say of it still remains far from exhausting its inner meaning, like the idea of God/Allah itself. He is Omnipresent, everywhere but nowhere as well. It is no wonder that classical Muslim jurists never agreed to write unanimously one full book of sharia where Muslims can find their answers and solace. It is for this reason sharia remains a path toward the source, and for that an interpretation of the path toward the source: the First and the Last, the Inner most and the Outermost. The Sufis, the Muslim mystics, too have developed many ways of grasping and approaching this all-encompassing love. The German literary master Goethe expressed it well, to show that the search for the Eternal Being is not only an Islamic or Eastern matter but also Western; it is human. This he expressed in his *West-East Divan* (1819), in the first pages of which he writes the following:

> To God belongs the Orient,
> To God belongs the Occident!
> The Northern and Southern lands,
> Resting tranquil in His hands![11]

Faith, however, is the most intimate aspect of a religion. The latter is a developed and sophisticated apparatus that tries to bring together the major pillars of a faith into an organized form. If the Prophet or Messenger of a faith tradition does not live long to establish an organized community and to canonize certain rituals and forms and public relations, then his followers do that so as to maintain the faith and fidelity to it. There is no faith tradition that has reached us today that has not turned into an organized religion, with religious scholars, hierarchies of scholars, and spiritual guides as its fundamental defenders, besides politicians and ordinary human beings who also adopt it and defend it. Faith then cannot sustain itself without an apparatus, an organized framework. It is, in this sense, like any other idea, or ideology; no idea or ideology can sustain itself and live if it does not organize itself through an apparatus of individuals, scholars, politicians, pedagogues, and institutions. Faith, like anything else human beings do and defend in life, is both an ordinary and extraordinary power that moves people and histories. That is why empires, kingdoms, and republics throughout history have been attentive to the power of faith and have found ways to embrace it or at least respect it as much as possible, to save their thrones and positions, lest it is abused and used against them. It is for this reason that faith is an inviolable right in human rights narratives. It is the store of incomprehensible and immense human powers. It is the reservoir of human liberation and dignity, which are the most sacred values for any human being. That is why people also believe and maintain faith; it is their life; it is Life for them; it tells them how their *being* should be, so as to come closer to the ideal *Being*, the Source, they believe in. It gives them guidance in Life; it positions them in human history; it tells them that they count, whether old or young, male or female, rich or poor, black or white or brown, and that they have dignity and can realize great things in their short-lived life, which can impact human history and Life at large. Islam as the Abrahamic faith most rational and universal in its view of the universe, human diversity, and human innate liberty and equality expresses the meanings of faith in different ways, the most fundamental of which are liberty in belief, good deeds that benefit the others' free will and moral responsibility.

The past, present, and future of a world religion like Islam can only be better understood from a triadic perspective, which I have developed and used elsewhere: world, society, and individual axes.[12] Being in the world/universe requires belief or nonbelief in an idea or faith, so that the human being feels their place in the world and in existence. Being in society requires good deeds not only to become an integral part of society but to raise one's sense of humanity through altruistic services. Being an autonomous individual means that one holds a moral compass that makes the self-assured and balanced in its inner and outer comportment. Immorality means an inner feeling of disharmony between what one does and what one feels in the bottom of their heart, irrespective of how utilitarian the outcome of an act may be.

Put differently, Islam speaks of the universe, nature, earth, and animate and inanimate beings; these are all part of the larger life the believer has to ponder over, enjoy, and take care of as well. This is the meaning of spiritual caliphate (vicegerency) of human beings on earth mentioned in the Qur'an. Islam speaks also of the family, the community, society, and humanity. Their diversity is intrinsic to this world, and it is another sign to ponder over, recognize, and respect. It ultimately speaks of the self, the ego, and the individual. It speaks of the most generous and humble levels human beings can reach through good deeds; good deeds are the measurement of true faith; faith without good acts is useless, vain, and at the end non-existent; it is not faith that is not based on good acts in society and the world and that could be egotism, pomposity, and arrogance, and not genuine faith. The Quran repeatedly says that God looks—that is, judges—at our acts and not at our faces, wealth, or intelligence. Rational rituals tame human arrogance and appetite for sovereignty over other human beings. They are the sports that cultivate and elevate the ego to higher levels of humanity. Rituals lead to piety and its different levels that "higher Sufism"—to use the term of Iqbal—has excelled in practicing and describing. If only one axis of these three is centralized at the expense of the other, then only a partial view of the Islamic worldview is begotten. The moderation (waṣatiyya) the Quran speaks of aims at balancing the view of these three axes so that human beings as individual believers feel the coherence between what they believe and what they do, at least minimally if not maximally, depending on the level of their faith.

Moreover, it is the comprehensiveness described above that has made religions like Christianity and Islam world religions. The universality of Islam lies in its adaptability to different contexts, times, and spaces, for the last fifteen centuries. It is this trilogy also that has made it a living tradition—a "discursive tradition" according to Talal Asad or a "lived Islam" according to Kevin Reinhart[13]—in constant metamorphoses, even when these metamorphoses appear to be slow or decadent, if compared to other traditions in certain historical moments. What Tareq Oubrou calls "geotheology," a theology in context for Muslims in Europe, is how Islam has already been lived, in different spaces and times.[14]

There are many voices within a faith tradition. To take the case of Islam, our concern here is that there are at least six major trends; each one of them can be divided into other sub-trends: Popular Islam, Sufi Islam, Intellectual Islam (or Theologic and Philosophic Islam), Political Islam, State Islam, and Othered or Biased-Orientalist Islam (Space does not allow going into details on each here).[15] Each of these has built a tradition of centuries of interpreting, living, and perceiving the tradition. Each one of them has built legitimate arguments for how it interprets the faith. While I am concerned with lived Islam, I am mostly concerned with theoretical issues, philosophical and theological. I am interested in why human beings need faith, how they interpret it, and also what faith does to them, and how it influences them. Political questions are secondary here in the sense that they are results of higher theoretical issues.

THICK AND THIN SHARIA

The ongoing potentiality of elasticity and flexibility in Islamic thought is based on two major messages of the faith, which scholars have discussed and prioritized differently over time: morality, or ethics writ large, and social justice; the first targets the individual and the second targets society. It is these messages that make it ahistorical and atemporal, thus cosmopolitan and universal. These two messages or themes are found in every influential Islamic classical or modern text. Ethics move human beings and societies, and so does the need for social justice. But the way Muslim scholars and thinkers have interpreted them has varied and has thus expressed diversity of what it means to be Muslim and Islamic. The fact that there is no one single authority that speaks for Islam ("no Muslim Pope") has made this diversity a blessing in the past, and it has apparently become a source of tensions in the modern times of nation states and their rivalries over the monopoly of legitimacy, religious authority, and institutions.[16]

Sharia as the path of God was for over a millennium diverse, and plural, even when certain ideas became mainstream. It is erroneous to equate current sharia debates with premodern sharia life and interpretations. Current sharia is often rigid, nationalized, territorialized, and focuses mostly on aspects of political sovereignty and leadership, private matters of marriage and divorce, and increasingly also on the emerging "Islamic economics and finance." It is no surprise that the media in the East and West do equate sharia now with only law—which is a sort of fallacious reductionism. "Classical sharia" is the human interpretation of the Divine Sacred Book of the Quran and the Prophetic Tradition; sharia in this sense is multiple, dynamic, and contextualist. Classical sharia is comprehensive and covers business, public relations, international law, and diplomacy, to name these major spheres. When it ruled comprehensively in its high days, it worked successfully; that was the case for about twelve centuries, until the late eighteenth and early nineteenth centuries, when a stronger modern legal framework emerged in Europe and reached Muslim-majority societies and its minorities in the beginning. "Modern Sharia" is a deformation of this classical advanced ethical and legal worldview; it is hybrid; it has been forcefully merged into modern national legal systems of independent nation states that do monopolize a good part of Muslim religious institutions in Muslim-majority societies.¹⁷ States where Muslims are a minority are trying to monopolize this sharia narrative and frameworks as well. This is often being met with resistance in both majority and minority contexts. This does not mean that classical religious establishments that gained respect over the centuries do "de-Islamize" all the modern nation state and its important achievements. Rather, the rivalry over who monopolizes the religious discourse has to do with more complicated sociocultural and ethical issues that neither the state alone nor religious institutions alone—in all faith traditions—can resolve. As some scholars have already done, borrowing the terms of "thin/thick" from Bernard Williams (d. 2003), one can speak here of "thick" and "thin" sharia,¹⁸ or "solid" and "liquid" sharia: the first is comprehensive and covers all fields of life, based not only on the halal/haram differentiation but also on the permissible, recommended, and abhorred legal categories, as "classical sharia" classified acts, while "thin sharia" is limited in scope and influence to often private fields, like marriage, divorce, and the custody of children, and centralizes more ethical and aesthetics aspects instead of their legal aspects; this is the "modern sharia."

Muslim feminists—including male scholars – move in this orbit of the morals of sharia and its ontological justice (i.e., all are created equal) to speak of egalitarian laws now for Muslim women in modern times. Despite their diverse paths and engagements, these, among many others, have given new power to the female voice and female scholarship in Islamic thought: earlier names like Huda al-Sha'rawi, Zaynab al-Ghazali, and Aisha Abderrahmane (known as Bint al-Shati'), to the contemporary ones like Fatema Mernissi, Amina Wadud, Asma Barlas, and Ziba Mir-Hosseini. Female imamship advocates in Western Europe and North America, as I note later below, are inspired by these leading modern figures. However, scholars like Wael Hallaq see in terms like the "Islamic state" based on modern sharia as an aberration, an impossibility, and a contradiction in terms, since the modern nation state and the sharia it adopts in Muslim-majority societies has nothing to do with the classical "ethical sharia" that permeated society in the first place.¹⁹

This distinction between the classical and modern sharia is not abrupt and definite in time or space; they do intertwine, since the debate on how to adapt to modern challenges is still alive in contemporary Islamic legal and moral thought for the last two centuries or so. This also does not mean that in the future only one of them will survive the challenge, and the other elapses to history; religious traditions survive in different ways, and even when sharia legal thought is "reformed"—that is simply contextualized—some minor classical aspects will always remain, chiefly on personal matters (*'ibādāt*), since they are the reminder of the past, of the tradition, and recall the classics, and the roots. The Catholic Church, for example, has been modernizing for the last 150 years, but it still bears traces of premodern times and of its deep past in some of its "juridical" or "dogmatic" (dogma = creed) views. The same applies to the Jewish tradition, or any other comprehensive world tradition that has reformed but has also retained aspects of the past. Without the past, the tradition cannot be a tradition. Without memory, there is no present.

This transformation of sharia from a thick into a thin reference has not been smooth and is still evolving. No tradition that flourished and governed human affairs for a millennium can smoothly transform itself into a minor reference without challenges, predicaments, resistances, and also radicalizations. The revival of Islamic thought in all sectors from the 1800s until now has not taken a smooth course—and all ideas that target human affairs do not find smooth ways to their realization, since they encounter other established traditions and habits that human beings cling to. Various internal and external factors and stakeholders have interfered in the process and have made the labor toward a refined sharia model nearly an impossible mission in modern times. The progressive revivalist salafiyya—in opposition to regressive salafiyya à la Wahhabiyya—of the late nineteenth and early twentieth centuries, led by influential religious scholars like Muhammad Abduh, Jamal al-Din al-Qasimi, Muhammad al-Tahir Bin Achour, Abdelhamid Ben Badis, Allal al-Fassi, among many others, did not live long, mostly because of the political situation of colonialism and the rise of authoritarian secularism and militarism especially in the Middle East where this revivalist movement first appeared, that is, in Egypt and Greater Syria, and afterward in the Maghreb—similar movements of revivalism appeared before or during this same period in the rest of the so-called Muslim world.[20] Instead, the rise of political Islam with its various branches from the mainstream moderate to the tiny radical branches that destroy lands and people has become the challenging fate of progressive revivalism so far. However, this predicament cannot last forever; it will elapse, sooner or later. Two centuries in the lives of universal traditions is not a long period. A different, brighter, side of the tradition will rise again, seeing the work being done toward this end; there are plenty of scholars and institutions working for it, though with immense difficulties.

Reformist or critical Islam is part of this process of polishing the house, but it cannot make it alone; it should work closely with the mainstream conservative-moderate scholars and institutions that have historical legitimacy over interpretating the tradition, besides direct contact with the believers through mosques, sermons, and publications. Reforms can only come out from these orthodox classical institutions, like al-Azhar in Cairo, or its equivalents of smaller size but of international importance, like al-Qarawiyyin in Fez, al-Zaytuna in Tunis, Umayyads Grand Mosque in Damascus, Jombang Mosque of Nahdlatul Ulama and Muhammadiyah Society in Indonesia, among other similar institutions worldwide. Historians of ideas and historians of religions can tell us that radically new ideas are often, if not always, hard at first to penetrate societies and intellectual or religious spheres. Western Europe that has been modernizing for at least five centuries still harbors premodern ideas within many of its intellectual and religious circles. Changing minds takes centuries. This is not because it is the sole responsibility of religion, but because this is linked to other factors that intertwine with religion, that is, politics, nationalism, race, wealth, economy, and political power and authority.

Though religious scholars appear to be the first responsible of either conservatism or reformism, it is, however, other stakeholders that either block or encourage change, based on the benefits this change can bring them. For an illustration, even when a few figures of Muslim religious scholars in modern and contemporary times try to be reformist and progressive, they are not allowed by their peers or by other competing religious institutions or movements or by the "secularreligious"[21] states that monopolize religious authority and discourse in most Muslim-majority societies.[22] International intervention and Islamophobia also contribute to making smooth change difficult, since a culture of defense grows to defend not only the faith and the religion at stake but also the culture, the people, and the societies under oppression, neocolonialism, cultural aggression, "diabolization," and othering.

Elsewhere I have spoken of four authorities that block change: two are internal and two are external.[23] The internal powers are represented by state apparatuses that monopolizes religious discourse, besides the regressive or stagnant religious authorities themselves. As to the external blocking powers, they are the colonial and postcolonial hegemonies as well as biased Orientalism studies that developed a negative picture of Muslim societies, their cultures and faith traditions, their sciences, and ultimately their history, which, for Wael Hallaq's most recent argument, remains entangled in Western linear history that does not see any resuscitation potential in it or in any other Oriental tradition, like that of China, India, or Latin America.[24] A lot of these nurture right wing and Islamophobic feelings toward Muslims worldwide and enforce the narrative that Islam is anti-Western and anti-democratic, a narrative which is not only close to the radical jihadis and salafis but also it is a narrative that has influenced some Muslims' own view of modernity and Islamic intellectual and social history.

Since 9/11 (2001) terrorist events in the United States, some political narratives emerged to underline the role of mosque-imams and the need to train them to solve current predicaments and radicalizations. That is certainly a needed step, since the mosque-imams are the closest to the community of believers and non-believers and are the most able to channel through a renewed message of adaptation and genuine co-existence among all faith interpretations and inter-faith differences. They can underline the differences between thin and thick sharia, so that believers, especially the young ones with little knowledge of the tradition, understand the in-depth of the faith outside its only legalistic aspects that are often underlined without contextualization and elaboration of the ethical weight lying behind it. However, mosque-imams cannot solve political and geostrategic problems that contribute to the predicament. The narrative of female-imams, which I refer to as female imamship, is no exception here; while it is an important step in the diversification of Islamic religious authority, through the empowerment of female voices, and local male-imams, it is a field full of challenges, and it needs to be treated case-by-case, or according to contexts, whether it is Muslim-majority context or minority context, as is the Western one for Muslims.[25]

MORALITY AND ETHICS

Morality seems to be the main aim of any faith and religion—the latter being the extended corpus and interpretations formed over the years and centuries of the former. Morality targets the profoundest levels of human psyche to transform them into moral, that is, good, human beings, based on a particular worldview. Each moral worldview has ways to teach individuals how to reach these levels of goodness and virtuousness, from basic rituals to laws pertaining to some parts of life or to all its aspects. When these teachings touch human relations, and not the individual alone, they move from being moral teachings to being ethical ones, since they aim larger and wider. In history, and whenever circumstances allow, these moral teachings that find space in the public create a polity and enlarge it to become local, regional, or imperial. Christianity and Islam are examples of such faith traditions that navigate easily between the private and the public when circumstances allow them. There are plenty of internal interpretations within these faith traditions and the limits or limitless domains of their moral and ethical teachings. Details aside, now with modernity and the concept of the nation state, the imperial ambitions of faiths have been tamed with so-called "secularism," that is, the separation of religious and political powers and the creation of a "neutral state" that rules based on the will of the people, and not on the will of some divinity or one single ideology.[26] With scientific developments and human rights, the "secularization" of societies at large has grown further. Of course, there is no single state that is fully neutral, nor is there one single society that is fully just one thing, one identity, or one faith, or one block of some idea; there is hidden diversity even in the most authoritarian and oppressive regimes. Moreover, secularization does not necessarily mean the death of religion or faith traditions, though it does lead to strong limitations on the influence of religion in the management of socioeconomic and political affairs in society. Rather, it means their reinterpretation to fit new human needs and their intellectual and spiritual needs, beyond classical orthodoxies and rigid rationalism, which Charles Taylor refers to as the "middle condition" that the modern self aspires to, away from emptiness.[27] Human beings have always lived with interpretations. Their moral traditions are interpretations of a morality that resides in the past and strives to live in the present and future. Human beings are intrinsically hermeneutical beings.

The point here is that while morality is fundamental for stirring change in the individual, it is ethics that carry this internal urge to the public. The public does not necessarily mean the political; it means the shared sphere that can host different, and also opposing, faith traditions and philosophies, and their possible ideological interpretations. The public is the space where real identities should be fully expressed without fear, and where moral choices are tested and measured, with reference to the social contract as stipulated in the constitution of the political entity where one thinks and acts. Morality without an impact in the public sphere is egoistic, individualist, and not humanist in the larger sense of the term; it has its vital value for the individual, but it is a limited value, since it does not urge the self to perform morality discourse in the public sphere for the larger community and society. Morality is individualist salvation. This is negative morality. Its opposite is positive morality.[28]

Morality that is positive is altruist; it is shared with the other, especially the different other; it is public; it is applied. When morality moves from the private to the public, it becomes ethical, and this is the distinction I am building here to argue for the potentiality of faith and religion to the future *homo ethics* and shared civilization of ethos. Morality becomes ethical when it is concerned with public issues, with global issues, when it moves from negativity to positivity, or from neutrality or inaction to action. To refer to the faith tradition that influenced Mahatma Gandhi and his public as well as political engagement, he says the following in the last sentences of his autobiography *The Story of My Experiments with Truth* (1927):

> my devotion to Truth has drawn me into the field of politics; and I can say without the slightest hesitation, and yet in all humility, that those who say that religion has nothing to do with politics do not know what religion means.[29]

This argument is not different from Iqbal's political engagement, based on his faith tradition as a religion for public use, or from other religious leaders in the Islamic world that equipped themselves and their fellows with liberation theology teachings to combat colonialism, as did Emir Abdelkader in Algeria, Muhammad Abduh in Egypt, and Allal al-Fassi in Morocco, to name but a few.

SPIRITUALISM AND SPIRITUALITY

Muslim-majority societies have experienced important juridical changes and adaptations during the last two centuries, and most modern international laws and conventions in all fields have been incorporated in national legal traditions of modern states in these societies, based on different methods of selection found in the classical legal tradition itself, like adopting whatever is beneficial to the community and the public good, easing what is difficult, and permission of the detestable or disliked when necessity requires. Marriage and divorce laws, inheritance issues, the custody of children, and the halal-haram food products remain the visible aspects of classical sharia legal apparatus in many of these societies. In Muslim-minority contexts as in liberal societies, Muslims abide by the laws of the land as part of their moral religious duty to honor contracts, that is, Constitutions and Citizenship requirements. In cases of not being citizens of liberal lands, then international law agreements and bilateral agreements of the lands they come from and the lands they reside in are applied. Europe and the "West" at large are now actually parts of the "Islamic world," the way the Islamic world is part of the West. Past and present interconnections make this fact more and more visible and more established. This is to say that Muslims in Muslim-majority societies are also experiencing transformations in their faith the way their co-believers experience them in liberal contexts. Similar transformations do not mean that they are identical; often they have different rhythms and different minute explanations and effects.

Like the concepts of morality and ethics, whose denotations and connotations change over time to unveil their relevance in each era, spirituality as a concept does too. Over the centuries, faith traditions has become more traditional, difficult to change or reform, and they challenge changes through classical lenses of spirituality and its past masters and models. Reformists, however, believe that spirituality is as changeable as morality is.

Often, the graduates of the modern universities are more liberal because they feel more freedom in their context than those surrounded by the conservatives and the ultra-conservatives in classical religious seminaries, madrassas, and traditional universities and colleges. Among some of the liberals has appeared a trend of interpreting classical Islamic Sufism in a more flexible form that appeals to the modern liberal context and individual freedoms discourse, based on the idea that every Muslim has the right as well as the duty to reinterpret the Sacred Text and the whole tradition as they see fit to their spiritual needs and level of faith.

Based on the earlier distinction between morality and ethics, another distinction can be built here between spiritualism and spirituality (*al-rūḥāniyyāt* and *al-rūḥiyyāt*, respectively, in Arabic).[30] Spiritualism is growing as a side-effect of the reformations faith traditions have been undergoing in modern times to replace religion, while spirituality is the classical and orthodox path of seeking the Ultimate Reality and Truth, irrespective of the political or intellectual paradigm that governs human societies; it is that search for "a larger life"—in the words of Iqbal—based on genuine belief, and true exertion to reach the profoundest senses of being and connection with the Real. Spiritualism is liberal, and spirituality is conservative. Spiritualism is self-gratifying, proud, and sometimes shows-off, while spirituality is modest, decent, humble, and often discrete. A spiritualist says he (or she) is spiritualist, and a rational believer, while a spiritual does not say anything and keeps his spirituality to himself and lets it speak through his comportment. Spiritualism creates its own rituals, while spirituality follows orthodox ones that have proven to be corrective of human morality and elevating human ethics and behavior. Spiritualism is an expression of private morality, while spirituality is an expression of public morality and engaged ethics. Spiritualism claims that it knows God or the Ultimate Reality and preaches this knowledge, while spirituality seeks God humbly, confidently, and does not claim that it knows God; it seeks God. Spiritualism is a civic philosophy that can become an ideology, and spirituality is a lived and living civic path that can correct civic ethics when they become blind ideological schemes of tutelage and hegemony. Both are of different levels: when the level of spiritualism increases, it becomes a dogma, rationally narrow-minded, while spirituality becomes more humble, more open, more accommodative of diversity when its mystic levels increase. Spiritualism wishes to enforce agreement among human beings while spirituality tries to find humane solutions to their diversity that it does not deny. Spiritualism can be regressive, while spirituality is always progressive, morally speaking.

This distinction, however, does not mean that they are exclusive of each other in the public sphere; they have more intertwining territories, and they can cooperate for the shared common, and the public good, since they both speak of altruism and serving humankind. They could complement each other despite their profound differences about the conception of life and the origins and end of humankind and of the universe—this is so because spiritualism is often scientist (for scientism) and secular (this-worldly), while spirituality is rooted in an orthodox faith tradition of the past, and antique philosophies of transcendence and eternity (i.e., Perennial Philosophy). These differences between the two impact their views on morality and ethics, and the need or not of faith traditions and their institutions.

Iqbal was very critical of popular manifestations of Sufism, which at times contradict the Tawhidic pillar of Islam, and so was Fazlur Rahman, Abdolkarim Soroush, Mohammed Abed al-Jabri, and Muhammad Abduh, and many others before them. This did not lead them to call for new rituals as a form of rationalizing faith. As a modernist believer and poet-philosopher, Iqbal speaks of three stages of religious life: faith, thought, and discovery. As humans move from rituals to metaphysics, they ultimately discover real religious life in their deepest inners; he speaks here of the psychology of the believer and his ability to communicate with the Ultimate Reality. He says:

> In the third period metaphysics is displaced by psychology, and religious life develops the ambition to come into direct contact with the Ultimate Reality. It is here that religion becomes a matter of personal assimilation of life and power; and the individual achieves a free personality, not by releasing himself from the fetters of the law, but by discovering the ultimate source of the law within the depths of his own consciousness.[31]

Note that while he emphasizes "higher experience" and "higher sufism" in fathoming the intent of faith—which he calls religion—he does not do without the law, "not by releasing himself from the fetters of the law," as he writes. Iqbal here is aware that the liberation faith teachers have to pass by training and exertion. It is not easy to reach the in-depth knowledge that could allow one to understand or see Ultimate Reality. He, in earlier chapters of his work cited above, speaks of the signs of *al-Anfus* (the inner ego as well as the soul) and the signs of *al-Āfāq* (the horizon, universe). Being erudite in Islamic theology and philosophy, Iqbal knows well that the rationalization of faith he calls for is not easy to reach; it is a process and is demanding, which is not what shallow spiritualism promises, I believe. Spiritualism claims, like ultra-orthodox literalists, that it knows what the Ultimate Reality is and that whatever the rational ego says, so be it; there is no need for psychological and intellectual "pain" (i.e., quest for the divine, *'ishq*) to go through. Spiritualism sells spiritual enlightenment without exertion. Spirituality, instead, demands both an intellectual and spiritual path. Genuine modern spirituality, in the Islamic tradition, I believe, has to meet – at least some of—the high standards of the classic Sufi masters, if we wish that it transforms the moderns into moralist and ethicist human beings. The levels of mystic enlightenment (*maqāmāt*) are infinite and take serious engagement and exertion. The Sufi master Al-Junaid (d. 910) defined Sufism as such, "Sufism is the recollection of God at a gathering [of like-minded people], ecstasy at the hearing [of this recollection], and action in compliance with the Divine Law." He also said, "Sufism is a struggle with no truce"; "If you see a Sufi who is concerned about his appearance, you should know that his inner self is rotten (*kharāb*)."[32] It is this intellectual spirituality, anchored in the tradition and engaged with modernity, that contemporary Muslim philosophers see as the antidote to arrogant self-gratification at the expense of altruistic service.[33]

Intellectual criticism is great but is not enough. Only spiritual self-criticism that transforms humans from the bottom of their heart can save us.[34]

IDEALISM AND REALISM

The background behind the defense of "spiritual self-criticism" as presented in this essay is an idealism—or more precisely Transcendent morality and ethicality—rooted in modern partial secularism (i.e., non-materialist secularism) and rationalism. This secularism is administrative, epistemological and not ontological. The world, according to this view, is not just what we see, but is also what we do not see, the world of inspiration and moral guidance that profound faith traditions can teach us; Islam belongs to these rich faith traditions; rather, it is classical Arab-Islamic philosophy that philosophized Abrahamic faith and turned it into a rational practice, besides its ritualistic and mystic sides. The secularism adopted here is open, historicist, and forward looking but is also traditional in the sense that it looks back to the moral richness of the past and its great masters, from prophets to influential spiritual and philosophic-theologic figures. It is, according to Abdelwahab al-Massiri (d. 2008), "partial secularism," and not "full secularism."[35] Full secularism is indiscreetly atheist, or in the least, it gives space to the divine only as much as this divine serves its egoistic and individualistic aspirations, and not the aspirations of humanity at large. As to rationalism, it is not purely materialist; full materialism echoes atheism, but rationally spiritual materialism often reflects free human beings who follow basic experimental methods, but which may often be pushed for by innate human belief in the future and in a metaphysical world. While exact sciences may be very neutral, the scientists cannot; they are human beings who hold ideas and are ready to engage the larger community and society, and are rooted in a living tradition which influences them and their lives, and possibly their work as scientists. Classical exact scientists in the Islamic civilization were methodically meticulous and rigorous, but this did not close their hearts and minds to faith and its teachings. This is the case for scientists in modern times. The defenders of bioethics are scientists who hold high moral standards that they have learnt from their faith or community traditions. Their scientist spirit does not eclipse their morality nor their ethicality. That is where faith and science meet. Ibn Sina and Ibn Rushd's medical expertise, for instance, do not eclipse their mastery of philosophy or their faith. Similarly, for the moderns, Descartes' mathematical genius did not eclipse his faith, nor did Kant's pure reason or Einstein's physics eclipse their amazement at the universe and its mysteries—its metaphysics.

In other words the above argument appears to strick a "middle way" between being idealist and being realist. Middle positions are always hard to form and maintain, since human societies, when they seek change, often move more toward the right or toward the left; if they choose the middle, that means that they have not solved the predicament they are in, and that reflects the balance of power in society and its intellects as well as the fear that a profound social change might destroy the essence the past holds, i.e. the tradition holds. This then means that too much of a move toward the future is hazardous, perilous, and who knows where it leads, to a Godless world, be it good or bad, or to a world of God, be it good or bad, or to that middle ground human beings often seek to live the good and still feel the divine vibrance in their lives! Often the middle way is taken after a revolutionary moment has taken place; this revolution may be spiritual, or intellectual, or political, or all of these. Some need a moment to shake them, and some go through it with more tranquility.

This middle ground in modernity is not easy, apparently, since secularism has become a dominant worldview, especially in the "West," empowered by "pure" rationalism, scientific achievements, industrialization, high technology, economic prosperity, and modern human rights. Charles Taylor, who was quoted earlier, calls our times a "secular age." And as a way out of the "disenchantment" we moderns are in, he proposes what he calls the "immanent frame" or "immanent order," and also "middle condition," whereby we can replace God and the Transcendent with some human rational order that preserves its love for freedom without truly smashing God or the Transcendent at the end.[36] This is the same middle ground I have invoked. It is not easy to maintain it in current modernity, though it is not impossible either. Abdennour Bidar's idea of "Self Islam" or an "existentialist reading of the Quran" is similar to this Taylorian perspective, a perspective that is Iqbalian in the first place, post-Iqbalian to be more precise. I have called such a middle ground a "Muslim Promethean" ground or option. The Orthodox God is not killed, but His Laws that have to do with immediate mundane issues are gently reformed because human intellect and needs require change. A life without Divine perfume is unbearable, according to this perspective. Meaning in life stems from this link with the Divine.[37] Widespread atheism is not sustainable by individual human beings—and by political entities as well—absolute sovereigns in human history ruled either as Gods or against God; in both cases, the idea of God was present.

Human beings need moral compass and need identity formation, which is first of all psychological, internal, existential, and only some higher moral order can satiate this identification. Still, modern secularism is a paradigm human beings have to cope with, as long as it leaves space for faith and religion, that is, as long as it is not radical secularism that smells of atheism, as Fazlur Rahman would say. That is why tradition in general, and the Islamic tradition in focus here, remains fundamental for constant rational and spiritual criticism. Reason and faith are complementary, not contradictory, and at certain levels identical in objectives. Spirituality in the Islamic worldview is not a space outside the material world; it is part and parcel of the material; that is why I think it holds that middle path of idealism and realism. And that is why reformation here is not only not applicable since there is no central authority (Pope-like) but especially because a reformation would require choosing between either idealism or realism, the ascending or the descending, the Transcendent or the mundane. Both are vital for human beings; they are complimentary, the way morality and ethics are. It is in this sense that religion and politics, or reason and revelation, or theology and philosophy are complementary. But this requires first steps of separation for abstraction and "intellectual judo" as well as profound psychological and moral transformations before their ideals meet on the ground, in this concrete world.

When George Hourani richly argues that Muslims may better re-start from where the rationalist Mu'tazilite intellectual tradition stopped if they wish to revive their theological and philosophical thinking,[38] he most probably unconsciously thinks that if religious thought becomes fully rational, through emphasis of the objectivism of moral values, that could solve current sociocultural, political, and economic issues in Muslim-majority societies. That is a view a lot of secular-liberal scholars of Muslim faith also hold. I only partially agree with this view. The Muslim world might have got into the current predicaments of modernity centuries earlier than the European-American moment, if they had endorsed the Ma'tazilite thought at the mainstream level since the eleventh century. Now the task is about who can get out of current modernity and its global malaise while remaining modern, differently modern.

Cultures and civilizations rotate in leadership in world history. The so-called Muslim world exhausted its circle after about five to six centuries of high culture—and a millennium of living history guided by the same paradigm—even though it adopted the Ash'arite thinking worldview in the majority Sunni world, a theological-philosophical view considered moderate, reconciliatory, in the middle, neither fully rational nor fully *divinical*—not to say "divine." The Ash'arite's use of reason is balanced, and keeps space to the Transcendent, the Divine, to intervene in the interpretation of human acts through causality, against arbitrariness, and in the interpretation of how humans can always aspire for better lives through utopic/divine attributes that are a moral compass for people to imitate (i.e., liberty, peace, justice, beauty, mercy, solidarity, gratitude, humility, confidence, among other attributes that teach values). It is a mediatory position that can still teach a lot. As to what can be retained most from the Mu'tazilites' rationalist tradition, it is their defense of pure reason and its ability to reach objectively what is good and evil, right and wrong, and most importantly their first two out of the five pillars of their doctrine: the idea of Justice and Oneness of God (*al-'adl wa al-tawhid*), which are the basis of liberation theology for the people, free will and accountability. Abdolkarim Soroush, who identifies himself as a Neo-Muʻtazilite, presents a rationalist but also idealist-moralist interpretation of Islamic theology and philosophy that remains friendly to the Divine, since he centralizes spiritual experience, though his views on the role of Prophet Muhammad in Quranic wording is controversial. In their philosophies of religion, Sayyed Hussein Nasr and Shabbir Akhtar, too, stand on this rational ground, but with clear affinity to the idea of the Transcendent and the Divine. Nasr links it to Perennial Philosophy, and Akhtar to the Muʻtazilites, who, however rationalist they were, remained believers and bound by Sharia legal prescriptions. Sincerity of intent here remains fundamental. I would say they are my antecedent fellows on this path of the "middle way" I have tried to outline here, the way Iqbal, Fazlur Rahman, Ali Izetbigovic, Hassan Hanafi, Taha Abderrahmane, Mohammed Abed al-Jabri, among others, have tried in their robust philosophical projects. To borrow the terms from Louay Safi and use them for this context, they are Muslim "rational idealists" whose rationalism recognizes human limitations and human need for a moral compass that is external to man—a corrective compass, so to call it. As to their counterparts who hold different views on the role of faith, and religion at large, in public life, they have a different view on the sources of morality and the meanings of ethics. Broadly, for them, morality is a very intimate issue, very private, and ethics are a public affair, negotiated based on public good, without a need to refer to faith in that public sphere, since it is a secular sphere. For them, the individual is divisible, they can have private morality that is different from its public manifestation or public ethics. What is right is abiding by the agreed upon public ethics, as to the goodness or not or moral private behavior, that remains a private choice as long as it does not violently disrupt public agreed upon choices.[39]

Overall, these two great traditions of the Ashʻarites and the Muʻtazilites have a lot to teach the moderns from all faith traditions, and Muslims in particular. However, I do not think that it is religion alone, or faith in particular, that needs to be reformed to enjoy modern "progress" and "prosperity." There are other internal and external political and economic factors that influence the flourishing or not of a tradition. Fundamentally, any tradition that defends human existential freedom and social justice is an ideal tradition to maintain, and this is defended by the mainstream Islamic tradition and its diverse sects and schools—violent radicals aside—since they are neither scholarly nor influential to be followed in mass. And this is the view of an important theologian, jurist, and philosopher like Ibn Rushd/Averroes, a reason for which he is championed by many modernists and contemporaries in the Arab and Muslim world. Prophets, according to him, are exemplary because of the *sharaʾiʿ* (pl. of shariʾa/worldview/rules) they brought to humanity, and which worked well for human beings especially in their formative period and for centuries afterward. More importantly, it is his balanced view on both philosophy and theology (sharia) as two independent pathways to Truth that makes his ideas most relevant in societies where a separation of the spheres of influence of authorities (secular/religious) have not developed clearly yet, or have developed but have not contributed to the aspired for change and "socioeconomic development." But development can have other sources of failure and success beyond the question of faith, secularism, and religion issues, as mentioned earlier. Other internal and external factors do make a faith tradition a strong contributor to social change or a barrier to it.

Again, only spiritual self-criticism can save us! That is, morality has to overcome the test of sincerity in the public through ethics; it needs to manifest itself beyond its private realm to bolster public ethics and competition for the good. This requirement of sincerity and consistency in moral and ethical action, if pursued globally, would also form a civilization of ideal-realist tension, a civilization of ethos manifested in authentic rational idealists of the sort Louay Safi articulates in *Islam and the Trajectory of Globalization* (2022). While privatizing the moral energies of faith traditions has become the norm for the stabilization of the social contracts of consolidated (liberal) democracies, this call of bringing the moral energy to the public does not aim at disrupting such an order, but at correcting its shortcomings that affect individuals, society, and world affairs—as succinctly noted in the beginning of this essay. To live a life worth living, human beings need to wash themselves by themselves, perpetually, as Rumi says, "Be melting snow/Wash yourself of yourself."[40]

NOTES

1. This chapter is based on the communication delivered in a roundtable discussion for *Islam in the 21st Century Second Conference*, organized by *Islam in the 21st Century* Network (Paris) and was hosted by UNESCO Palace in Paris, 16–17 February 2022.

2. Louay Safi *Islam and the Trajectory of Globalization: Rational Idealism and the Structure of World History* (London and New York: Routledge, 2022).

3. Zygmunt Bauman and Leonidas Donskis, *Moral Blindness: The Loss of Sensitivity in Liquid Modernity* (Cambridge UK: Polity Press, 2013).

4. More on this in due time below.

5. In English, see Wael Hallaq, *Reforming Modernity: Ethics and the New Human in the Philosophy of Abdurrahman Taha* (New York: Columbia UP, 2019); Mohammed Hashas and Mutaz al-Khatib, ed., *Islamic Ethics and the Trusteeship Paradigm: Taha Abderrahmane's Philosophy in Comparative Perspectives* (Leiden: Brill, 2021). In Arabic, see, for instance, Taha Abderrahmane, *The Question of*

Ethics—A Contribution to Ethical Criticism of Western Modernity (Casablanca and Beirut: Arab Cultural Center, 2000).

6. Jurgen Habermas, "Modernity: An Unfinished Project," in *Habermas and the Unfinished Project of Modernity: Critical Essays on The Philosophical Discourse of Modernity*, eds., Marissio Passerin D'Entrèves and Seyla Benhabib (Cambridge: MIT Press, 1997) 38–48,

7. Muhammad Iqbal, *The Reconstruction of Religious Thought in Islam* (1930), ed. M. Saeed Sheikh, intr. Javad Majeed (California: Stanford University Press; Lahore: Iqbal Academy Pakistan, 2012), 105, 143, 147.

8. "Mindscape" is a concept developed by the Scottish poet-philosopher Kenneth White (b. 1936) in his open world project of "geopoetics." For an introduction, see Mohammed Hashas, *Intercultural Geopoetics: An Introduction to Kenneth White's Open World* (New Castle: Cambridge Scholars Publishing, 2017).

9. Khaled Abu El Fadl, *Reasoning with God: Reclaiming Shari'ah in the Modern Age* (New York and London: Rowman and Littlefield, 2014), 395.

10. Wilfred Cantwell Smith, *The Meaning and End of Religion* (New York: The New American Library of World Literature, 1964).

11. Johann Wolfgand von Goethe, *West-East Divan [1819]: The Poems, with "Notes and Essays": Goethe's Intercultural Dialogues*, trans., intr., comm., by Martin Bidney, "Notes and Essays" trans. By Martin Bidney and Peter Anton von Arnim (Albany NY: State University of New York Press, 2010), 5.

12. See Mohammed Hashas, *The Idea of European Islam: Religion, Ethics, Politics, and Perpetual Modernity* (London and New York: Routledge, 2019).

13. Talal Asad, "The Idea of an Anthropology of Islam," Occasional Paper, *Georgetown University Center for Contemporary Arab Studies* (1986); Kevin Reinhart, *Lived Islam: Colloquial Religion in a Cosmopolitan Tradition* (Cambridge: Cambridge UP, 2020).

14. Hashas, *The Idea of European Islam*, 117–39.

15. It is difficult to refer to one or some works that try to cover with study all these disciplines at length; however, attempts through anthologies from different perspectives have been made by scholars, in English language here, like Ibrahim Abu Rabi', Seyyed Hossein Nasr, Omid Safi, Charles Kurzman, John Esposito, Richard C. Taylor, Peter Adamson, Sabina Schmidt, Lloyd Ridgeon, among others.

16. The case of the current theologico-political system ruling in the Islamic Republic of Iran since 1979 can be considered an exception; its *vilayet-e-faqih*/Supreme Leader theory looks like the hierarchy of the Roman Catholic Church and figure of the Pope.

17. The terms "modern" and "classic" here are descriptive, and do not hold positive or negative connotations, though in common use one may praise modern human rights achievements and say the "modern" is more advanced than the "classic"/ premodern world. The past was full of moral teachings and had its merits that in some fields are superior in achievements to modern times. "Family," "solidarity," and "hospitality" are some major "classical" virtues that are being demolished in some modern contexts because of excessive self-interest, irrational consumerism, and fear of the neighbour and the Other. There is no nostalgia for the past here; the

past still influences our modern comportment in many ways, despite its pastness and remoteness. And the present is not all-evil as some may argue. Human history has never been perfect, nor will be. This said, one can also say that one century of human modernity, the twentieth century of two devastating world wars, among other regional wars against colonialism, is the worst of all human known history. The measure here is simple: how many people die because of wars. Wars bring out the worst in humankind. Maybe if classical human beings were industrialized, they could have been worse centuries, too, and the ethical they now invoke may be because the weaponry was not industrialized and devastating as it is now. Still, one major difference remains: premodern times valued values most, while modern times value the material most. And that makes a whole difference of epistemes and conception of the world, society, and the individual.

18. See Jan-Erik Lane and Hamadi Redissi, R*eligion and Politics: Islam and Muslim Civilization* (Surrey and Burlington, VT: Ashgate, 2009), 277–83. Abdolkarim Soroush also distinguishes between thin and thick reality, the first is this-worldly, and the second is other-worldly, and includes the metaphysical; he also speaks of positive and negative pluralism, essentials and accidentals of religion, minimalist and maximalist religiosity; see, Soroush, *The Expansion of Prophetic Experience, The Expansion of Prophetic Experience: Essays on Historicity, Contingency and Plurality in Religion*, trans., Nilou Mobasser, ed., Forough Jahanbakhsh, Leiden: Brill, 2009).

19. Wael Hallaq, *The Impossible State: Islam, State, and Modern Predicament* (New York: Columbia University Press, 2013).

20. These important volumes give a good picture of the early dynamics of modern Islamic thought and societies: Charles Kurzman, ed. *Liberal Islam: A Sourcebook* (Oxford and New York: Oxford University Press, 1998); Charles Kurzman, ed. *Modernist Islam 1840–1940: A Sourcebook* (Oxford and New York: Oxford University Press, 2002); for the Arab world in particular, these are major texts: Albert Hourani, *Arabic Thought in the Liberal Age 1798–1939* ([1962] Cambridge: Cambridge University Press (22nd printing), 2013); Ibrahim Abu Rabi', *Contemporary Arab Thought: Studies Post-1967 Arab Intellectual History* (London and Sterling, VA: Pluto Press, 2004), Suzanne Kassab, *Contemporary Arab Thought: Cultural Critique in Comparative Perspective* (New York: Columbia University Press, 2010). To decentralize the Arab world in Islam studies, Shahab Ahmed proposed looking at the Balkan-Bengal complex/horizon of Muslim-majority societies and their intellectual productions in philosophy, theology, sufism, and literatue: Shahab Ahmed, *What Is Islam? The Importance of Being Islamic* (Princeton: Princeton University Press, 2016).

21. The term was first used by Asef Bayat, *Life as Politics: How Ordinary People Change the Middle East* (Amsterdam UP, 2010).

22. The case of Sheikh Muhammad Abduh (d. 1095), the Grand Mufti of Egypt and pioneering figure of the so-called Arab-Islamic Nahda/Awakening is often quoted as a prominent example; his attempts to reform education in al-Azhar was met with resistance.

23. See Mohammed Hashas, "The Arab Possible State: from al-Tahtawi to al-Jabri," in *Islam, State, and Modernity: Mohammed Abed al-Jabri and the Future of*

the Arab World, eds. Zaid Eyadat, Francesca Corrao, and Mohammed Hashas (New York: Palgrave: 2018), 271–302.

24. Wael Hallaq critiques the knowledge produced by both Orientalists' Orientalism and anti-Orientalists à la Edward Said in *Restating Orientalism: A Critique of Modern Knowledge* (New York: Columbia University Press, 2018).

25. Mohammed Hashas, Jan Jaap de Ruiter, Niels V. Vinding, eds., *Imams in Western Europe* (Amsterdam: Amsterdam UP, 2018); Hashas, "On Female Imamship in Europe," preliminary title, forthcoming paper, 2024.

26. Secularism as a form of separation of powers can become itself a staunch ideology that could be used to target manifest differences based on religion in the public sphere. French *laïcité* and the "Muslim question" is the most prominent example here. The literature on secularisms and religion in the public sphere is vast; for instance, see: José Casanova, *Public Religions in the Modern World* (Chicago and London: Chicago University Press, 1994); Linell E. Cady and Elizabeth S. Hurd, eds. *Comparative Secularisms in a Global Age* (New York: Palgrave, 2010); Abdullahi Annaim, *Islam and the Secular State: Negotiating the Future of Shari'a* (Hardvard, MA, and London: Harvard University Press, 2008).

27. See Charles Taylor's magnum opus *A Secular Age* (Cambridge, MA, and London: The Belknap Press of Harvard University Press, 2007).

28. Positive and negative distinction here is borrowed from Isaiah Berlin's famous essay "Two Concepts of Liberty," in his *Four Essays on Liberty* (Oxford University Press, 1969). In Arabic, morality, which is sometimes translated as or rendered equivalent to *ḍamīr* (conscientiousness), can also be translated as *akhlāq jawwāniyya* (internal ethics), and ethics as *akhlāq barrāniyya* (external ethics). Not to make a point into it here, another more original Arabic translation, with modifications in meaning, can be rooted on the juridical lexicon used in Hadith sciences, i.e. *akhlaq li-thātihā* (intrinsic morals) and *akhlāq li-ghayrihā* (extrinsic morals).

29. Mahatma Gandhi, *The Story of My Experiments with Truth* (1927), trans. Mahadev Desai (Ahmedabad: Navajivan Publishing, n.d.).

30. This Arabic distinction goes to Taha Abderrahmane, and my distinction here is inspired by his overall work, though my mapping of modern Islamic thought at large has also contributed to forming this distinction here.

31. Iqbal, op. cit, 143.

32. As quoted by Abu'l-Qasim al-Qushayry, *Al-Risala al-Qushayriyya fī 'ilm al-Taṣawwuf/ Al-Qushayry's Epistle on Sufism*, trans. Alexander D. Knysh, rev. Muhammad Eissa (Reading, UK: Garnet Publishing, 2007), 290–91.

33. For instance, in an exchange with John Hick in 1994, Seyyed Hossein Nasr emphacized the role of revelation in the future of faith and human salvation from the predicaments of rational modernity, instead of scientist spirituality and human reason alone, or what I have referred to here as spiritualism; for him mysticism is fundamental in the guidance of the intellect; in Adnan Aslan, *Religious Pluralism in the Christian and Islamic Philosophy: The Thought of John Hick and Seyyed Hossein Nasr* [1994] (London: Routledge, 2004), xii–xiii.

34. "Spiritual self-criticism" is here put as the equivalent of al-Tazkiyya in Arabic. See our work on Taha Abderrahmane for the philosophic dimensions of this Sufi

concept in the secular age: Hashas and al-Khatib, eds., *Islamic Ethics and the Trusteeship Paradigm*, op. cit.

35. Abdelwahhab al-Massiri, *Al-'ilmāniyya al-juz'iyya wa al-'imāniyya al-shāmila* (Partial and Full Secularism) 2 vols (Cairo: Dar al-Shuruq, 2002).

36. Taylor, *A Secular Age*, op. cit.

37. Hashas, *The Idea of European Islam*, 140–61.

38. George Hourani, *Reason and Tradition in Islamic Ethics* (Cambridge: Cambridge UP, 1985).

39. The prominent figures of this camp include Abdellah Laroui, Mohammed Arkoun, Sadek Jalal al-Azm, Abdelmajid Charfi, Bassam Tibi, Abdennour Bidar, among others.

40. Coleman Barks, and John Moyne, trans., *The Essential Rumi* (Edison, NJ: Castle Books, 1997), 13.

REFERENCES

Abderrahmane, Taha. *su'āl al-akhlāq: musāhamatun fi al-naqd al-akhlāqī li al-ḥadātha al-gharbiyya* [The Question of Ethics—A Contribution to Ethical Criticism of Western Modernity]. Casablanca and Beirut: al markaz athaqāfī al'arabī, 2000.

Abderrahmane, Taha. *The Question of Ethics—A Contribution to Ethical Criticism of Western Modernity*. Casablanca and Beirut: Arab Cultural Center, 2000.

Abu El Fadl, Khaled. *Reasoning with God: Reclaiming Shari'ah in the Modern Age*. New York and London: Rowman and Littlefield, 2014.

Abu Rabi', Ibrahim. *Contemporary Arab Thought: Studies Post-1967 Arab Intellectual History*. London and Sterling, VA: Pluto Press, 2004.

Ahmed, Shahab. *What Is Islam? The Importance of Being Islamic*. Princeton: Princeton University Press, 2016.

Al-Massiri, Abdelwahhab. *Al-'ilmāniyya al-juz'iyya wa al-'imāniyya al-shāmila* (Partial and Full Secularism) 2 vols. Cairo: Dar al-Shuruq, 2002.

Al-Qushayry, Abu'l-Qasim. *Al-Risala al-Qushayriyya fi 'ilm al-Taṣawwuf/Al-Qushayry's Epistle on Sufism*, trans. Alexander D. Knysh, rev. Muhammad Eissa. Reading, UK: Garnet Publishing, 2007.

Ali Izetbigovic, Ali. *Islam between East and West* (1984), 3rd ed. Oil brook, IL: American Trust Publications, 1993.

Annaim, Abdullahi. *Islam and the Secular State: Negotiating the Future of Shari'a*. Hardvard, MA, and London: Harvard University Press, 2008.

Asad, Talal. "The Idea of an Anthropology of Islam," Occasional Paper, *Georgetown University Center for Contemporary Arab Studies* (1986), 1–30.

Aslan, Adnan. *Religious Pluralism in the Christian and Islamic Philosophy: The Thought of John Hick and Seyyed Hossein Nasr* [1994]. London: Routledge, 2004.

Bauman, Zygmunt and Leonidas Donskis, *Moral Blindness: The Loss of Sensitivity in Liquid Modernity*. Cambridge UK: Polity Press, 2013.

Bayat, Asef. *Life as Politics: How Ordinary People Change the Middle East*. Amsterdam UP, 2010.
Berlin, Isaiah. *Four Essays on Liberty*. Oxford University Press, 1969.
Cady Linell E., and Elizabeth S. Hurd, eds. *Comparative Secularisms in a Global Age*. New York: Palgrave, 2010.
Cantwell Smith, Wilfred. *The Meaning and End of Religion*. New York: The New American Library of World Literature, 1964.
Casanova, José. *Public Religions in the Modern World*. Chicago and London: Chicago University Press, 1994.
Coleman Barks, and John Moyne, trans., *The Essential Rumi*. Edison, NJ: Castle Books, 1997.
Gandhi, Mahatma. *The Story of My Experiments with Truth* (1927), trans. Mahadev Desai. Ahmedabad: Navajivan Publishing, n.d.
Goethe, Johann Wolfgand von. *West-East Divan [1819]: The Poems, with "Notes and Essays": Goethe's Intercultural Dialogues*, trans., intr., comm., by Martin Bidney, "Notes and Essays" trans., by Martin Bidney and Peter Anton von Arnim. Albany NY: State University of New York Press, 2010.
Habermas, Jurgen. "Modernity: An Unfinished Project," in *Habermas and the Unfinished Project of Modernity: Critical Essays on The Philosophical Discourse of Modernity*, eds., Marissio Passerin D'Entrèves and Seyla Benhabib. Cambridge: MIT Press, 1997, 38–48.
Hallaq, Wael. *Restating Orientalism: A Critique of Modern Knowledge*. New York: Columbia University Press, 2018.
Hallaq, Wael. *Reforming Modernity: Ethics and the New Human in the Philosophy of Abdurrahman Taha*. New York: Columbia UP, 2019.
Hallaq, Wael. *The Impossible State: Islam, State, and Modern Predicament*. New York: Columbia University Press, 2013.
Hashas, Mohammed and Mutaz al-Khatib, ed., *Islamic Ethics and the Trusteeship Paradigm: Taha Abderrahmane's Philosophy in Comparative Perspectives*. Leiden: Brill, 2021.
Hashas, Mohammed, Jan Jaap de Ruiter, Niels V. Vinding, eds., *Imams in Western Europe*. Amsterdam: Amsterdam UP, 2018.
Hashas, Mohammed. "The Arab Possible State: from al-Tahtawi to al-Jabri," in *Islam, State, and Modernity: Mohammed Abed al-Jabri and the Future of the Arab World*, eds. Zaid Eyadat, Francesca Corrao, and Mohammed Hashas. New York: Palgrave: 2018. 271-302.
Hashas, Mohammed. "Vers une civilisation de l'éthique: de l'Homo Moralis à l'Homo Ethicus." *Revue L'Islam au XXIème Siècle/Journal of Islam in the 21st Century*, no. 7 (2022), 20–46.
Hashas, Mohammed. *Intercultural Geopoetics: An Introduction to Kenneth White's Open World*. New Castle: Cambridge Scholars Publishing, 2017.
Hashas, Mohammed. *The Idea of European Islam: Religion, Ethics, Politics, and Perpetual Modernity*. London and New York: Routledge, 2019.
Hourani, Albert. *Arabic Thought in the Liberal Age 1798-1939* ([1962]. Cambridge: Cambridge University Press, 2013.

Hourani, George. *Reason and Tradition in Islamic Ethics*. Cambridge: Cambridge UP, 1985.

Iqbal, Muhammad. *The Reconstruction of Religious Thought in Islam* (1930), ed. M. Saeed Sheikh, intr. Javad Majeed. California: Stanford University Press; Lahore: Iqbal Academy Pakistan, 2012.

Kurzman, Charles. Ed. *Liberal Islam: A Sourcebook*. Oxford and New York: Oxford University Press, 1998.

Kurzman, Charles. Ed. *Modernist Islam 1840-1940: A Sourcebook*. Oxford and New York: Oxford University Press, 2002.

Lane, Jan-Erik and Hamadi Redissi. R*eligion and Politics: Islam and Muslim Civilization*. Surrey and Burlinghton, VT: Ashgate, 2009.

Reinhart, Kevin. *Lived Islam: Colloquial Religion in a Cosmopolitan Tradition*. Cambridge: Cambridge UP, 2020.

Safi, Louay. *Islam and the Trajectory of Globalization: Rational Idealism and the Structure of World History*. London and New York: Routledge, 2022.

Soroush, Abdolkarim. *The Expansion of Prophetic Experience, The Expansion of Prophetic Experience: Essays on Historicity, Contingency and Plurality in Religion*, trans., Nilou Mobasser, ed., Forough Jahanbakhsh. Leiden: Brill, 2009.

Suzanne Kassab, *Contemporary Arab Thought: Cultural Critique in Comparative Perspective*. New York: Columbia University Press, 2010.

Taylor, Charles. *A Secular Age*. Cambridge, MA, and London: The Belknap Press of Harvard University Press, 2007.

Part II

GLOBAL CONFLUENCE IN THE MUSLIM SOUTH

Chapter 7

Muslim Intellectuals and Global Justice

A View from Southeast Asia

Khairudin Aljunied

What do Muslim intellectuals have to say about global justice? In a book written by a productive and no-less-controversial scholar, Abdullahi Ahmed An-Na'im advances a pioneering and "theoretical approach to global justice from an Islamic perspective."[1] What he means by this is a reimagining of global justice in ways that reinterprets the *shari'a* (Islamic ethical and legal code). A newly conceptualized *shari'a* in tune with contemporary human problems is urgently needed. For An-Na'im, such a reconceptualization can only be possible when Muslims readily embrace the idea that secularism is the best organizing principle for statecraft and, by implication, for the realization of global justice. That is to say, "the policy and law enforced by the state must always respect the equal fundamental constitutional and human rights of the totality of the population, Muslims and non-Muslims, men and women."[2] Only when states in Muslim countries are secular and only when these states acknowledge the functional and not totalizing place of the *shari'a* within the larger framework of human life that justice, both local and global, be fully achieved.

For An-Na'im, much of the extant Muslim scholarship lacked an in-depth take into issues pertaining to global justice because it is stifled by ideological standpoints. He castigates Muslim liberals, socialists, and fundamentalists for their inability to engage with civility on the question of justice. To An-Na'im, such internal discourse within Islam and with other traditions can eventually lead to "an overlapping consensus on commonly agreed principles, even despite disagreement on our respective reasons for that shared commitment."[3] An-Na'im is not always true to his plea. His text lacks inclusivity toward ideas outside his primary regions of concern. While claiming to provide a pluralistic standpoint, An-Naim's excursus relies almost wholly on ideas drawn from Anglo-American as well as Middle East and North African (MENA) thinkers. To wit, his theory and substantiations of global justice are based primarily on the ideological edifice developed by his revered Sudanese teacher, Mahmoud Mohammed Taha (1909–1985). While An-Na'im is open "to accepting any alternative methodology that will achieve what I believe to be the necessary degree of Islamic reform,"[4] much of his deliberations on global justice are, to a large extent, Arabocentric expressed within the vocabulary and grammar of liberalism. Indeed, his ideas are for the most part bracketed within, for the lack of a better term, the Taha-ist paradigm which argues for "the key notions of 'absolute individual freedom' and 'total social justice,' which together represent the cornerstone of his [Taha] theory of a second message of Islam."[5]

This chapter builds on the salient points raised by An-Na'im in his absorbing book. It addresses An-Na'im's limited horizons and fills a yawning gap in existing works on Muslims and global justice. While recognizing the many contributions made by scholars in the MENA region to discourses on justice, I argue that such ideas ought to be provincialized as but one of the many strands of thought that we should consider. Provincializing the MENA region does not entail downplaying their significance. Rather, what I am attempting to do here is to encourage scholars to adopt a wider frame of reference: one that conceives ideas in the MENA and other parts of the sprawling Muslim world as equally important in any analysis of global justice. To be sure, in order for us to expand the scope of discussions on global justice and its implications on Muslims, we must take into account what Richard Bulliet describes as "the view from the edge." By this, he means a new way of seeing the Muslim world and the ideas that define it from centrifugal and multi-nodal perspectives rather than the usual core–periphery framework. Such vantage point demands according equal importance to ideas that grew from Muslim domains outside the MENA region. It necessitates moving away from the presumptions that the intellectual cultures and traditions that grew in the wider Muslim world are second-tier derivatives, mere borrowings, or creative extensions of great traditions. Instead, the view from the edge entails seeing such ideas as attempts by non-Arab Muslims at expanding the repository of Muslim thought in their own unique ways that can inform us how Muslims had spawned many different centers of Islamic intellectualism, each of which is distinctive in their own right, most of which drew from the same mainspring of knowledge: The Qur'an.[6]

I wish to bring to the fore the rather neglected ruminations of an erudite Malay scholar-activist, Hamka (abbreviation and pen-name of "Haji Abdul Malik bin Abdul Karim Amrullah," 1908–1981). Author of over 118 books, Hamka was more than an armchair theorist of justice. He was one of the leaders of Indonesia's largest Muslim social movement—the Muhammadiyah—during its most difficult years striving to reform Muslim societies from its backwardness. He served as one of the founders of the Islamic party, Masyumi (Partai Majelis Syuro Muslimin Indonesia, or The Council of Indonesian Muslim Associations), and was an active participant during the revolutionary struggles for Indonesia's independence from 1945 to 1949. Hamka was also the first chairman of the Majlis Ulama Indonesia (MUI, or Indonesian Islamic Scholars' Council). Hamka's concern with global justice encompasses areas which Erin Wilson handsomely outlined:

> as focusing primarily on issues of extreme poverty, hunger, conflict, mass human rights abuses, and, increasingly, unequal use of and damage to the global environment as well as unequal exposure to the consequences of global environmental change. I also understand global justice as the promotion of equality, social justice and reconciliation, diversity, democracy, nonviolence, solidarity, ecological sustainability, and planetary citizenship.[7]

For Hamka, it is incumbent upon all Muslims to be attentive and vigorous defenders of global justice. Upholding global justice is a core part of their responsibility toward humanity.[8]

I argue here that Hamka's ideas of global justice could be termed as a dialogical conception of global justice. John Rawls, in his classic *Theory of Justice*, defines conceptions of justice as "the outgrowth of different notions of society against the background of opposing views of the natural necessities and opportunities of human life."[9] It follows then that Hamka's conception of justice was shaped by his dialogue with various notions of global justice which was dominant during his time, be it those espoused by Muslims or non-Muslims. He was well acquainted and yet critical of the materialist and parochialist viewpoints. His conception of global justice also involves a reformist reinterpretation of key concepts in Islam. For him, the concepts of *khalifatullah fil 'ard* (vicegerents of God on earth), *amanah* (sacred trust), *shura* (mutual consultation), and *maslahah* (general welfare) are among the most important in constructing a new thinking about global justice. To put it succinctly, Hamka's standpoint considers the interplay between texts and evolving contexts and the interfaces between ideas drawn from Islamic and supra-Islamic sources. His fresh understanding of global justice is rooted in the Islamic tradition, and yet pragmatic and responsive to shifting global vicissitudes. In that sense, Hamka shares some of An-Na'im's viewpoints. Both urge Muslim scholars to cultivate a deep appreciation of the Islamic tradition and how it may inform contemporary approaches to global justice. Both were also acquainted with Western thought without being overly captivated by it. They were equally keen on reaching an overlapping consensus between different conceptions of global justice and seeking ways to go beyond such ideas. The two differ however in the sense that Hamka was against any permutations of secular thought and reasoning while An-Na'im viewed secularism as a useful ideological instrument that could be used to manage human affairs.

CRITIQUING DOMINANT CONCEPTIONS OF GLOBAL JUSTICE

The conceptions of global justice that dominated the minds of Muslim intellectuals since the 1920s were an upshot of staggering global events. The Great Depression, the two world wars, the struggles for independence, and the subsequent founding of new nation-states spawned ideational and social movements that agitated for equality and the restoration of human rights. These movements highlighted problems of underdevelopment, unemployment, inequality, and deprivation that characterized societies across the world.[10] Muslim intellectuals were cognizant that although many Muslim lands were eventually free from colonial rule, most Muslims were living in abject poverty. They were wretched in their own homeland, caught in between the heavy hand of the state, the ruling elites, and the exploitative schemes of transnational corporations. Muslims were becoming increasingly divided between many camps—religious, secular, socialist, capitalist, anticolonial, and elitist. The most serious problem confronting Muslims during this phase of human history, as seen through the eyes of the Algerian thinker Malek Ben Nabi, was intellectual bankruptcy. Their understanding of justice, civilization, and development was influenced by ideas that were alien to their traditions and hence detrimental to their societies.[11]

Hamka concurs with Ben Nabi's castigation of Muslim intellectual backwardness. He criticizes prevailing conceptions of global justice. Such critiques, according to Benjamin McKean in his illuminating book that exposes the ills of the neoliberal conception of global justice, are necessary on the road toward developing an "alternative orientation" that "puts existing inequality in perspective, enabling us to identify and act against injustice more effectively."[12] One conception of global justice that came under Hamka's sharp analytical knife was the "materialist" conception. To Hamka, the materialist conception of global justice could be divided into two branches.

The most dominant is the capitalist idea that free-market forces can bring about global justice. Such a belief, according to Hamka, was based on the capitalists' conviction that men are rational beings. Their material pursuits would not necessarily dissuade them from becoming responsible members of society. From this line of reasoning, the capitalists contend that states and other governing institutions should not play a direct role in regulating society. Rather, these institutions should act as facilitators for market forces to run smoothly and to structure society so as to achieve equilibrium and harmony, which capitalists recognize as essential to the growth of the economy.[13] Hamka's view of the capitalist conception of global justice is rather simplistic. In reality, purveyors of capitalism do believe in some form of governance that would ensure justice. Markets, as Daniel Halliday and John Thrasher explain,

> are, however, not fully spontaneous as governance is needed for various assurances and other enabling conditions. And prices cannot always be relied on to get the job done, as in the cases of alleged market failure that we've discussed. The invisible hand—the tendency of some spontaneous market orders to deliver mutual advantage and greater justice—usually requires certain background conditions.[14]

In Hamka's defense, however, even if certain checks and balances have been placed to ensure that markets do not necessarily have a free hand, the reality is such that global capitalism has bred widescale injustices. Most severe of all has been toward the natural environment as seen climate change and deforestation caused by the exploitation of multi-national companies.[15] For the same reason, Hamka believes that the promises of a capitalist conception of global justice were illusory and deceitful. Capitalism exploits human beings and nature through the agency of profit-driven establishments such as banks and corporations. History bore testimony to the reality that these establishments funded European colonial schemes, which led to the domination over and abuse of non-European peoples. Colonial capitalism widened the gaps between the haves and the have-nots in colonized societies. Colonial capitalism laid the foundations for the creation of the *masyarakat riba* (society of usury), which encouraged the poor to believe that they too could be like the rich by living on borrowed cash, without realizing that they had been enslaved by banks and credit firms.[16]

These points were reinforced by a Malaysian scholar's study of the impact of colonial capitalism on the Malay world. In *The Myth of the Lazy Native*, published in 1977 during the same period when Hamka was actively writing about global justice, Hussein Alatas states that colonial capitalism had ravaged almost all aspects of Southeast Asian life, from the moral to the economic to the spatial, from health to the spiritual. Colonial capitalism led to the growth of many diseases such as malaria, tuberculosis, venereal disease, and dysentery.

> The hasty development of settlements, the crowding of people, bad sanitation and sewage, prostitution, injurious habits such as opium smoking and drinking

amongst those of modest means, had resulted from the opening of the mines and estates with its attendant urbanization.[17]

Hamka's trenchant critique of capitalism as a negating force on global justice gives us the impression that he was leaning toward the Marxist, communist, and socialist conceptions of justice that were making a comeback during the 1950s. But this was not the case. He criticizes the writings of Muslim socialists who preceded him, such as Abdul Rahman al-Kawakibi (1855–1902). Charles Tripp argues that al-Kawakibi

> portrayed Islamic principles of social justice and ethical economic organisation as identical with those of modern socialism. By his account, therefore, Islamic law and principles called for economic equality for all, for the public ownership of the means of production and for the right and indeed duty to work for the good of all.[18]

Hamka observes some affinities between Islam and socialist ideas but he emphasizes the stark differences between them.

For him, the Marxists, communists, and socialists committed the error of conceiving global justice narrowly from the perspective of materiality. They believed that social justice could be delivered when capitalism was thoroughly dismantled and when people were rewarded equally regardless of their position in society. From Hamka's perspective, such visions are utopian, as seen in the case of Stalin's Russia, where justice was denied to the most vulnerable people.[19] Marx's theory of historical materialism and other related postulations also downplayed the importance of religion in the reformation of society. Marx "viewed religion as an invention of the economy, and in some instances [maintained that] religion is an enemy that would obstruct the emergence of the dictatorship of the proletariat and the Global Revolution!"[20] But unlike the conservative Muslims who saw that there is nothing to be gained from Marxist and communist ideas, Hamka concedes that some of Marx's ideas are congruent with the Islamic conception of social equality. Communism has brought some good to many societies. But the overall thrust of Marxist and communist theories, in Hamka's estimation, is problematic. These ideas are regressive and obstacles to global justice.

Hamka caricatures Marxist and communist conceptions of global justice as ideologies that regarded human beings "as things, that happen to have the intelligence to breathe . . . as if they are creatures that gravitate around the economy only."[21] He is right to state that Marx was suspicious of religions and denounced it throughout his life. Even so, Marxists, communists, and socialists do give primacy to non-material factors as determinants of global justice. It takes into account religions as motor forces of society. Grounded in Marxist thought, the global liberation theology movement, for example, acknowledges the importance of religious values and morality in the construction of a just world.[22]

It is obvious that Hamka censured Marxist and communist conceptions of justice as he was of the capitalist variant. If capitalism had brought about stark inequalities in society and did not fulfill its aims of achieving global justice through market forces, Marxism and communism resulted in the making of dictatorships. These dictators justified autocratic rule by reasoning that communism could be realized only when human beings were conditioned and coerced to act justly toward one another. But Hamka did not reserve his critiques for materialist conceptions of global justice alone. He rebuked Muslims who comprehended justice in a narrow and parochial way and who maintained there was nothing to be learned from non-Muslims. This was a position taken by renowned writers, such as Abul A'la Maududi (1903–1979). Maududi, for example, confidently asserts that "justice is the only objective of Islam," and that "there is justice in Islam only."[23] Hamka sees their stances toward Western and non-Muslim thought as too parochial.

From Hamka's perspective, Western and other non-Muslim thinkers, intellectuals, organizations, and movements offered conceptions and practices of justice that Muslims could benefit from as long as they were in keeping with the ethical guidelines provided by Islam. He gives the example of the Universal Declaration of Human Rights (UDHR), adopted in 1948 by the United Nations. Although the declaration was largely drafted by Europeans at a time when many countries were still subjected to Western colonialism and although the Europeans had not lived up to the articles in the UDHR, Hamka contends that all except articles 16 and 18 were in line with the spirit of Islam and could aid in the process of enforcing global justice. Muslim must enter into a critical dialogue with these conceptions of global justice and construct alternatives that are grounded in their religious conviction. In other words, Hamka envisions a new conception of global justice that is at once universal and rooted in Muslim religiosity, thus bridging the chasm between secular and Islamic thought. Such chasm is to him unproductive in a globalized world where peoples of all faiths and convictions are equally striving to safeguard the sanctity of human dignity, liberty, and equality.[24] The reconciliation and harmonization of secular and Islamic ideas in Hamka's writings bring closer to An-Na'im theorization of global justice.

A DIALOGICAL CONCEPTION OF GLOBAL JUSTICE

Hamka sought to fuse diverging conceptions of global justice and transcend their constrictions; a methodology that is somewhat similar to An-Na'im. He defines justice as "doing good to others with commitment and sincerity, defending humanity, loving the homeland, upholding morality, [encouraging] charity and ensuring equal rights.... Doing what is necessary to uphold the rights of other human beings, and doing what is appropriate to ensure the protection of one's own rights."[25] The opposite of justice, Hamka added, is *zulm* (injustice). According to Fazlur Rahman, "All Arab philologists assure us that *zulm* in Arabic originally meant "to put something out of its proper place," so that all wrong of any kind is injustice."[26] Hamka's idea of *zulm* was congruent with Fazlur Rahman's. He extended this rendering of *zulm* to explain that the word implies darkness in the soul of human beings, which leads to a few consequences: individualism and selfishness, defending what is morally wrong, exploiting other human beings to serve one's greed and causing disharmony and destruction to society.[27]

From this definition, Hamka argues that global justice must rest on four key concepts: *khalifatul fil'ard*, *amanah*, *shura*, and *maslahah*. These concepts are not mere abstractions or figments. They are what could be described as practical concepts, which Hamka used to explain the pillars which global justice in Islam rests upon. All expositions on global justice are defective without acknowledging that human beings are *khalifatul fil'ard*, which, according to Hamka, has a scriptural basis in the Qur'an. It is found in the chapter "The Cow," verse 30, which reads,

And, when your Lord said to the angels, "Indeed, I will make upon the earth a vicegerent," they said, "Will You place upon it one who causes corruption therein and sheds blood, while we declare Your praise and sanctify You?" Allah said, "Indeed, I know that which you do not know."

This verse, according to Hamka, indicates that human beings are chosen as vicegerents of God on earth because they are endowed with the necessary intelligence and intellect that are not found in the rest of creation. Human beings are therefore obligated to fulfill two main responsibilities: to live in accordance with divine ordinance as enshrined in the sacred sources and to devise ways to uphold human dignity, equality, and freedom in society.[28]

The reality of life on earth, however, is that not all human beings will feel obliged to accomplish the functions of the vicegerent of God, even if they are Muslims. Human beings are often swayed by their *nafs* (desires), which inhibit their innate realization of the need to uphold justice. The task of reminding human beings of this duty lay squarely on the shoulders of the true believers of God. These were select group of responsible human beings who are cognizant that global justice is an *amanah*. When amanah was neglected, corruption in society would soon follow.[29]

Hamka's ideal types of persons who upheld justice were the prophets. On this score, his ideas are in line with those of Ibn Qayyim, who wrote:

> Justice is the supreme goal and objective of Islam. God has sent scriptures and messengers to establish justice among people . . . any path that leads to justice is an integral part of the religion and can never be against it.[30]

According to Hamka, the prophets were aware of the "sacred trust, and the consciousness of gravity of the sacred trust becomes the stimulus to reform society into becoming just and prosperous."[31] They fulfilled the sacred trust of justice because it was one of the means by which human beings could live together harmoniously and was a factor that would allow the message of God to be disseminated more effectively. Little wonder then that all prophets were unjustly persecuted. Their call for the restoration of justice threatened the rule of despotic rulers in all times and places, from the pharaohs right up to the *jahilliyya* (ignorant) society during the era of Prophet Muhammad.[32]

Hamka posited that *shura* is also a linchpin in the process of creating a just global society. According to Ilyas Ba-Yunus, no "sociological approach to the understanding of Islam can afford to ignore the meanings and implications of shura, which seems to be a dynamic process of seeking solutions to the problems of living in a plural society."[33] Hamka shares this position and feels that shura must exist at many levels for justice to be in full operation. At the basic level, shura refers to open and respectful discussions between common people of diverse views and backgrounds—siblings, spouses, friends, and neighbors—regarding matters affecting everyday life. This is a form of shura that has minimal impact upon the larger society. More decisive than that is shura in the arena of politics. Hamka expresses his contempt for all forms of autocratic, authoritarian, and tyrannical tendencies in political leadership that stifle mutual consultation among elites and between elites and the masses. Muslims should not be quietists, therefore allowing despots and tyrants to reign at the expense of the masses, but they should also not fall into the trap of becoming perpetrators of instability in their attempts to reclaim justice. Here, Hamka leans closer to Ibn Taymiyya (1263–1328) whom he referenced in many of his works. Ibn Taymiyya was against selected forms of rebellion (*baghy*), even against cruel Muslim rulers. But he did not encourage quietism. The best approach to overcoming injustices, to him, is through discursive disobedience. Failing that, one should adopt a policy of non-participation toward unjust practices and policies of rulers for this would ensure that chaos (*fitna*) is avoided. When all of these strategies have been expended and proved to be futile, then armed rebellion is permissible within the strict constraints of the shari'a.[34] Hamka took this stand. He participated in the armed revolution against the Dutch because injustice under colonial rule was endemic and no attempts at rectifying such inequities were effective. However, under Sukarno (1901–1970), the first president of Indonesia, Hamka was imprisoned for two years for false charges of being part of an anti-state subversive movement. At no point during these difficult moments did Hamka urge Muslims to violently rebel against the Sukarno regime. He firmly believed in ensuring order for the benefit of the masses. He emphasized that peace was of higher priority than resisting injustice meted out by Muslims against other Muslims. This view was challenged by many Muslim intellectuals and activists during his era.[35]

Actualizing *shura*, according to Hamka, necessitates dynamism putting it in practice in accordance with changing times. This is in line with the Prophetic tradition: "You know best the affairs of your worldly life."[36] One of the political systems that could enable *shura* to take root was democracy. Hamka enjoins Muslim scholars to embrace democracy and respect political leaders as and when they abided by democratic principles. Political leaders, in turn, must consult the scholars and the masses in matters of governance and allow freedom of expression. Still, for Hamka, democracy as the West understood it was not shura because, in the European countries, divine laws were made subservient to secular laws. The type of democracy that came close to shura was one that utilizes the Qur'an and the Hadith as sources of policymaking without having to establish a theocratic state or an Islamic state. Hamka calls it "God-conscious democracy (*demokrasi taqwa*)."[37]

Hamka's notion of a God-conscious democracy was in part a reaction against the *Demokrasi Terpimpin* (Guided Democracy) enforced by President Sukarno from 1959 till 1966. To him, guided democracy was a veiled form of totalitarianism. The idea of God-conscious democracy was also emblematic of the discourses of Muslim reformist thinkers during his time that theorized alternatives to Western ideas of democracy. These thinkers called for a comprehensive evaluation of the ideas of democracy as against the Islamic understanding of *shura*. They were divided into three camps: the rejectionists, who saw democracy as alien to the Islamic political system; the accommodationists, who viewed aspects of democracy as compatible with Islam and looked for means to marry democratic ideals with shura; and the secularists, who wholeheartedly embraced Western democracy and saw that there was no need to return to the concept of shura, to use divine laws as the basis of the legal and political order.[38] Hamka belonged to the second group. He was optimistic about infusing the practical concept of shura into modern ideas of democracy to deliver global justice. Democracy with the divine left out, Hamka wrote, would lead to greed, oppressiveness, and the chasing of positions and status among elites. The masses would be rendered helpless and exploited. For Hamka, this was the sickness that had affected Muslim societies in the modern world.[39]

We can draw parallels here between Hamka's God-conscious democracy with the concept of "Muslim democracy" recently espoused by the Tunisian democrat, Rashid Al-Ghannouchi. Both underline the importance of *shura* in modern statecraft. Both emphasize fluidity in defining the term and translating it into just politics that ensure that religion does not become the instrument of the state or that the state becomes an unjust instrument of religious functionaries. Hamka would have agreed with Al-Ghannouchi's point that "no political party can or should claim to represent religion and that the religious sphere should be managed by independent and neutral institutions. Put simply, religion should be nonpartisan."[40]

The culmination of *shura* is the achievement of *maslahah* (general welfare). Hamka emphasizes that not only Muslims but also all human beings stood to benefit from *shura*. He departed from many traditional thinkers by interpreting *maslahah*, a concept derived from the *usul al-fiqh* (principles of Islamic jurisprudence), in a universalist sense. For him, the

> objective of Islam is not to bring good to the lives of one group only. The objective of Islam is to bring good to the life of everyone. . . . Islam is not the property of Muslims. It is born out of God's Revelation for the goodness of all mankind.[41]

Individualism is not tolerated in Islam, for all individuals must see themselves as part of the larger society and must work toward the fulfillment of public good.

The practical concept of *maslahah* is also important because it guides Muslims to be context-driven in their implementation of justice. Some punishments, programs, and policies may lead to the general welfare at a given time but not in others.

Hamka gives the example of the punishment of cutting off the hands of robbers and thieves. Although prescribed in the Qur'an and a medium that could uphold justice, such a punishment must take into consideration the general welfare of the community before it can be implemented. In times when a country is experiencing economic difficulties and when the person who is prosecuted for theft is known to be in poverty, a moratorium should be imposed on such a ruling in view of the wider problems affecting the community in general. *Maslahah* is a useful thinking and analytical tool to determine whether a stated punishment, policy, or program can indeed bring about the common good or run contrary to it.[42] Clearly, Hamka's ideas on *maslahah* were built on Mahmud Shaltut's discussions of *maslahah* in his classic *Al-Islam: Aqidah wa Syariah*. Shaltut maintains that *maslahah* is a useful intellectual mechanism for deriving, and in fact revising, age-old laws and scholarly consensus (*ijma'*) to meet the changing contexts and circumstances faced by Muslims in the modern world. By considering, above all, the welfare of the masses, Muslim scholars and legislators would be compelled to rethink laws and reformulate policies that are already in operation and thereby relieve undue burden upon societies.[43] If operationalized on a wider scale and explained in ways that are universal and fathomable to both Muslims and non-Muslims, to Hamka, *maslahah* is one of the bedrocks of global justice.

CONCLUSION

A major fissure in contemporary writings on global justice is the marginalization of religion. Religion is often ignored or downplayed because of its assumed irrational tendencies and absolutist claims. Religion is cast aside because most scholars deem its commitment to the salvation of a given community of faith as antithetical to the ideals of global justice.[44] This chapter defends the view that Islam stands for global justice and that Muslim intellectuals have played significant roles in deliberating on the subject matter. These Muslim intellectuals are conscious that global justice can be a far-fetched ideal in a world defined by the sovereignty of nation-states. They are mindful that "a sovereign global state" cannot be easily established and, as Amartya Sen aptly describes it, mere "loose talk" in the current world order.[45] Any efforts at realizing some form of alternative transnational coalition would succumb to the pressures of dominant superpowers that have been influential in decisions made by the United Nations. These superpowers are unfazed by any critiques of their violent interference into the affairs of Muslim nations as seen in the invasions of Afghanistan and Iraq and in the support they render toward authoritarian regimes throughout the Muslim world.

Sensitive to the contextual realities of his time, Muslim intellectuals such as Hamka propound their conceptions of global justice with the hope such ideas would someday become the ideological framework of most states and societies. A versatile thinker Hamka utilizes the sacred sources of Islam and ideas from various thinkers as the foundations of his new interpretation of global justice. For him, the return of Islam as a force in the contemporary world must begin with the reinstatement of a dialogical conception of global justice in the minds of Muslims.

Majid Khadduri, in a pioneering study of the Islamic conceptions of justice, argues that modern-day Muslim theorists of justice could be divided into two opposing camps. The first was the modernist camp. They argue that justice should be conceptualized by way of reason and through a deep understanding of the contextual needs of the people. For the modernists, there is no need to draw upon the sources of Islam for guidance and inspiration. On the contrasting side are the revivalists. They in turn underline the importance of revelation in the rethinking of social justice in the modern world. Until the 1980s, when Khadduri wrote his classic text, no synthesis between the two groups had emerged.[46]

Where did Hamka fit in between these two camps? At first glance, he seemed to be closer to the revivalists, in that revelation was the starting point of his conception of justice. But he did not reject the use of reason in the reformulation of justice, nor did he ignore the actualities on the ground. In that sense, he shared some common ideas with the modernists. Indeed, if

Khadduri had looked beyond the Arab world in his study of justice and analyzed what Southeast Asian scholars such as Hamka had written, he would have found the amalgamation of revivalist and modernist ideas of justice through the eyes of a local Muslim intellectual. Hamka, unlike many Arab thinkers, was able to bring together opposing conceptions because his views were not stifled by the divisions that characterized Islamic discourses of his time. All these make Hamka a fascinating and highly original Southeast Asian thinker that ought to be considered seriously by scholars working on global justice. The view from Southeast Asia can cast new light on how Muslim intellectuals from outside the MENA region engage with the problems of inequality and injustice that besiege us all.

NOTES

1. Abdullahi Ahmed An-Naʿim, *Muslims and Global Justice* (Philadephia: University of Pennsylvania Press, 2011), 2.

2. An-Naʿim, *Muslims and Global Justice*, 2.

3. An-Naʿim, *Muslims and Global Justice* (Philadephia: University of Pennsylvania Press, 2011), 236.

4. An-Naʿim, *Muslims and Global Justice* (Philadephia: University of Pennsylvania Press, 2011), 194.

5. Mohammed A. Mahmoud, *Quest for Divinity: A Critical Examination of the Thought of Mahmud Muhammad Taha* (New York: Syracuse University Press, 2007), 137.

6. Richard W. Bulliet, *Islam: A View from the Edge* (New York: Columbia University Press, 1993).

7. Erin K. Wilson, "Beyond Dualism: Expanded Understandings of Religion and Global Justice," *International Studies Quarterly* 54, no. 3 (2010): 735.

8. Hamka, *Tafsir Al-Azhar, Vol. 3* (Jakarta: Gema Insani, 2018), 612.

9. John Rawls, *A Theory of Justice* (Cambridge, MA: Harvard University Press, 1999), 9.

10. David West, *Social Movements in Global Politics* (Cambridge: Polity, 2013), 56.

11. Malik Bennabi, *The Question of Ideas in the Muslim World, Ed. and Trans. Malik Mohamed El-Tahir El-Mesawi* (Kuala Lumpur: Islamic Book Trust, 2003).

12. Benjamin L. McKean, *Disorienting Neoliberalism: Global Justice and the Outer Limit of Freedom* (New York: Oxford University Press, 2020), 11.

13. Hamka, *Keadilan Sosial Dalam Islam* (Kuala Lumpur: Pustaka Antara, 1966), 85.

14. Daniel Halliday and John Thrasher, *The Ethics of Capitalism: An Introduction* (New York: Oxford University Press, 2020), 79–80.

15. Rogene Buchholz, *Restructuring Capitalism: Materialism and Spiritualism in Business* (London: Routledge, 2017), 1–92.

16. Hamka, *Tafsir Al-Azhar Vol. 1* (Pustaka Panjimas, 1982), 672.

17. Hussein Alatas, *The Myth of the Lazy Native* (Frank Cass, 1977), 226.

18. Charles Tripp, *Islam and the Moral Economy: The Challenge of Capitalism* (Cambridge: Cambridge University Press, 2006), 36.

19. Hamka, *Revolusi Agama* (Djakarta: Pustaka Antara, 1949), 75.

20. Hamka, *Keadilan Sosial Dalam Islam*, 24.

21. Hamka, *Keadilan Sosial Dalam Islam*, 131.

22. Lilian Calles Barger, *The World Come of Age: An Intellectual History of Liberation Theology* (New York: Oxford University Press, 2018).

23. Syed Abul A'la Maududi, *Economic System of Islam* (Lahore: Islamic Publications, 1984), 104.

24. Hamka, *Hak Asasi Manusia Dalam Islam Dan Deklarasi PBB* (Selangor: Pustaka Dini, 2010), 281–95.

25. Hamka, *Falsafah Hidup* (Kuala Lumpur: Pustaka Antara, 1977), 256 and 289.

26. Fazlur Rahman, *Major Themes in the Qur'an* (Kuala Lumpur: Islamic Book Trust, 1989), 25.

27. Hamka, *Falsafah Hidup*, 284.

28. Hamka, *Tafsir Al-Azhar Vol. 1*, 163.

29. Hamka, *Keadilan Sosial Dalam Islam*, 10.

30. Ibn Qayyim al-Jawziya, *Al-Turuq al-Hukmiyya Fi'l-Siyasa al-Shari'yya* (Cairo: Mua'assa al-'Arabiyya li'l-Taba'a, 1961), 16.

31. Hamka, *Keadilan Sosial Dalam Islam*, 11.

32. Hamka, *Khutbah Pilihan Buya HAMKA: Juma'at, Idul Fitri & Idul Adha* (Jakarta: Pustaka Panjimas, 2005), 78.

33. Ilyas Ba-Yunus, in *Ideological Dimensions of Islam: A Critical Paradigm,"* in *Interpreting Islam, Ed. Hastings Donnan* (London: Sage, 2002), 106.

34. Khaled Abou El Fadl, *Rebellion and Violence in Islamic Law* (Cambridge: Cambridge University Press, 2001), 271–76.

35. Hamka, *Falsafah Hidup*, 394.

36. Hamka, *Tafsir Al-Azhar, Juz 25*, 6521.

37. Hamka, *Khutbah Iftitah Ketua Umum Majelis Ulama Indonesia* (Jakarta: Sekretariat Majelis Ulama Indonesia, 1978), 9.

38. John L. Esposito and Yvonne Y. Haddad, *The Islamic Revival Since 1988: A Critical Survey and Bibliography* (Westport, CT: Greenwood Press, 1997), xiii.

39. Hamka, *Pelajaran Agama Islam* (Kelantan, Malaysia: Pustaka Aman Press, 1967), 94.

40. Rached Ghannouchi, "From Political Islam to Muslim Democracy: The Ennahda Party and the Future of Tunisia," *Foreign Affairs* 95, no. 5 (2016): 63.

41. Hamka, *Keadilan Sosial Dalam Islam*, 26.

42. Hamka, *Keadilan Sosial Dalam Islam*, 52–60.

43. Mahmud Shaltut, *Al-Islam: 'Aqidah Wa Shari'ah* (Cairo: Dar al-Syuruq, 2001), 546.

44. Claudia Baumgart-Ochse et al., "Faith in Justice? The Role of Religion in Struggles for Global Justice," in *The Role of Religion in Struggles for Global Justice*

Faith in Justice? Ed. by Peter J. Smith, Katharina Glaab, Claudia Baumgart-Ochse, and Elizabeth Smythe (London: Routledge, 2018), 2.

45. Amartya Sen, *The Idea of Justice* (Cambridge, MA: The Belknap Press, 2009), 25.

46. Majid Khadduri, *Islamic Conception of Justice* (Baltimore: Johns Hopkins University Press, 1984), 218–19.

REFERENCES

Abou El Fadl, Khaled. *Rebellion and Violence in Islamic Law*. Cambridge: Cambridge University Press, 2001.

Alatas, Hussein. *The Myth of the Lazy Native*. Frank Cass, 1977.

An-Na'im, Abdullahi Ahmed. *Muslims and Global Justice*. Philadephia: University of Pennsylvania Press, 2011.

Barger, Lilian Calles. *The World Come of Age: An Intellectual History of Liberation Theology*. New York: Oxford University Press, 2018.

Baumgart-Ochse, Claudia, Katharina Glaab, Peter J. Smith, and Elizabeth Smythe. "Faith in Justice? The Role of Religion in Struggles for Global Justice." In *The Role of Religion in Struggles for Global Justice Faith in Justice?* Ed. Peter J. Smith, Katharina Glaab, Claudia Baumgart-Ochse, and Elizabeth Smythe, 1–7. London: Routledge, 2018.

Ba-Yunus, Ilyas. In Ideological Dimensions of Islam: A Critical Paradigm." In *Interpreting Islam*, Ed. Hastings Donnan, 99–109. London: Sage, 2002.

Bennabi, Malik. *The Question of Ideas in the Muslim World, Ed. and Trans. Malik Mohamed El-Tahir El-Mesawi*. Kuala Lumpur: Islamic Book Trust, 2003.

Buchholz, Rogene. *Restructuring Capitalism: Materialism and Spiritualism in Business*. London: Routledge, 2017.

Bulliet, Richard W. *Islam: A View from The Edge*. New York: Columbia University Press, 1993.

Esposito, John L., and Yvonne Y. Haddad. *The Islamic Revival Since 1988: A Critical Survey and Bibliography*. Westport, CT: Greenwood Press, 1997.

Ghannouchi, Rached. "From Political Islam to Muslim Democracy: The Ennahda Party and the Future of Tunisia." *Foreign Affairs* 95, no. 5 (2016): 58–67.

Halliday, Daniel, and John Thrasher. *The Ethics of Capitalism: An Introduction*. New York: Oxford University Press, 2020.

Hamka. *Falsafah Hidup*. Kuala Lumpur: Pustaka Antara, 1977.

———. *Hak Asasi Manusia Dalam Islam Dan Deklarasi PBB*. Selangor: Pustaka Dini, 2010.

———. *Keadilan Sosial Dalam Islam*. Kuala Lumpur: Pustaka Antara, 1966.

———. *Khutbah Iftitah Ketua Umum Majelis Ulama Indonesia*. Jakarta: Sekretariat Majelis Ulama Indonesia, 1978.

———. *Khutbah Pilihan Buya HAMKA: Juma'at, Idul Fitri & Idul Adha*. Jakarta: Pustaka Panjimas, 2005.

———. *Pelajaran Agama Islam*. Kelantan, Malaysia: Pustaka Aman Press, 1967.

———. *Revolusi Agama*. Djakarta: Pustaka Antara, 1949.
———. *Tafsir Al-Azhar, Juz 28*. Jakarta: Pustaka Panjimas, 1985.
———. *Tafsir Al-Azhar Vol. 1*. Pustaka Panjimas, 1982.
———. *Tafsir Al-Azhar, Vol. 2*. Jakarta: Gema Insani, 2018.
Jawziya, Ibn Qayyim al-. *Al-Turuq al-Hukmiyya Fi'l-Siyasa al-Shari'yya*. Cairo: Mua'assa al-'Arabiyya li'l-Taba'a, 1961.
Khadduri, Majid. *Islamic Conception of Justice*. Baltimore: Johns Hopkins University Press, 1984.
Mahmud Shaltut. *Al-Islam: 'Aqidah Wa Shari'ah*. Cairo: Dar al-Syuruq, 2001.
Maududi, Syed Abul A'la. *Economic System of Islam*. Lahore: Islamic Publications, 1984.
McKean, Benjamin L. *Disorienting Neoliberalism: Global Justice and the Outer Limit of Freedom*. New York: Oxford University Press, 2020.
Mohammed A. Mahmoud. *Quest for Divinity: A Critical Examination of the Thought of Mahmud Muhammad Taha*. New York: Syracuse University Press, 2007.
Rahman, Fazlur. *Major Themes in the Qur'an*. Kuala Lumpur: Islamic Book Trust, 1989.
Rawls, John. *A Theory of Justice*. Cambridge, MA: Harvard University Press, 1999.
Sen, Amartya. *The Idea of Justice*. Cambridge, MA: The Belknap Press, 2009.
Tripp, Charles. *Islam and the Moral Economy: The Challenge of Capitalism*. Cambridge: Cambridge University Press, 2006.
West, David. *Social Movements in Global Politics*. Cambridge: Polity, 2013.
Wilson, Erin K. "Beyond Dualism: Expanded Understandings of Religion and Global Justice." *International Studies Quarterly* 54, no. 3 (2010): 733–54.

Chapter 8

Toward a Justice-Based Foreign Policy

Farid Senzai

After the Cold War ended in 1991, promoting liberal democracy seemed poised to replace containment as the guiding principle of U.S. foreign policy. Flouting the primacy of its military and the universal appeal of its liberal values, Washington embraced the idea that democratization could become its next mission. Over the next three decades, it began to spread its liberal values aggressively and to engage in social engineering "nation-building" projects in the Middle East and elsewhere. Many policymakers agreed that spreading democracy—especially liberal democracy—benefits citizens making international peace more likely and serves U.S. interests. Similarly, the two dominant international relation schools within academic circles, realism, and liberalism have tried to navigate and make sense of this post-Cold War era.

The realists contended that the U.S. invasions of Afghanistan and Iraq were motivated by a desire to punish those implicated in 9/11, whereas the liberals emphasized promoting democracy and freedom in the region. Yet, in both the cases, this foreign policy, rooted in power politics and self-interest rather than achieving peace, often led to instability and violence. Washington's ill-informed invasions, subsequent occupations, and continued support for authoritarian Middle Eastern regimes have brought neither peace nor stability; rather, they have cost trillions of dollars and countless innocent lives. In short, policies driven by liberal ambitions to promote democracy were often simultaneously mired in supporting autocratic regimes. Is there any alternative to this paradox? Is it even possible for a government to pursue ethical principles?

This chapter argues that the United States should pursue a more principled foreign policy, one that incorporates various understandings of justice, especially in the Middle East and Muslim-majority countries (hereinafter the Muslim world). Advancing such a foreign policy will inevitably invite a vigorous debate over how—or even whether—ethics and justice should be factored into its foreign policy. Critics may also point to the urgency of domestic challenges, relative to foreign policy ones, or the fear of overextension abroad to argue that an ethics-based foreign policy rooted in justice is unwise or simply impossible. Devising such an approach will certainly not be easy; however, it is the most appropriate course for the Muslim world.

SUPPORT FOR AUTHORITARIAN REGIMES

Washington's relationship with and support for authoritarian regimes has often been the norm. For nearly five decades, its foreign policy was principally driven by the realists' struggle against communism. Given that all of its decisions on the international stage were based on a zero-sum game against the Soviet Union, the latter's collapse has largely replaced this approach with a worldwide liberal devotion to democracy and the free-market system. Yet, in many developing countries, the United States supported authoritarian leaders as long as they professed anti-communism, despite their inability or unwillingness to promote modernization.[1] "He may be an S.O.B., but he's our S.O.B." This maxim is attributed to President Franklin D. Roosevelt as he was describing Nicaraguan dictator Anastasio Somoza and has frequently served as a credo for U.S. foreign policy. During the Cold War, the United States made common cause with countless dictators. Jeanne Kirkpatrick, the U.S. ambassador to the United Nations, embraced this maxim to such an extent that it later came to be known as the Kirkpatrick Doctrine. In a 1979 essay, "Dictatorships and Double Standards," Kirkpatrick showed herself to be a staunch advocate of supporting authoritarian leaders.[2] Using it to justify supporting Third World anti-communist dictatorships, she claimed that the Soviet bloc and other Communist states were totalitarian regimes, whereas pro-Western dictatorships were merely "authoritarian" ones.

According to her, totalitarian regimes were more stable and self-perpetuating and thus had a greater propensity to influence neighboring states. In Asia, Latin America, and Africa, the United States was often solidly on the side of the most brutal, visionless, corrupt, and unpopular regimes: the Somoza dynasty (Nicaragua), Ferdinand Marcos (the Philippines), Fulgencio Batista (Cuba), Mobutu Sese Seko (Zaire; now the Democratic Republic of Congo), Emperor Haile Selassie (Ethiopia), Syngman Rhee (South Korea), Suharto (Indonesia), and others. This paradox largely accounts for a simplistic (Cold War) explanation of Washington's cozy relationships with authoritarian regimes across the global South.[3]

The United States often sided with the Muslim world's authoritarian leaders. For example, it led the first military coup d'état in the Middle East against

Syria's elected government in 1949. The CIA's toppling of democratically elected governments in the region was on display in 1953, when it and Britain's MI6 replaced the popular and freely elected Prime Minister Mohammad Mosaddegh with Mohammad Reza Shah, who governed as an absolute monarch until he was ousted by the 1979 Iranian revolution.[4]

The 1949 coup in Syria, which soon became the model, was "studied in CIA training classes for the next two decades."[5] CIA director Allen Dulles repeated a similar coup in Egypt in 1951 against King Farouk.[6] Elsewhere, the United States supported Pakistan's Mohammed Zia ul-Haq, its decades-long support for such military-led authoritarian leaders as Egyptian presidents Hosni Mubarak and Abdel Fattah el-Sisi, and the many-decades-long support of ruling dynasties in Jordan and the Arabian peninsula is evidence of our friendly ties with autocratic monarchs. Similarly, Washington's invasion of Iraq, its broader failure to oppose the autocrat-led counter-revolution in the wake of the Arab Spring, and its long historical record of supporting dictators complicate its attempts to make a credible case for supporting the people's will.

Take, for example, the Bush administration's post-9/11 invasion of Afghanistan. From a geopolitical standpoint, this decision was simply unwarranted in terms of the stated mission: dealing with an extremist group's presence and influence. Furthermore, its foreign policy obsession with taking out key extremist leaders like Bin Laden while launching attacks nationwide was problematic because doing so only creates a breeding ground for new and potentially even more extreme leaders (i.e., ISIS).

The justifications for war were minimal but legally sustained and legitimized through an international judicial standard known as "Jus ad Bellum" (the right to go to war). The criteria embedded in this just war theory outline the importance of a justified "cause" to intervene, along with a "reasonable hope for peace" as the expected outcome. Afghan women were presented as a primary "cause," and the West's version of women's rights would be implemented with ease as the "hope for peace." Paradoxically, war and intervention "inevitably involve the use of force," which detracts from this operation's legitimacy. Therefore, this short-sighted, ill-informed U.S.-led invasion continues to have long-term implications for innocent Afghan civilians. Notably, 63% the casualties were women.

For scholars such as Louay Safi, Western-backed interventions are examples of Washington's pursuit of power politics and self-interest in the Middle East at the expense of liberty and democracy. Western-backed dictators understand this contradiction and shrewdly represent themselves as the defenders of liberal values against reform movements, which they accuse of undermining freedom and free choice.[7] Less appreciated is that many dictatorships have provided the breeding grounds for extremist movements. In short, rather than helping to expand a liberal ethos, they undermine freedom and distort the image of liberal democracy. They pretend to support it by employing an iron-fist strategy against internal justice-oriented opposition groups. Safi is correct that Western democracies tout classical liberal values yet engage in neoliberal and neorealist policies by backing authoritarian states and the practices of police states and autocratic leaders.[8]

LIBERAL HEGEMONY

Classical liberalism and the European Enlightenment's philosophical foundation are rooted in the thought of Immanuel Kant (1724–1804). For many, Kant remains liberalism's most influential philosopher. His thought is typically understood as a political philosophy that asserts the universality of rights based on rational precepts equally available to all people, over and above the particularism of tradition.[9] Similarly, his ideas have profoundly impacted international relations theory and the policies pursued by liberal policymakers to this day. One reason that Kant became famous was his vision of perpetual peace.[10] His liberal conception of international peace continues to impact thinking about the practice of international politics.[11]

Writing in *Metaphysics of Morals*, he argued, "in their external relationships with one another, states, like lawless savages, exist in condition devoid of right." For him, achieving perpetual peace, in the sense of transcending the fragile security arrangement provided by the balance of power, requires a transformation of individual consciousness. He further posits that promoting constitutional republics would lead to virtuous politics, namely, politics based on principles and institutions that today would be identified as a liberal democracy.[12]

Given this reality, democracies, being pacific and less inclined toward war, would build permanent international peace among themselves,[13] for

> if the consent of the citizens is required to decide that war should be declared . . . nothing is more natural than that they would be very cautious in commencing such a poor game, decreeing for themselves all the calamities of war.[14]

People living in democracies would logically prefer to avoid the costs of war, the painful rebuilding associated with it, and the sustained national debt that comes with an extended military mobilization. Kant believed that all people inherently desire peace and that reasonable people would seek it via representative democracy and placing popular constraints on leaders.[15]

Some contemporary scholars of international relations, such as Robert Kagan, suggest that today's neoliberal foreign policy strategy is in line with the historic legacy of Kant's Enlightenment. "After World War II, because of

America's unrivaled power," Kagan writes, "those Enlightenment principles suddenly enjoyed a force behind them that they had never before possessed."[16] In his estimation, the Enlightenment principles of liberalism and democracy (as well as capitalism) go together and should be promoted.[17] Liberalism's defenders are deeply embedded throughout Washington's foreign policy establishment, including the most prominent think tanks. Proponents "believe it will make the world more peaceful and ameliorate the dual problems of nuclear proliferation and terrorism. It will reduce human rights violations and make liberal democracies more secure against internal threats."[18]

But Safi and other critics argue that neoliberalism integrates liberalism with neorealism. Traditionally, classical liberalism's egalitarian and optimistic inclination stands in stark contrast to neorealism's power-centered and pessimistic worldview. This divergence seems to have changed due to the recent mutations in the two major doctrines of international relations.[19] Safi argues that neoliberalism and neorealism are in general agreement. At the same time, however, they differ at the macro-theory level but share a common approach to international politics. Shaped by constructivism, they are more in line at the policymaking level.[20] For Safi, they share an epistemology firmly rooted in rational positivism,[21] even though they are incompatible with the rational idealism that guides liberalism's advocates[22] and view the international arena as anarchic.

The difference is that neoliberals, while agreeing that the international system lacks an overarching authority, are more optimistic of the states' capacity to engage in economic cooperation rather than, as realists suggest, in constant animosity and warfare. Interestingly, the neoliberals–neorealists' manipulative environment is the result of their mutual rejection of creating an ethical foundation upon which to engage in politics.[23] Safi correctly suggests that this frame of reference makes it hard for states to develop world peace. It is equally problematic to assess the unscrupulous foreign policy actions taken by Western democracies on the global stage, for these raise concerns about neoliberalism's disruptive impact on global politics.[24]

Furthermore, given that neoliberalism encompasses politics and economics, unlike classical liberalism, it highlights economic policies, markets, and the ideas that influence the economy. Neoliberals often emphasize private enterprise and seek to transfer the control of economic factors from the government to the private sector. Many of their policies are concerned with the efficient functioning of free-market capitalism and focus on limiting government spending, regulation, and public ownership. From this standpoint, neoliberalism can also be attributed to Prime Minister Margaret Thatcher and President Ronald Reagan. At the time, neoliberals promoted the "Washington Consensus" policies of austerity to cut government spending on social programs for developing countries.

After the Cold War and the Soviet collapse, the United States, as the sole superpower, was positioned to promote this "neoliberalism," or what John Mearsheimer has called a "liberal hegemony."[25] The American foreign policy establishment's embracement of this liberal hegemony has made it the most prominent vision of American foreign policy for the twenty-first century. It aims to support and expand the number of liberal democracies while also fostering an open global economy and building formidable international institutions.[26]

This neoliberal foreign policy, initially introduced by President Bill Clinton as part of a "democratic enlargement," was followed by George W. Bush's administration's more strident and militaristic neoconservative "freedom agenda" after 9/11. President Bush articulated it best in his second inaugural address:[27]

> America's vital interests and our deepest beliefs are now one. From the day of our Founding, we have proclaimed that every man and woman on this earth has rights, and dignity, and matchless value, because they bear the image of the Maker of Heaven and Earth. Across the generations, we have proclaimed the imperative of self-government, because no one is fit to be a master, and no one deserves to be a slave. Advancing these ideals is the mission that created our Nation. It is the honorable achievement of our fathers. Now it is the urgent requirement of our nation's security and the calling of our time. So, it is the policy of the United States to seek and support the growth of democratic movements and institutions in every nation and culture, with the ultimate goal of ending tyranny in our world.[28]

In this speech, he outlined a vision that was focused on and appealed to American values and ideals as a basis of foreign policy. Although such an approach was not new, it did, however, reflect a shift from a Cold War-oriented foreign policy based solely on a balance of power. Not only did this worldview incorporate idealism as a central tenant of engagement abroad, it also reflected a desire to maintain American primacy on the global stage while finding a way to spread American values and ideals.[29] The Obama administration returned to the neoliberal interpretation of promoting democracy while continuing with the previous administration's military-led policies.[30]

These (primarily Democrats) neoliberals focused much of their attention on American power as a source for promoting democracy and advocating for human rights abroad, whereas neoconservatives (primarily Republicans) supported similar ideas but did so by also asserting U.S. military dominance abroad. As Sean Kay points out, this high-end level of common sentiment does not apply to all contemporary idealists or realists, as there are many variations between them. But at the general level, the liberal–neoconservative divide is primarily one of means, not of goals.[31] In his view:

[n]eoconservatives tend to part from liberals over whether the exercise of American power requires the legitimacy of international law or whether America should act unilaterally. Neoconservatives generally argue that if America leads, its actions are legitimate because of what America stands for. Liberals prefer gaining legal, or at least political, legitimacy from international institutions like the United Nations and operating multilaterally.[32]

Thus, for example, liberals generally view a United Nations-backed agreement to constrain Iran's nuclear program—achieved in late 2013—as a victory for advancing America's search for security while holding Iran to hard commitments to future change via sustained international sanctions. Neoconservatives tend to view such a deal as appeasing a dangerous threat. Both approaches, however, see Tehran's ideology as inconsistent with the values held by Americans and thus prefer policies that require a change before full relations are restored. Both views appeal to the idealistic tradition in American foreign policy and have justified a post-Cold War narrative that the world benefits from the country's primacy in the international system.[33]

This was evident from the left when at the time, Secretary of State Hillary Clinton described America as the world's "indispensable nation" and that:

[T]he United States is still the only country that has the reach and resolve to rally disparate nations and peoples together to solve problems on a global scale, we cannot shirk that responsibility. Our ability to convene and connect is unparalleled, and so is our ability to act alone whenever necessary. So, when I say we are truly the indispensable nation, it's not meant as a boast or an empty slogan. It's a recognition of our role and our responsibilities.[34]

This combination of faith in democracy, freedom, and the spirit of commerce contributed to a popular belief, consolidated over time, that God has blessed the United States. It is ironic that religion (i.e., Christianity) prominently shaped America's sense of its place in the world, given that separating church from state was one of its founding principles. Nevertheless, a sense of "uniqueness"[35] in its self-image reflects a belief that the natural rights and blessings Americans enjoy are God-given. This view contrasts starkly the despotic claim of "old Europe" monarchs' claims to their divine right to rule, against which the Americans had rebelled.

As journalist John B. Judis notes, the missionary rhetoric of American leaders included a belief that America is "God's chosen nation"; that it has a unique duty and mission to transform the world; and that because of who and what it represents, the United States is inherently a force for good versus forces of evil. This concept coalesced into the nineteenth-century vision of Manifest Destiny as America became a continental power and a political rationale for its expanding search for security. To oppose such a patriotic vision was, logically, to oppose the country's greatness. Thus, those who wielded exceptionalism carried a powerful political tool.[36]

Some prominent realists such as John Mearsheimer and Stephen Walt[37] suggest that this liberal post-Cold War foreign policy is increasingly outdated and destined to fail. Similar arguments have been made by Stephen Wertheim,[38] who argues that these more expansive conceptions of liberal foreign policy aim to increase the prevalence of *liberal* democracies.[39]

As this suggests, realists generally see liberal expansionism abroad as a natural extension of the universalist tendencies inherent in liberalism. If we accept the premise that liberalism is not neutral, then, like any ideological orientation, it will have trouble restricting its application. It will want more for itself. On this, they have a point.[40]

For Mearsheimer, the "strategy invariably leads to policies that put a country at odds with nationalism and realism," which ultimately, he contends, "have far more influence on international politics than liberalism does." In his view, this

> basic fact of life is difficult for most Americans to accept. The United States is a deeply liberal country whose foreign policy elite have an almost knee-jerk hostility toward both nationalism and realism. But this kind of thinking can only lead to trouble on the foreign policy front.[41]

Mearsheimer suggests that "American policymakers would be wise to abandon liberal hegemony and pursue a more restrained foreign policy based on realism and a proper understanding of how nationalism constrains great powers."[42]

Some scholars have more recently posited that liberalism has fallen on hard times, with realists such as Mearsheimer suggesting that "liberalism has failed"[43] and that we now live in a "post-liberal age."[44] According to Susannah Black, "While most scholars and practitioners agree that the liberal order built after 1945 is in crisis, or at least facing unprecedented challenges, they are sharply divided over the question of how these challenges might be addressed."[45]

Other scholars argue that the solution is more liberalism on the grounds that the post-1945 norms and institutions still provide sufficient benefits to motivate key international actors to defend them.[46] For them, defending liberal–democratic norms and protecting multilateral institutions as the bedrock of liberal interdependence generate incentives and opportunities for international cooperation, thereby facilitating the peaceful resolution of conflicts. In short, "The best news for liberal internationalism is probably the simple fact that more people will be harmed by the end of some sort global international order than will gain"[47]

Yet this can only be good news for liberalism's defenders if there is sufficient international determination to protect progressive liberal norms while also recognizing and finding more effective ways of addressing the problems and abuses associated with some of the practices conducted in liberalism's name. Often at fault is the inconsistent and selective application of the principle of global justice. In recent years, however, even optimistic liberal scholars have hardened their assessment of the difficulty involved in securing support for liberalism's defense. Thus, "the future of this liberal order hinges on the ability of the United States and Europe—and increasingly a wider array of liberal democracies—to lead and support it."[48] This, in turn, depends on the major liberal democracies' ability to build new coalitions of allies among developing democracies and to find effective solutions to current problems. More profoundly, it requires that liberal democracies "remain stable, well-functioning and internationalist."[49]

Others have proposed the existence of a growing sense that neoliberalism both undermines the very principles of democracy and liberty as well as undercuts the long-term economic growth of countries that come under their influence. Neoliberalism, the argument goes, threatens the "livelihoods, social cohesion, and environmental conditions" of those societies subjected to its philosophical outlook.[50] Neoliberal policies tend to create unequal development and growth not only among nations but also within the societies in which it prevails.[51]

Rather than advancing the liberal tradition that emphasizes equal opportunities for all people and conforming to a form of government that represents the citizenry and protects their civil and human rights, neoliberalism has developed into an elitist platform concerned with perpetuating the political and economic privileges of global elites who have gradually moved from striving for human liberation to seeking political domination.[52] Nowhere is this more true than in Muslim societies.

JUSTICE IN MUSLIM SOCIETIES

Islam's concept of justice is especially important today as we witness the tumultuous and, at times, violent changes occurring in the Muslim. This is the age of political transitions, as many countries have shed their colonial past and are trying to cast off the subsequent secular-oriented despotic regimes in the hope of embracing a new system of government based on the tenets of Islam and justice. Subsequently, Muslims are formulating new constitutions and building new institutions rooted in Islamic values. In this regard, reverting to Islam's basic teachings about good governance and a just society can greatly help them create a governance structure that is both acceptable to the country's leaders and can produce positive results for the masses.

Good governance is often situated at the intersection of religious doctrine, social ethics, and cultural norms, all of which continue to evolve as the religious text is understood and reinterpreted so that it can be applied to the situations in which countries find themselves. Within the confines of a polity or a state, good governance generally refers to the authorities' ability to exercise coercive and/or motivational power to effectively direct the resources and energies of the polity's members or the state's citizens in order to ensure their continued survival and advancement. Thus, this relative term refers to the efficiency and effectiveness of decision-making designed to serve the people's interests by formulating an appropriate governing system.

More generally, governance is defined as a government's ability "to make and enforce rules, and to deliver services, regardless of whether that government is democratic or not."[53] In this initial conceptualization, as Francis Fukuyama correctly points out, "the quality of governance is different from the ends that governance is meant to fulfill. That is, governance is about the performance of agents in carrying out the wishes of principals, and not about the goals that principals set."[54] Therefore,

> the government is an organization that can do its functions better or worse; governance is thus about execution, or what has traditionally fallen within the domain of public administration, as opposed to politics or public policy. Hence, an authoritarian regime can be well governed, just as a democracy can be maladministered.[55]

Governance rooted in justice becomes Islamic when it is motivated and driven by the norms and morals that constitute what might be considered "Islamic conduct," namely, imposing upon the governors and the governed those ideals that reflect obedience to an authority beyond that of the governors, the polity, and the people. Amr G. E. Sabet refers to the religiopolitical conduct that anchors an Islamic government: "Irrespective of any number of structural forms that it may take, Islamic governance becomes the reflection of a continuum of internal and external behaviors infused with religiopolitical norms and imperatives which distinguish it from other exclusively politically guided regimes."[56]

For Muslims, a just government is anchored in a set of divinely ordained morals and ethics. Note that this does not necessarily presume a theocracy, defined as those individuals with the necessary authority to interpret the Divine Will or un-interpreted commandments of God govern. This latter situation recognizes God as the supreme ruler and the priests who claim the divine authority to interpret His laws. Tamara Sonn, for instance, contends that Islam espouses a nomocracy, "a state governed by a codified system of laws,"[57] the ideal state being governed by individuals or bodies bound by Islamic law. Pursuant to this argument, an Islamic state is a state governed by laws codified by qualified scholars and justly enforced by capable governors.

Noah Feldman sees the following potential: "If the new Islamic state can find an institution to fill the role traditionally played by the scholars, it has a reasonable chance of establishing political justice and, through it, political legitimacy."[58] He also suggests that principles of constitutional democracy can still guide those governing structures that emerge from traumatic interventions: "Whatever the disastrous practicalities of governance in Iraq or the limitations of the central government in Afghanistan, the constitutional process in these two countries demonstrate that a constitutional democracy is indeed possible."[59]

Many Muslim societies today are in turmoil, often violent, from Iraq and Syria to Yemen and Afghanistan, with dramatic transformations taking place across Muslim world. In some cases, Western powers have nudged or supported nation-building ventures (e.g., Iraq, Afghanistan, and Libya) with hopes of transitioning such countries into Western-style liberal democracies for others to emulate. Jocelyn Cesari of Harvard University's Middle East Center argues that such nation-building exercises have turned Islam into a modern national ideology and "led to an unprecedented politicization of Islam."[60]

For most Muslims, just governance is about leadership as much as it is about institutions and the moral conduct that anchors them. The Qur'an makes the following foundational reference to leadership:

> And remember that Abraham was tried by his Lord with certain commands, which he fulfilled: He said: "I will make thee an Imam to the Nations." He pleaded: "And also (Imams) from my offspring!" He answered: But My Promise is not within the reach of evil-doers. (2:124)

Three principles of leadership emerge from this exchange: (1) Abraham could not be appointed leader unless he had proven his qualifications by passing a test; (2) human nature desires for one's progeny what one has; and (3) while heredity successions may not be completely ruled out, the determining criterion is not heredity but rather the individual passing a test and possessing the necessary leadership qualifications.

More importantly, the Islamic concept of leadership is rooted in the institutionalization of principles rather than personalities. The inaugural speech of the first caliph, Abu Bakar al-Siddiq, provides some insight and describes some of good governance's fundamental characteristics. Immediately after being elected by the community to succeed the Prophet, he said:

> I have been given authority over you, although I am not the best of you. If I do well, help me; and if I do wrong, set me right. Loyalty is, to tell the truth to a leader; treason is to hide it. The weak among you will be powerful in my eyes until I secure his rights if Allah so wills. The strong among you shall be weak in my eyes until I get the right from him. If people do not follow in the way of Allah, He will disgrace them. Obey me as long as I obey Allah and his Prophet, and if I disobey them, you owe me no obedience.[61]

Inherent in this statement is the cardinal principles of good governance, such as honoring the people's will, freedom of expression, the rule of law, and judicial independence.[62]

Just governance demands more than a capable and benevolent leader. In fact, it requires institutions that can respond to the people's cultural and ethical urges, as well as an ideology that anchors the ruler's conduct and relationship with the ruled. In an Islamic context, good governance must be based on a set of rules—laws and regulations—that normalizes the ruler–ruled relationship: "Those, when given authority in the land, establish (system of) *salah*, give *zakah* and enjoin what is good (*ma'ruf*) and forbid what is wrong (*munkar*)." (Quran, al-Hajj, 22:41). It further states: "O you who believe, stand up as a witness for Allah in all fairness and do not let the hatred of people deviate you from justice (*'adl*). Be just, this is closest to piety." (Quran, al-Ma'idah, 5:8)

Other qualifications are that "good governance" (1) strives to achieve justice in society; (2) aspires to maintain the dignity of men and women and protect group freedom, regardless of religious or national affiliation; (3) steers individuals toward achieving a means of sustainable livelihood before aspiring for other luxuries; (4) encourages virtue, limits vice, and rejects compulsion in matters of religion; and (5) achieves its aims through consultation, participation, representation, accountability mechanisms, and legal conventional regulations in *all* social formations.[63]

Through its principles and percepts, Islam created a unique system of government that both legitimized and sustained its institutions, practices, and values. The Prophet and his immediate successors derived laws from Islam's foundational sources and had the authority to enforce them on a willing population. Their successors faced a different environment, for the abilities to derive and then enforce rulings and laws became separated. Scholars issued rulings, but only rulers could enforce them. In the earlier period following the Rightly Guided Caliphs, rulers deferred to scholars because they derived their authority to rule from the latter's endorsement. Over time, the scholars became deferential to the rulers and were soon marginalized within the government's systems and institutions.

The Islamic concept of justice is understood in terms of philosophy, theology, sociology, economics, and institutions of state and society.[64] As the idea played out over time, it was affected by both intrinsic and extrinsic factors. Necessarily, therefore, it becomes subject to change and evolution. Certain of its core notions appear to be permanent, even though they also subtly change with time and place. One example of this is the idea that justice is correlated to the degree and extent to which one abides by divinely sanctioned commands in societies with an overtly religious culture. In the Western world, these have metamorphosed over time from justice as the appropriate observance and fealty to duties to justice becoming, in part, a matter of acknowledging rights. An inversion, therefore, takes place: rights assume the place of duties. This now almost universal phenomenon replaces traditional concepts of justice with desacralized understandings.[65]

The other vector of Islam's concept of justice points to the Absolute, to the One from whom all manifestations of existence flow. This is an altogether different field of understanding.[66]

The word justice in the Qur'anic Arabic is rendered as *'Adl*. The word itself has a multiplicity of meaning. In its common usage, it can mean "even" "to determine with evenness," "to be equal to," and "to attribute value." It is also the opposite of inequity and unfairness. In the Qur'an, however, the word is used with further shades of meaning. There are five basic usages of the word in the Qur'an. The first implies an offering or recompense.[67] The second implies expiation or amendment.[68] The third implies fairness, the opposite of inequity.[69] The fourth implies setting right.[70] Lastly, it implies equalizing.[71]

At another level, though, the text warns against hoarding riches and condoning massive discrepancies in material wealth between individuals and nations.[72] We all share in God's bounty of being brought into existence, but the disparity in living circumstances is a product of *zulm*, the opposite or absence of justice. Tolerating oppressive inequalities (*zulm*) on account of *tafdhil* (the claim of being awarded a higher measure by God) is not an acceptable outcome for the just person.[73]

Establishing justice also requires a scale (*mizan*). The scale of the divinely revealed law is the weighting of the two pans and the presence of an indicator and a lever. In the Qur'an, God has given the scale's power to humanity and warned people to weigh justly. The Shari'ah's scale is one—but not the only—measure of the scale. The scale *as a whole* is a scale of *qist* (the just scale). So, justice cannot be defined as the outcome of weighing facts and judgments, following precedent, or the automatic outcome of transgressing the Shari'ah's boundaries. Rather, it is an inherent quality of the scale itself. Humanity achieves justice by holding up the scale at all times and putting everything in its appropriate place. In turn, justice is enhanced by wisdom, defined as acting appropriately and pursuant to a deep commitment to the principle of equal dignity of all human beings. In fact, wisdom takes precedence over *all* rankings and hierarchies. Anyone who acts wisely and is driven by the just scale exhibits the correct courtesy (*adab*) toward the Creator. In regular steps, the just person progresses to the rank of *wali Allah* (friend of God).[74]

The inner dimensions of Islam's definition of justice echo throughout Hossein Askari and Abbas Mirakhor's new work and infuse their profound dissection of it as an element of just governance.[75] Setting out to demonstrate how Islam's concept of justice underlies any serious debate on inequality, poverty reduction, fair governance, and institutional arrangements, they establish that this concept is best served within the context of basically self-governing autonomous units. In this regard, they depart radically from the conventional discourse, which locates justice within the framework of the large, centralized state. For example, Rawls' theory of distributive justice requires the intrusive and controlling power of the state to essentially affect the outcome in the direction sought.[76]

A corollary of the just state in Islam is, in fact, that the just community and the just individual are self-correcting and bound by an internally consistent set of rules, principles, and values.[77] The state's role is that of a referee and social agent rather than an initiator and executor. Needless to say, this is a far cry from the modern states found in the Muslim world, which combine the worst aspects of the domineering state with dysfunction and abysmal governance. What they also imply is that Islam's concept of the state has to be radically rethought if it is to reflect the imperative of providing a canopy of just rule for, rather than over, society. This is an altogether admirable synthesis and exploration into an area of immense significance that has exercised Muslim minds for centuries.[78]

A MORE ETHICAL AND JUSTICE-ORIENTED FOREIGN POLICY

For a long time, but particularly in the past century, the West has tried to shape Muslim societies in general and Middle Eastern societies in particular. The approach employed had nothing to do with promoting a set of political values rooted in dignity and justice but with superimposing what Safi refers to as "the European modernization experience" on developing societies along the lines proposed by modernization theory, even if that meant empowering dictators.[79]

Realists and liberals alike imposed these modernization ambitions on the Middle East. On the economic front, these efforts were often rooted in the Washington Consensus,[80] while politically, the efforts focused on liberalism and democracy. While these ideas are conceptually laudable, the efforts have rarely been translated into good governance for the region's people. In most cases, U.S. foreign policy has been driven by narrow self-interests (e.g., oil and Washington's security concerns), rather than a more accountable and transparent government. Additionally, the results of American interventions claimed to be based on humanitarian principles have often been lackluster and demonstrated a weak resolve to see them through, as witnessed in Syria, Iraq, Yemen, Somalia, and Afghanistan.

In the hope of addressing the resulting skepticism and lackluster results, Shadi Hamid suggests a middle path. He recommends decoupling democracy from liberalism so that the United States might prioritize democracy over liberalism, especially in the Middle East. In his estimation, Washington's foreign policy establishment faces a "democratic dilemma": it wants democracy in theory but not necessarily its outcomes in practice.[81] This is a uniquely American dilemma, for the country insists on promoting democracy as a core aspect of its foreign policy aims and is also one of the few countries with the clout to do something about it. Hamid proposes "democratic minimalism" as a path to resolving this democratic dilemma: The spread of liberalism across the Middle East is unlikely, for liberalism obviously requires liberals, of which there are few in the region. Moreover, it is hard to imagine that the majority of Egyptians, Iraqis, Saudis, or Afghans will decide to become liberals anytime soon.[82] "Liberalism may garner some sympathy in the margins, [but] the vast majority of religiously conservative Muslim-majority countries remain much more resistant."[83]

Hamid correctly poses that, at its core, the American conception of democracy is one of self-government and privileging choice and agency, which Americans insist on for themselves, should be extended to other polities. Democracy, as a system and a set of procedures that enables the regulation of politics without predetermining its outcomes, would allow Arabs and Muslims to decide their own course(s) and determine which values are the most important to them.[84] To compel non-Westerners to become Western-style liberals is a mark of hubris, for it is bound to be either ineffective and/ or unrealistic because it is self-negating. In short, if democracy is a form of government, then liberalism is a form of governing. Putting it like this helps clarify the distinctions between asking a country to be democratic and asking it to become liberal. The latter is more invasive—in both reality and perception—for it requires electorates to, in effect, repurpose their substantive ends and rethink their conception of what is just and good.[85]

Liberals insist that their approach provides a "neutral public space" in which individuals can freely express their beliefs and religious preferences. However, this supposed neutralism can only be accepted within a liberal framework.[86] Political liberalism, as expounded by Rawls, is based on the "veil of ignorance"—the notion that a new polity's founders are free to construct their own society without any distinctive set of preferences or values.

But as Lenn Goodman, one of his most perceptive critics, reminds us, "even neutrality, in Rawls's scheme, is not neutral. . . . Every one of Rawls's choosers is trapped in a liberal society. . . . They are not free to construct a value system for themselves."[87]

Furthermore, a foreign policy that truly understands the hopes and aspirations of Muslims can only emerge by listening and understanding what most of them insist upon for themselves: respect, dignity, and peace. They seek good governance from their public officials, namely, governance that is morally grounded and supports justice. When asked about the type of government they envision, most of them often put justice front and center. Islam commands its followers to create a just society, meaning one that looks after its people's welfare and betterment. Yet for centuries, Muslims have grappled with the concept of an "Islamic polity" and what might constitute "good governance." Ever since the time of Prophet Muhammad, Muslim leaders, scholars, political activists, and Islamists have sought to imagine and articulate what such a polity might look like in both conceptual and practical terms.

While those groups continue their fierce debates, these issues also have real-life implications for Muslims living in societies where the debates around Islam's role in the public sphere have, at times, become violent. The majority of Muslims insist that Islam should play some role in politics. From Iraq and Syria to Egypt, Libya, and Yemen; from Turkey to Afghanistan and Pakistan; and even all the way to Malaysia and Indonesia, one finds that a popular desire in the Muslim world gives voice to Islam in public life, of course in different forms and to varying degrees.

The ongoing upheaval in many of these countries simply reflects the restlessness and heightened aspirations of the Muslim public to elucidate what might constitute such a polity. Muslims have different views of Islamic governance: from their historical heritage to taking pride in the hope for a future that merges Islamic elements with what they regard as "rational" in the contemporary Western model.[88] The details of such a mixture differ. Some want to "Islamicize" modernism, while others seek to link Islamic foundations to various applications borrowed from the modernist model.[89]

Liberalism, as both a value system and a set of premises about the primacy of reason and progress over revelation, speaks to foundational questions about the good life and the purposes of government. Due to liberalism's inevitable clash with a religious doctrine that, in its various mainstream iterations, has guarded its jurisdiction over such ultimate questions,[90] one must assess its appeal and interest in the Muslim world. Hamid argues that "If democracy is part of a package that includes within it ontological premises about the nature of progress, human nature, and ultimate ends, then it is less likely to be accepted in societies where those premises are not shared."[91] As political theorist Joseph Kaminski puts it, Islam and liberalism "operate on fundamentally different baseline assumptions about the nature of reality itself."[92]

With this in mind, American policymakers would be more convincing if they focused on means rather than ends while engaging with the Middle East. If the ends of politics revolve around existential questions, then outsiders cannot answer them.[93] Coming to terms with this reality means that they should be far more cautious and limited in their efforts to promote liberal democracy. Supporting democracy abroad cannot be treated as a project of ideological and cultural transformation, nor should it be Washington's job to refashion sociopolitical institutions from the ground up.[94]

All Middle Eastern countries except Israel and Lebanon profess Islam as their state religion. Whether simply in words or in actuality, Islam is woven into their societies' fabric and thus affects everything from their political systems to their social, financial, and economic systems.[95] Islam is a rules-based system, for its collected rules constitute those of its institutions that seek to establish just societies. Allah commands Muslims to behave fairly and justly with everyone in order to protect the rights of others, as well as to be just in business dealings, honor agreements and contracts, help and be fair to the needy and orphans, and be just even to one's enemies. He also orders them to establish just societies, be governed by just rulers, and stand up for the oppressed.[96] This is why Muslims say that justice is the heart of Islam. In the same vein, the state (policies) must step in to restore justice whenever and wherever Muslims fail to comply with divine rules. According to this understanding, government intervention must enhance justice.[97]

NOTES

1. Osita G. Afoaku, "U.S. Foreign Policy and Authoritarian Regimes: Change and Continuity in International Clientelism," *Journal of Third World Studies* XVII, no. 2 (Fall 2000); Social Science Premium Collection, 13.

2. Jeanne J. Kirkpatrick, *Dictatorships and Double Standards: Rationalism and Reason in Politics* (New York: American Enterprise Institute, 1982), 49–50. For a critique of this doctrine, see Ted Galen Carpenter, "The United States and Third World Dictatorships: A Case of Benign Detachment," Cato Policy Analysis No. 58, August 15, 1985.

3. Afoaku, "U.S. Foreign Policy and Authoritarian Regimes," 13.

4. Louay Safi, *Islam and the Trajectory of Globalization: Rational Idealism and the Structure of World History* (Routledge, 2022), 252.

5. See Louay Safi, *Islam and the Trajectory of Globalization*.

6. Safi, *Islam and the Trajectory of Globalization: Rational Idealism and the Structure of World History* (Routledge, 2022), 42.

7. Safi, *Islam and the Trajectory of Globalization*, 43.

8. Ibid., 44–45.

9. M. Anthony Mills, "Liberalism and the Common Good," September 28, 2020, https://lawliberty.org/liberalism-and-the-common-good/

10. Immanuel Kant, *Political Writings,* ed. H. Reiss (Cambridge, UK: Cambridge University Press, [1797] 1991), 102.

11. Alexandra Gheciu, "Liberalism and Peaceful Change," in *The Oxford Handbook of Peaceful Change in International Relations,* ed. T.V. Paul et al. eds. (Oxford: Oxford University Press), 112.

12. Gheciu, 113.

13. Sean Kay, *America's Search for Security: The Triumph of Idealism and the Return of Realism* (Rowman & Littlefield Publishers, 2014).

14. Immanuel Kant, "Perpetual Peace," in *Conflict after the Cold War: Arguments on Causes of War and Peace,* 2nd ed., ed. Richard K. Betts (New York: Longman, 2002), 103.

15. Kay, *America's Search for Security.*

16. Robert Kagan, (will provide footnote)

17. Shadi Hamid, *The Problem of Democracy: America, the Middle East, and the Rise and Fall of an Idea* (Oxford University Press, 2022), 7.

18. John J. Mearsheimer, *Great Delusion: Liberal Dreams and International Realities* (Yale University Press, 2018), vii–xiv. JSTOR, https://doi.org/10.2307/j.ctv5cgb1w.3.

19. Safi, *Islam and the Trajectory of Globalization,* 33.

20. O. Waever, "The Rise and the Fall of the Inter-Paradigm Debate," in *International Theory: Positivism & Beyond,* eds. K. Booth et al. (Cambridge: Cambridge University Press, 1996), 163.

21. S. Smith, "Positivism and Beyond," in *International Theory: Positivism & Beyond,* eds. K. Booth et al. (Cambridge: Cambridge University Press, 1996), 17.

22. Safi, *Islam and the Trajectory of Globalization.* 34.

23. Ibid.

24. Ibid.

25. Mearsheimer, *Great Delusion,* vii–xiv.

26. Ibid.

27. Kay, *America's Search for Security.*

28. George W. Bush, "2nd Inaugural Address," Washington, DC, 20 January 2005.

29. Kay, *America's Search for Security.*

30. Fawaz A. Gerges, The End of America's Moment?: Obama and the Middle East, (Palgrave Macmillan: 2012).

31. Kay, *America's Search for Security.*

32. Ibid.

33. Ibid.

34. Hillary Clinton, "Speech at the Council on Foreign Relations," Washington, DC, 1 February 2013.

35. Kay, *America's Search for Security.*

36. Ibid.

37. John Mearsheimer, *The Great Delusion: Liberal Dreams and International Realities*, Stephen Walt, *The Hell of Good Intentions: America's Foreign Policy Elite and the Decline of U.S. Primacy* (New York: Farrar, Straus and Giroux, 2018).

38. Stephen Wertheim, *Tomorrow, The World: The Birth of U.S. Global Supremacy* (Cambridge, MA: Belknap Press, 2021).

39. John Mearsheimer, *The Great Delusion*, 123.

40. Hamid, *The Problem of Democracy*, 9.

41. Mearsheimer, *Great Delusion*, vii–xiv.

42. Ibid.

43. Patrick J. Deneen, *Why Liberalism Failed* (Yale University Press, 2018).

44. Susannah Black, "Our Post-Liberal Moment" April, 19, 2020, https://spectatorworld.com/topic/our-post-liberal-moment/

45. G. John Ikenberry, The End of Liberal International Order?, *International Affairs*, 94, no. 1 (January 2018): 7–23; G. John Ikenberry, "Why the Liberal World Order Will Survive," *Ethics & International Affairs*, 32, no. 1 (2018): 17–29.

46. Francis Fukuyama, *Liberalism and Its Discontents*.

47. Ikenberry, "The End of Liberal International Order?" 23; G. John Ikenberry, Why the Liberal World Order Will Survive, *Ethics & International Affairs*, 17–29.

48. Ibid., 22.

49. Ikenberry, "The End of Liberal International Order?," 22.

50. Adrian Smith, Alison Stenning, and Katie Willis (eds.), *Social Justice and Neoliberalism Global Perspectives* (London and New York: Zed Books, 2008). As referenced in Louay Safi, *Islam and the Trajectory of Globalization*, 31.

51. Safi, *Islam and the Trajectory of Globalization*, 31.

52. Ibid., 33.

53. Francis Fukuyama, "What is Governance?" *Governance* 26, no. 3 (July 2013): 347–68.

54. Ibid.

55. Ibid.

56. Amr G. E. Sabet, *Islam and the Political: Theory, Governance and International Relations* (London and Ann Arbor, MI: Pluto Press, 2008), 101.

57. Tamara Sonn, "Political Thought in Classical Islamic Thought," *The American Journal of Islamic Social Sciences*, 13, no. 3 (Herndon, VA, International Institute of Islamic Thought), xx.

58. Ibid.

59. Noah Feldman, *The Fall and Rise of the Islamic State* (Princeton, NJ: Princeton University Press, 2008), 14.

60. Jocelyn Cesari, *The Awakening of Muslim Democracy* (New York: Cambridge University Press, 2014), 279.

61. Abu Jaʿfar al-Ṭabarī, *Tārīkh al-Ṭabarī* (Cairo: Dār al-Maʿārif, 1969), 3:224.

62. Abdullah al-Ahsan and Stephen B. Young (eds.), "Guidance for Good Governance Explorations in Qur'anic, Scientific and Cross-cultural Approaches" (Kuala Lumpur: International Islamic University Malaysia and Caux Round Table 2008), 19.

63. Hashem, "Islamic Roots of Good Governance," *Arab Insight* 1, no. 163–71.

64. Ali Allawi writing the Forward to Askari and Mirakhor's book provides a concise summary of Justice in Islam which I cite extensively here. Askari and Mirakhor Conceptions of Justice, forward, ix.

65. Ali Allawi as cited in Askari and Mirakhor *Conceptions of Justice,* forward, ix.

66. Ibid., xi.

67. Qur'an (2:48).

68. Qur'an (5:95).

69. Qur'an (4:58).

70. Qur'an (82:7).

71. Qur'an (6:1).

72. Ali Allawi as cited in Askari and Mirakhor *Conceptions of Justice*, forward, xii.

73. Ali Allawi as cited in Askari and Mirakhor *Conceptions of Justice,* forward, xii.

74. Ibid.

75. Ali Allawi as cited in Askari and Mirakhor *Conceptions of Justice*, forward, xii.

76. Ibid., xii.

77. Ibid. xii.

78. Ibid., xiii.

79. Ibid., 252.

80. John Marangos, "The Evolution of the term 'Washington Consensus,'" *Journal of Economic Surveys*, 23, no. 2 (April 2009): 350–84.

81. Hamid, *The Problem of Democracy,* 5.

82. Ibid., 16.

83. Ibid., 16–17.

84. Ibid., 17.

85. Ibid.

86. Ibid.

87. Lenn Goodman, "The Road to Kazanistan" American Philosophical Quarterly Vol. 45, No. 2 (Apr., 2008), pp. 81–106 (26 pages) Published By: University of Illinois Press.

88. Mazen Hashem, "Islamic Roots of Good Governance," *Arab Insight* 1, no. 1 (Spring 2007): 63–71.

89. Ibid.

90. Hamid, *The Problem of Democracy*, 16.

91. Ibid., 17.

92. Joseph Kaminski, *Islam, Liberalism, and Ontology* (New York: Routledge, 2021), 3.

93. Hamid, *The Problem of Democracy*, 17.

94. Ibid., 17.

95. Hossein Askari and Abbas Mirakhor, *Conceptions of Justice from Islam to the Present* (Palgrave, 2020), preface.

96. Ibid.

97. Ibid.

REFERENCES

Afoaku, Osita, "U.S. Foreign Policy and Authoritarian Regimes: Change and Continuity in International Clientelism," *Journal of Third World Studies*, XVII, no. 2 (Fall 2000); Social Science Premium Collection.
al-Ahsan, Abdullah and Stephen B. Young (eds.), "Guidance for Good Governance Explorations in Qur'anic, Scientific and Cross-cultural Approaches" (Kuala Lumpur: International Islamic University Malaysia and Caux Round Table 2008).
al-Tabarī, Abu Ja'far, *Tārīkh al-Tabarī* (Cairo: Dār al-Ma'ārif, 1969).
Alexandra Gheciu, "Liberalism and Peaceful Change," in *The Oxford Handbook of Peaceful Change in International Relations*, ed. T.V. Paul et al. eds. (Oxford: Oxford University Press).
Askari, Hossein and Abbas Mirakhor, *Conceptions of Justice from Islam to the Present* (Palgrave, 2020).
Black, Susannah, "Our Post-Liberal Moment" April, 19, 2020, https://spectatorworld.com/topic/our-post-liberal-moment/
Bush, George W., "2nd Inaugural Address," Washington, DC, 20 January 2005.
Carpenter, Ted Galen, "The United States and Third World Dictatorships: A Case of Benign Detachment," Cato Policy Analysis No. 58, August 15, 1985.
Cesari, Jocelyn, *The Awakening of Muslim Democracy* (New York: Cambridge University Press, 2014).
Clinton, Hillary, "Speech at the Council on Foreign Relations," Washington, DC, 1 February 2013.
Deneen, Patrick J., *Why Liberalism Failed* (Yale University Press, 2018).
Feldman, Noah, *The Fall and Rise of the Islamic State* (Princeton, NJ: Princeton University Press, 2008),
Gerges, Fawaz A., *The End of America's Moment?: Obama and the Middle East* (Palgrave Macmillan: 2012).
Hamid, Shadi, *The Problem of Democracy: America, the Middle East, and the Rise and Fall of an Idea* (Oxford University Press, 2022).
Hashem, Mazen, "Islamic Roots of Good Governance," *Arab Insight* 1, no. 1 (Spring 2007): 63–71.
Ikenberry, "The End of Liberal International Order?" 23; G. John Ikenberry, Why the Liberal World Order Will Survive, *Ethics & International Affairs*, 17–29.
Ikenberry, G. John, The End of Liberal International Order?, *International Affairs*, 94, no. 1 (January 2018): 7–23; Ikenberry, G. John, "Why the Liberal World Order Will Survive," *Ethics & International Affairs*, 32, no. 1 (2018): 17–29.
Kaminski, Joseph, *Islam, Liberalism, and Ontology* (New York: Routledge, 2021).
Kant, Immanuel, "Perpetual Peace," in *Conflict after the Cold War: Arguments on Causes of War and Peace*, 2nd ed., ed. Richard K. Betts (New York: Longman, 2002).
Kant, Immanuel, *Political Writings,* ed. H. Reiss (Cambridge, UK: Cambridge University Press, [1797] 1991).

Kirkpatrick, Jeanne J., *Dictatorships and Double Standards: Rationalism and Reason in Politics* (New York: American Enterprise Institute, 1982).

Marangos, John, The Evolution of the term 'Washington Consensus' *Journal of Economic Surveys*, 23, no. 2 (April 2009): 350–384.

Mearsheimer, John J., *Great Delusion: Liberal Dreams and International Realities* (Yale University Press, 2018), vii–xiv. *JSTOR*, https://doi.org/10.2307/j.ctv5cgb1w.3.

Mills, M. Anthony, "Liberalism and the Common Good," September 28, 2020, https://lawliberty.org/liberalism-and-the-common-good/

Sabet, Amr G.E., *Islam and the Political: Theory, Governance and International Relations* (London and Ann Arbor, MI: Pluto Press, 2008).

Safi, *Islam and the Trajectory of Globalization: Rational Idealism and the Structure of World History* (Routledge, 2022).

Sean Kay, *America's Search for Security: The Triumph of Idealism and the Return of Realism* (Rowman & Littlefield Publishers, 2014).

Smith, Adrian, Alison Stenning, and Katie Willis (eds.), *Social Justice and Neoliberalism Global Perspectives* (London and New York: Zed Books, 2008).

Smith, S., "Positivism and Beyond," in *International Theory: Positivism & Beyond*, eds. K. Booth et al. (Cambridge: Cambridge University Press, 1996), 17.

Sonn, Tamara, "Political Thought in Classical Islamic Thought," *The American Journal of Islamic Social Sciences*, 13, no. 3 (Herndon, VA, International Institute of Islamic Thought).

Stephen Wertheim, *Tomorrow, The World: The Birth of U.S. Global Supremacy* (Cambridge, MA: Belknap Press, 2021).

Waever, O., "The Rise and the Fall of the Inter-Paradigm Debate," in *International Theory: Positivism & Beyond*, eds. K. Booth et al. (Cambridge: Cambridge University Press, 1996).

Chapter 9

Religious Diversity in Arab Society
Myth, Conspiracy, and Reality
Mohammed Abu-Nimer

Managing diversity has emerged as one of the most valuable skills and competencies needed in the twenty-first century, especially with the massive technological advancement and changes that swept the globe since the end of the Cold War. New forms of communication, especially social media, have wiped out national boundaries and divides which in the past prevented people from comparing themselves with others outside of their own communities (national, ethnic, racial, religious, linguistic, cultural, etc.). In addition, there have been many rapid demographic changes due to migrants and refugees and due to mobility in general. Millions of people cross between the northern and southern hemispheres, as they attempt to start new life in search of a more secure living and better social and economic conditions.

These changes have resulted in significant transformation in the ethnic and religious composition of many societies and states. The Arab region is no exception. Its societies have experienced massive waves of protest movements and campaigns for political, social, and economic changes.[1]

Ethnic, tribal, and religious differences have been deployed by politicians and religious leaders alike to mobilize support and leverage to influence the national agenda and shape the public opinion in favor of their ideological preferences.

It is also well known and documented that ethnic and sectarian grievances were among the primary reasons that motivated and incited people to take to the streets, especially the youth who expressed resentment and anger over the existing failing political governance systems. These grievances exist despite the fact that celebrating religious harmony between Muslims and non-Muslims and among different Muslim sects is the primary discourse adopted and promoted by most Arab governments and regimes. Such discourse was essential and central for the Arab national movement that fought against colonial powers in the 1950s and 1960s. It was also deployed by the leaders of various military coups (Iraq, Syria, Yemen, Libya, Sudan, etc.). The dominant narrative of national unity was based on the domination of cultural and religious majority which was utilized to mobilize support against colonial powers' policies.[2]

This type of national unity suppressed any element, factor, voice, or agency that hinted to the need to recognize cultural and religious differences and or demanded a unique and special treatment of social groups due to their unique background. In fact, treason and foreign conspiracy were often the primary tools used by the gate keepers of Arab nationalists to prevent any serious consideration of the need for systematic inclusion of the various ethnicities, religions, sects, and marginalized cultural groups.[3]

The accumulated results of these policies of political, social, and economic marginalization, discrimination, and exclusion became clear in the demands of many groups prior to and during the Arab Spring revolts in Egypt, Lebanon, Yemen, Syria, Iraq, Bahrain, and so on. Many scholars and studies have linked the recent uprisings and political turmoil to the need for better arrangements to manage differences (age, gender, ethnicity, religion, culture, region, etc.) in every Arab society.

It should also be noted that there is a thread of discourse that has acknowledged cultural diversity and a basic level of coexistence and tolerance of cultural and religious practices in Arab societies and communities. This thread can be easily detected in the symbolic representation of cultural and religious diversity programs in many formal Arab governmental institutions. One will hear the statements "We have lived together for hundreds of years, and we eat and visit with each other. We do not differentiate between our people in our community"; and "We used to live together and celebrate our separate holidays and even exchange food and gifts in holidays." Such typical statements made by elders and others capture the story and narrative of cultural and religious harmony that existed during precolonial and a couple of decades of postcolonial periods.[4]

CORE PRACTICES OF MANAGING DIVERSITY

Managing diversity effectively and in an inclusive framework requires social, political, and cultural transformation of the local and national spaces, in a way that respecting and accepting diversity is placed in the center and not in the margins of the national agenda. Ethnic, religious, gender, and cultural differences become a source of richness to be celebrated and not feared or disdained by members of the dominant majority. Society reconfigures its institutions (educational, cultural, political, economic, media, etc.) to recognize the possible contributions that each of its national components can bring to the whole.

Globally, people and societies are still struggling to construct such systems to fully honor diversity and manage it in an ideal way, and some have made more progress in their efforts to respond to the needs of their diverse populations.[5] It is crucial to apply constructive diversity management in all spheres that affect the public and private lives of the citizens. Nevertheless, there are five essential core areas for the management of effective diversity:

1. Equal access to public spaces: members of the minority groups are able to relate to the public spaces and feel a sense of belonging and not exclusion. For example, the public square in the heart of the city not only has Quranic verses or Hadith, but it also has other religious groups' representation; the Airport has prayer spaces for Muslims, Christians, and other religious groups; streets and boulevard names reflect religious diversity too. Diverse representation in the public space is the rule, not the exception.
2. Inclusive education: formal educational curriculum on all levels prioritizes the principle of diversity. Such principles will be manifested in the teaching of history, religion, social sciences, math, chemistry, and so on. Mainstreaming diversity and inclusion in every subject allows young generations to become more inclusive in their approach, especially to cultural and religious differences.[6] For them, diversity becomes the rule and not the exception. Thus when celebrating national heroes, they are aware of the contribution of the diverse groups to the national project throughout their shared history. The challenges in implementing such principles, even after political peace agreements, can be observed in the case of Lebanon in which the formal public education system could agree on a unified curriculum of history or religion to be taught in the schools to students from all ethnic and religious affiliations. Since the Taef Agreement in 1991, the Lebanese Ministry of Education has struggled in implementing such a curriculum. Similar situation was in post-Saddam Iraq between 2003 and 2013, in which an inclusive civic education curriculum that reflects the principle of religious and ethnic diversity was debated and delayed.[7]
3. Common and equal access to citizenship: managing diversity constructively means that all the components of the society (of the nation state) have the right to equal representation in all the state's structures and institutions. Limiting the access and representation means reducing inclusion and perpetuating exclusion in the arena of civic rights. Thus, for example, the presidency or higher political offices are not exclusively limited to certain ethnic or religious groups; for example,

you do not have to be Muslim to become a president or prime minister, the minister of defense, the head of a national university, the director of official state media outlets, etc. For example, the Lebanese system continues to be based on sectarian proportional arrangements in a majority of its formal institutions; other Arab political regimes have their own criteria for restrictions on free access to political, religious, military, or other sensitive government positions. The mere fact that you are a citizen qualifies you to run or occupy any office in the state. However, for such a principle to be implemented, there is a need to challenge the hegemonic domination of ethnic, cultural, or religious majoritarian or sectarian systems in Arab society.

4. Religious freedom: all faith groups (individually and collectively) have the right and equal access to practice their faith in public and private settings. Thus, there is no restriction on building mosques, churches, temples, synagogues, etc. In addition, governmental and formal state agencies recognize such religious diversity and allocate resources to celebrate and respect it. Such a principle has been extremely challenging to implement in the Arab society context due to the domination of the Muslim discourse in both public and private spheres. This discourse is influenced by the Islamic religious heritage of Ahl Adhimma (Protected People),[8] which has in many ways dictated and shaped the formal and informal treatment of religious minorities in the Arab region, especially Christians and Jews. Although historically this principle provided Christians and Jews with relatively greater civic and religious rights than what the European protestant governance system provided to its minorities, there are major concerns in adopting such principles in our modern and global reality of today. In fact, raising such an issue has always been a sour diplomatic point between Northern Hemisphere policy makers and government officials in the Arab region. However, in the past decade, for a variety of reasons, there have been significant policy changes, especially in certain Gulf countries like UAE, Oman, and Bahrain in their position toward issues of religious freedom for Jewish and Christian minorities.[9] However, it must be noted that the small number of Jews and Christians in these Arab societies and states constitute no significant threat to the dominant discourse and structures of the state and society at large. Thus, it is not clear to what extent these policies are internalized and sincerely adopted or whether they will continue to be symbolic gestures to be utilized in the states' public relations and public diplomacy image.

5. National calendar and narrative: constructing an inclusive formal state and national calendar for celebrations. Such a principle is crucial to reflect the sincere commitment of the state in enforcing the diversity in

its symbolic and substantial spheres and practices, especially when state media and formal agencies (education, economic institutions, military, etc.) adopt such inclusive practice. In the Arab society context, this will have implications for national and religious celebrations in the public spheres, for example, Christmas trees in the mayor's offices, special programs on public TV recognizing and celebrating these religious events, special recognition by government officials of the diverse religious discourse of other groups than Muslim Shia or Sunni dominant groups. Obviously, in this limited essay, one cannot comprehensively identify and list all the public and private spheres and on both individual and collective levels of practice. Nevertheless, it is obvious that socioeconomic mobility and full integration in security and military forces are primary areas to ensure that diversity is indeed being institutionally respected. The religious and cultural identity of any individual or group should not be an obstacle to their advancement of acceptance in these institutions. For example, in the Arab society context, a Shai, Sunni, or any of the religious schools of thoughts (madhhab) should determine the opportunities for any individual advancement or acceptance in formal institutions.

OBSTACLES AND CHALLENGES TO DIVERSITY IN ARAB SOCIETY

The degree of success in implementing diversity measures in the above areas varies among different societies around the globe. Arab societies struggle with this issue as well. There are serious structural and cultural factors that impede the adaptation and implementation of such models of diversity. The processes of building institutions and practices that honor the principles of diversity and inclusion are being debated and manifested in the Arab region in many areas and in different ways, including academic debates, political movements, arts, social media campaigns, and religious voices. The dynamics of debating the limits of acceptance of diversity often reflects common sets of obstacles and challenges facing those who call for managing diversity in a more constructive and inclusive arrangement.[10]

When explaining the weak local and national capacities in managing diversity in the Arab society context, it is often attributed to a complex set of historical, economic, social, and political factors and forces. However, religious identities, both intrareligious and interreligious, can play a significant role in the process of undermining or strengthening the fabric of diversity in the various Arab communities.

This section will examine how these factors have utilized the religious identity to perpetuate the exclusive domination of certain ethnic, cultural, and religious agencies in Arab societies.

Authoritarianism: in a postcolonial period of the history of Arab societies, political and military leaders relied on authoritarian structures to form political, economic, and security institutions to consolidate their powers. Thus, ethnic and religious inclusivity was sacrificed in the name of building a unified nation as envisioned by the authoritarian regimes. Any opposition or questioning of such an approach was automatically labeled as treason and often punished by execution or long-term imprisonment.[11]

Tribal and ideological loyalty: in the process of stabilizing the newly formed Arab states (1950s), there was a pressing need for fostering political and military loyalty. Such loyalties were crucial for new regimes surrounded by internal and external threats and instability. Tribal and religious sectarian identities in Jordan, Iraq, Syria, Lebanon, Libyan, Gulf states, and others lent themselves easily to non-inclusive management of diversity. Thus, key governing institutions were entrusted to individuals with unwavering loyalty to ruling parties and dominant political ideologies, or to those with clear religious, sectarian, or tribal affiliation. For example, Baath party membership in both Iraq and Syria was used as a criterion for loyalty; tribal affiliation in Jordan was utilized by the Hashemite monarchy for governing the country, leading to the marginalization of Palestinian identity; similarly, Shia and Sunni identity in Gulf states and Arab and Berber cultures in North Africa become the criteria for awarding key positions within the government.

One of the direct consequences of these policies of exclusion was the lack of development of strong political and parliamentarian norms and cultures. Thus, when many of these regimes and their centralized institutions collapsed in the Arab Spring (beginning of 2010), there were no strong, credible, and well-established political alternatives to gain the trust of the various forces who competed for control.[12]

The paradox of merit versus tribal loyalty has existed in the Arab cultural context for many centuries and has been debated by many scholars as many argued it is rooted in the cultural fabrics of norms and values of tribalism.[13] In the context of religious diversity, it should be noted that constructive diversity management is undermined by the tribal, religious, or ethnic loyalty in all its shapes and forms. In fact, many forms of exclusion of religious minorities and other forms of exclusion are affected by this principle which is often practiced in formal and informal fashion in official government and non-government institutions.[14]

Instrumentalization of education: the process of legitimizing exclusion and marginalization of diverse constituencies in Arab societies has existed for centuries. It has been transferred from one generation to another through educational policies, structures, and institutions. Those have been utilized and instrumentalized by postcolonial regimes and leaders to perpetuate and maintain such exclusion of different ethnic, religious, and political groups. In fact, religious agencies have been agreed to be manipulated to justify such ideological practices. Thus Sunni and Shia clergies and institutions provided theological grounding for the exclusion of other religious minorities or other sects from their own dominant national majority public spaces.[15]

Such policies resulted in socializing younger generations with limited skills of critical thinking and lack of basic cultural competencies to deal with diverse reality. Thus, exclusion was normalized, and students, especially those who belong to the dominant majority or privileged groups, are desensitized to the pain and victimhood of marginalization from an early age. This mental frame was carried by their higher education, employment, and personal lives too.[16]

Structural violence: For the cultural practices of exclusion to be systematic and systemic and to gain legitimacy for their existence, socialization agents utilized fear and direct or indirect violence. Thus, military and security forces were deployed in postcolonial Arab regimes to ensure stability and order under the banner of protecting national unity. In the process of enforcing these state rules, policies of structural violence were designed and implemented—for example, harsh security measures against political, ethnic, religious, or other forms of opposition; weakening or abolishing any formal agency that calls for legal, economic, and political accountability. Surviving these forms of structural violence became the primary concerns of those who were marginalized and called for inclusion.[17] This tendency to suppress any political opposition through violent means also perpetuated the hegemonic domination of one ethnic, religious, or cultural group.[18] It also prohibited the development of healthy and constructive localized forms of managing religious diversity in the society. On the contrary, the system of violence punished and persecuted voices of opposition who called for reforms in the arena of religious diversity and who were labeled enemies of the state.

The Conspiracy Syndrome: Accusing and blaming foreign forces for all social and political ills in the social and political is central to the dynamics used by many religious and political leaders throughout human history. Disinformation is a key instrument used by leaders who want to silence internal dissent or discourage change in power relations. Undoubtedly, the external threat is often real and imposes tangible costs. The colonial legacy in the Arab region and the Israeli Zionist movement have played a huge and central role in being a real external threat that brought a great deal of destruction and victimhood in every Arab society.

However, such threat has been manipulated and utilized by political and religious agencies to justify the suppression of rights for many groups within these societies. In the name of protecting the nation and withstanding against the external threats, economic, political, religious, and marginalization policies were created and implemented. Conspiracy theory has become an integral tool utilized by leaders to prevent and suppress demands for better management of diversity.

The above are only selected few core factors that obstructed inclusivity and constructive management of diversity, there are many others that can be identified and explored. However, the remaining of this chapter will focus on current constructive responses to enhance capacities for the management of diversity in Arab societies.

CAPACITIES FOR CONSTRUCTIVE DIVERSITY MANAGEMENT

The process of adopting diversity norms and practices is not only the responsibility of policy makers but also an individual responsibility and life journey. Every person can go through various development stages in becoming culturally, religiously, and nationally sensitive to diversity.[19] However, this process requires certain capacities and skills that can be gained and practiced.

From denial to taking a stand: dealing with differences is at the core of managing diversity. Differences can be perceived as threatening, especially to those who have privileges to lose. For example, a male who enjoys the benefits of being a director of a legal firm in which women cannot be directors will be threatened by the calls for diversity and inclusion of women in such firm. Certain Buddhist monks who supported the dominance of Buddhism in Myanmar were threatened by the various religious and ethnic minorities call for inclusion. Similarly, white South Africans were threatened by calls for the inclusion of the black population and the end of apartheid. Similarly, the call to include Kurdish and other ethnic and religious minorities is faced by opposition by members of dominant religious and ethnic majorities in Arab societies.

Thus, recognizing the added value and importance of these cultural and ethnic differences is the first step to moving away from the state of denial which is often reflected in the belief that there are no important differences among the various diverse groups in the Arab society. Insisting on the discourse of unity and ignoring any form of diversity are obstacles in dealing with differences.

Once the person and group awareness recognized the existence of diverse ways of life and religious beliefs and practices, they developed different reactions to such diversity, as discussed below.

Superiority and defensiveness: Although the Muslim majority in the Arab societies are raised to believe in the notion of tolerance of other faiths, especially people of the book, they are also raised to believe that they are superior to them.[20] The arguments of why their faith is superior and more perfect than other faith groups are required and integral part of religious and popular informal education. Such beliefs are often translated into prejudice attitudes and even to discriminatory practices. When dealing with religious differences and diversity, there is an initial resistance to accept the validity of the other faith groups and allow a space for them to be fully recognized and practiced.

Passive acceptance of difference: in the process of gaining and recognizing diversity, individuals learn to accept the fact that there are others who are different from them and have the right to practice that difference. Those individuals can reach this realization or internalize this understanding from their own new and reformed understanding of their faith. For example, Muslims who have gone through this process often recite Qur'anic verse that encourages believers to respect the diversity of truth and religious practices.[21] This type of attitude is a passive acceptance in which the person is obliged to accept the differences because of the religious and legal ramifications of rejecting them.

Active acceptance of differences (pluralist): The profile of the active-accepting individuals is reflected in those who genuinely believed and internalized the principles that all humans have the right to culturally and religiously believe and practice their own identity in the way they choose without harming or damaging others. Obviously, there are many debates on the boundaries of these practices. The Geneva Haman Rights Declaration (1948) is one of those international agreements that attempts to regulate and define these boundaries. Nevertheless, the crux of this developmental stage of managing diversity constructively is that the individual accepts the fact that cultural and religious differences exist, need to be respected, and they are equal in their capacity to seek the truth. Thus, acceptance in this stage is not because of legal or religious laws only, but it stems from the belief that diversity is inherently good for human development, and it enriches individuals and collective beings.

In the previous stages of diversity management, the individual believed that he/she has the absolute truth, and his/her group path is superior to others, and therefore the society, state, and national space should be constructed in a way to reflect such superiority. However, in this stage of active acceptance, the absolute truth to this individual is not exclusive to any group or faith. All faith groups have truths, pieces of the truth, or there is no single truth. On the cultural differences, the individual in this stage relates to differences without assigning any value of judgment or preference, but all are viewed from the functionality and power relations perspectives.[22]

REFORMING POLICIES OF DIVERSITY MANAGEMENT

Although the above four developmental stages of management of diversity characterize the individual's journey of dealing with religious and cultural differences, state policies and societal norms and values can support or impede the process of gaining such competencies and skills. In current Arab societies, the political, religious, and social institutions have been struggling to manage diversity constructively, especially religious and ethnic diversity. The processes of reforming these institutions' policies and regulations have been interrupted by many internal and external forces; nevertheless, there is an urgent need to continue, promote, and advance these various efforts.

One of the venues to enhance the capacity of the current Arab societies to manage diversity is through the support and development of inclusive citizenship for all ethnic and religious communities. In the last two decades, there have been a number of campaigns and efforts, especially led by civil society and faith-based organizations to advocate for such policy reforms in religious and governmental institutions. Some of these recommendations can directly enhance capacities to manage diversity:[23]

Religious institutions (1) develop an institutional strategy for promoting inclusive attitudes among followers, especially for religious, ethnic, cultural, and gender diversity;[24] (2) reform existing formal religious narratives to support religious diversity, at least the passive acceptance of diversity directly and explicitly; (3) hold religious media accountable for their role in disseminating hate speech and incitement to violence against others; (4) establish programs and special units to institutionalize the efforts to engage with groups from the same and other faith and other faith groups; and (5) formulate and design explicit and direct strategy in support of equal citizenship for all diverse components in the Arab society.

Governmental institutions (1) design and formulate a national strategy to advance diversity management practices in all governmental institutions; (2) adopt regulations to prevent hate speech and incitement to violence and protect religious freedom norms and practices; (3) revise national curriculum to ensure that every student is sensitized to and equipped with basic skills and competencies of diversity management; and (4) support national and local diversity councils to ensure that policies of inclusion are being implemented on such levels.

CONCLUSION

The collective and individual development of institutions that manage diversity constructively in the Arab region certainly requires the engagement of all socialization agencies (religious, political, educational, cultural, media, legal, security, etc.). This is not a task that can be achieved by one of these agencies alone. In fact, a certain degree of coordination is necessary among and within these agencies in order for their efforts to be beneficial.

Within this construct for change, religious authority and institutions have an essential role to play due to the level of religiosity that exists within the fabric of the Arab society. For the development of diversity management systems based on the principle of acceptance and respect of differences, gaining the trust and credibility of religious agencies is central to unlock the hesitance and reduce resistance among various segments of the societies. Obviously working with such leaders does not exclude or negate the need to invest efforts with policy makers, media, and other sectors in the societies.

Finally, it is obvious that our emerging global economies and technologies have made it abundantly clear that all human societies and cultures have to learn to deal with differences and engage with the different other. In fact, for many groups, this has become an existential matter. The Arab societies are no exception to this rule. Reverting to primordial identities and retreating to narrow enclaves of tribal, ethnic, and religious identity circles and spaces have proven to be destructive and traumatic for many groups in the Arab region in the past two decades. Thus, the way forward is to develop the internal capacities for strengthening and celebrating commonalities and managing differences constructively.

NOTES

1. See Fahed al-sumait; Nele Lenze and Michael c. Hudson (eds.). *The Arab Uprisings Catalysts, Dynamics, and Trajectories* (Rowman and Littlefield, 2014).

2. See Mohammed Abu-Nimer, Amal Khoury, and Emily Welty. *Unity in Diversity: Interfaith Dialogue in the Middle East* (USIP, 2007).

3. Ibid.

4. Many scholars explain the deterioration in religious pluralism and policies of exclusion by the rise of political Islam in late 1960s and early 1970s. (See: Youssef M. Choueiri, *Islamic Fundamentalism* (London: Printer Press, 1990); Peter Mandeville, *Global Political Islam* (London: Routledge, 2007; John L. Esposito, *Islam and Politics (Contemporary Issues in the Middle East)* (Syracuse: University Press, 1998); Syed Hussain Shaheed. "Political Islam: A Rising Force in the Middle East." *Pakistan Horizon* 66, no. 4 (2013): 21–37. http://www.jstor.org/stable/24711513.

5. See: Synnøve Bendixsen, Mary Bente Bringslid and Halvard Vike, eds., *Egalitarianism in Scandinavia: Historical and Contemporary Perspectives* (London: Palgrave, 2018). See also UNESCO reports and special issue on managing diversity https://unesdoc.unesco.org/in/documentViewer.xhtml?v=2.1.196&id=p::usmarcdef_0000222319&file=/in/rest/annotationSVC/DownloadWatermarkedAttachment/

attach_import_1c2dbd45-461c-461f-ad92-93eafa1c6cd1%3F_%3D222319eng.pdf
&locale=en&multi=true&ark=/ark:/48223/pf0000222319/PDF/222319eng.pdf#%5B
%7B%22num%22%3A4%2C%22gen%22%3A0%7D%2C%7B%22name%22%3A
%22XYZ%22%7D%2Cnull%2Cnull%2C0%5D (accessed November 19, 2022).

6. See UNESCO special reports on efforts for inclusion of religion, gender, and cultural diversity in education: making content of textbook inclusive: A focus on religion, gender and culture. (2013). https://unesdoc.unesco.org/ark:/48223/pf0000247337.locale=fr (accessed November 19, 2022).

7. The author was involved for five years in a project to introduce civic education manual for Iraqi and Kurdish teachers through Salam Institute and USIP (United States Institute for Peace). The initiative also involved several exposure trips to the Lebanese Ministry of Education to learn about their post war experience in dealing with civic education for diversity and inclusion. In the Iraqi case, the ministry of education of the federal government and the KRG) (Kurdistan Region) agreed for the first time in their history to sponsor a common manual to train teachers in how to introduce issues of religious and ethnic diversity. The manual was printed by the Iraqi Ministry of Education and KRG Ministry of Education. (USIP project on Iraq Civic Education 2008–2013-unpublished report).

8. There are thousands of academic and theological resources debating the meaning and implementation of the Ahl Adhimma principle in Muslim society and history. The following is a one of the classic sources defining the status of Ahl ADhimma.

"According to Islamic law, the non-Muslims inhabited in the Islamic state were called *ahlu dh-dhimmati* (people of protection) or simply *al-dhimma* or *dhimmis.* They included the Christian, Jewish, Magian, Samaritan and Sabian. *Ahl al-dhimma* were prohibited in the Muslim state from holding public religious ceremonies, from raising their voices loudly when praying and even from ringing their church bells aloud. All schools agree that it is not allowed to build new churches, synagogues, convent, hermitage or cell in towns or cities of *Dar al-Islam* (Muslim lands). When these injunctions were disobeyed, the Muslim leaders were authorized to treat the offenders as dwellers in *Dar al-Harb* (non-Muslim lands) and not as *ahl al-dhimma* in *Dar al-Islam* (Muslim lands), vide *Subh al-A'asha fi Sina'at at al-Insha* (Cairo, 1922, 13: 356) by Qalaqashandi (d. 821/1418).

Also see: Ahl al-Dhimma", in: *Encyclopaedia of Islam, Second Edition*, edited by P. Bearman, Th. Bianquis, C.E. Bosworth, E. van Donzel, W.P. Heinrichs. Consulted online on 31 December 2022. http://dx.doi.org/10.1163/1573-3912_islam_DUM_0168 (2012).

9. Synagogues and churches were open ion such countries and symbolic gestures of inclusion were introduced in UAE and Bahrain, too.

See: Are the Arab Gulf States Improving Religious Liberty? By Steven Howard on October 7, 2019. https://providencemag.com/2019/10/arab-persian-gulf-states-religious-liberty/ (accessed in December 21, 2022).

10. See several cases and examples of managing religious diversity in the Arab region in: Mohammed Abu-Nimer and Ramy Atta (eds.). *Managing Religious Diversity in Arab Society* (KAICIID Publication, 2022). (Arabic).

11. See Abu-Nimer, et al, 2007.

12. Obviously, there are many other factors that contributed to the lack of political and parliamentarian c=norms and cultures the Arab societies such media, education, military and security, etc.

13. See recent report on:

14. See *Political Corruption in the Arab World* (Aman Transparency-Palestine. June 2014).

This report was prepared in partnership with: The Lebanese Transparency Association Transparency Morocco I Watch Organization- Tunisia Yemeni Team for Transparency and Integrity The Coalition for Integrity and Accountability- AMAN-Palestine Egyptians without Borders (EWB) Work Team: Main researcher: Dr. Ahmad Abu-DayyiaPalestine Ms. Hoda Ghosn- Lebanon Ms. Aya Jarad- Tunisia Dr. Ahmad Moufid- Morocco Dr. Abd-Albaqi Shamsan Qayed- Yemen Dr. Yosri 'Azbawi- Egypt

https://www.aman-palestine.org/cached_uploads/download/migrated-files/itemfiles/00641c6049323493a8bf87fa4df1054c.pdf (accessed November 22, 2022).

See also: Mohammed Abu-Nimer. *Nonviolence and Peacebuilding in Islamic Context* (University Press of Florida, 2003).

15. In Iraq Saddam Hussein regime utilized Sunni religious establishment to justify his suppression of Shia clergy who were not politically loyal. In Syria the Asad Regime utilized Alwaits clergy to justify his states exclusion of Sunni.

See: https://carnegieendowment.org/2016/01/07/shia-centric-state-building-and-sunni-rejection-in-post-2003-iraq-pub-62408 (accessed Dec. 2, 2022).

16. see Mohammad Shafique and Mohammed Abu-Nimer. Interfaith Dialogue: A guide for Muslims International Institute for Islamic Thought (IIIT), 2011.

Also, the author has led hundreds of dialogue and capacity building training with Arab religious leaders and youth from religious institutions. Based on this experience in Muslim intrafaith relations, there is a great deal of ignorance and misperception being injected in the religious education institutions in the Arab region regarding Sunni Shia relations. Participants always admit their lack of knowledge and any significant experience or exposure to the other side's discourse and narrative.

17. Many communists, Muslim brotherhood, and other opposition activists lost their lives in the prisons and were prosecuted by the regimes and their security forces.

18. وجيه كوثراني ؛ " هويات فائضة مواطنة منقوصة : فى تهافت خطاب حوار الحضارات وصدامها عربيا ؛ دار الطليعة للطباعة والنشر ؛ بيروت ؛ "
2004

Also See: ياكوب, جوزيف, مابعد الاقليات بديل عن تكاثر الدول, ترجمة حسين عمر, المركز الثقافي العربي, بيروت- الدار البيضاء, ط اولى, 2004.

19. See Abu-Nimer "Conflict Resolution, Culture, and Religion: Toward a Training Model of Interreligious Peacebuilding." *Journal of Peace Research,* 38, no. 6 (Nov. 2001): 685–704.

20. This sense of superiority is often linked to the religious interpretations supporting beliefs such as: Islam is the perfect religion; no other religions or prophets after Islam; Christians and Jews have strayed away from the righteous path, etc. Such set of beliefs and their supporting interpretations have prompted exclusion and fed a sense of justified policies of superiority among certain Muslims.

21. To You Your Religion and To Me Mine (Qur'an 109:1–6).

22. For more on this developmental stage, see Bennet 1993. And Abu-Nimer adaptation of this model in (2006).

23. The selective list of recommendations are adapted from various consultations (2019—2021) carried out by a consortium of Arab (Muslim and Christian) faith-based organizations convened for two years to create a common and inclusive citizenship charter. Another set of recommendations was developed by the Arab platform for interreligious dialogue created by KAICIID in 2014 and continued to operate in the region (see: www.kaiciid.org).

24. Abu-Nimer, Mohammed. 2017 "Engaging Interreligious Peacebuilding Agencies and Policymakers in Responding to Conflicts," in *Observatoire Géopolitique du Religieux*. Institut de Relations Internationales et Strategiques. February 2017. http://www.iris-france.org/wp-content/uploads/2017/02/Obs-religion-f%C3%A9vrier-2017.pdf; Abu-Nimer, Mohammed. 2017. "Injecting Morality in Conflict: The Role of Religious and Interreligious Actors in Peacebuilding and Policy Making," in the Berkley Forum. Georgetown University's Berkley Center for Religion, Peace, and World Affairs. 22 February 2017. https://berkleycenter.georgetown.edu/forum/the-vatican-and-peacebuilding-exploring-the-church-s-role-in-conflict-resolution/responses/injecting-morality-in-conflict-the-role-of-religious-and-interreligious-actors-in-peacebuilding-and-policymaking; Abu-Nimer, Mohammed. "Interreligious Peacebuilding: An Emerging Field of Research and Practice," in *Sustainable Security*, Sustainablesecurity.org, 16 March 2016. https://www.oxfordresearchgroup.org.uk/blog/interreligious-peacebuilding-an-emerging-field-of-research-and-practice

REFERENCES

Abu-Nimer, "Conflict Resolution, Culture, and Religion: Toward a Training Model of Interreligious Peacebuilding." *Journal of Peace Research*, 38. 6 (Nov. 2001): 685–704.

Abu-Nimer, Mohammed and Ramy Atta (eds.), *Managing Religious Diversity in Arab Society* [in Arabic] (KAICIID Publication, 2022).

Abu-Nimer, Mohammed, Amal Khoury, and Emily Welty, *Unity in Diversity: Interfaith Dialogue in the Middle East* (USIP, 2007).

Abu-Nimer, Mohammed. "Interreligious Peacebuilding: An Emerging Field of Research and Practice," in Sustainable Security, Sustainablesecurity.org, 16 March 2016. https://www.oxfordresearchgroup.org.uk/blog/interreligious-peacebuilding-an-emerging-field-of-research-and-practice

Abu-Nimer, Mohammed. 2017 "Engaging Interreligious Peacebuilding Agencies and Policymakers in Responding to Conflicts," in *Observatoire Géopolitique du Religieux. Institut de Relations Internationales et Strategiques*. February 2017. http://www.iris-france.org/wp-content/uploads/2017/02/Obs-religion-f%C3%A9vrier-2017.pdf

Abu-Nimer, Mohammed. 2017. "Injecting Morality in Conflict: The Role of Religious and Interreligious Actors in Peacebuilding and Policy Making," in the

Berkley Forum. Georgetown University's Berkley Center for Religion, Peace, and World Affairs. 22 February 2017. https://berkleycenter.georgetown.edu/forum/the-vatican-and-peacebuilding-exploring-the-church-s-role-in-conflict-resolution/responses/injecting-morality-in-conflict-the-role-of-religious-and-interreligious-actors-in-peacebuilding-and-policymaking;

Al-sumait, Fahed, Nele Lenze, and Michael c. Hudson, eds., *The Arab uprisings catalysts, dynamics, and trajectories* (Rowman and Littlefield, 2014).

Bendixsen, Synnøve, Mary Bente Bringslid and Halvard Vike, eds., *Egalitarianism in Scandinavia: Historical and Contemporary Perspectives* (London: Palgrave, 2018).

Choueiri, Youssef M. *Islamic Fundamentalism* (London: Printer Press, 1990).

Esposito, John L., *Islam and Politics* (Contemporary Issues in the Middle East) (Syracuse: University Press, 1998).

Mandeville, Peter, *Global Political Islam* (London: Routledge, 2007).

Mohammed Abu-Nimer. *Nonviolence and Peacebuilding in Islamic Context* (University Press of Florida, 2003).

Political Corruption in the Arab World (Aman Transparency-Palestine. June 2014).

Qalaqashandi (d. 1418), *Subh al-A'asha fi Sina'at at al-Insha* (Cairo, 1922).

Shafique, Mohammad and Mohammed Abu-Nimer. *Interfaith Dialogue: A guide for Muslims* (International Institute for Islamic Thought (IIIT), 2011).

Shaheed, Syed Hussain, "Political Islam: A Rising Force in the Middle East." *Pakistan Horizon* 66, no. 4 (2013): 21–37. http://www.jstor.org/stable/24711513.

Wajih kawtharani, *hawiyat fa'ida wa muwatana naqisa* [Excessive Identities and Incomplete Citizenry] (Beirut, Lebanon: Dar al-Tali'a, 2004).

Yaqub, Joseph, *Ma Ba'da al-Aqaliyat* [After Minorities] (Beirut, Lebanon: Center of Arab Culture, 2004).

Chapter 10

Arab Authoritarianism and Western Complacency

Louay M. Safi

The United States led in 1945 a concerted effort to set a world order based on international law that honors the human rights and dignity of all peoples, prevents future conflicts and aggressions, and respects the rights of nations to decide their own internal affairs. To make sure that communication, negotiation, and collaboration among nation states are given priority over the use of naked force, the United States succeeded in establishing the United Nations Organization to serve as an administrative and collaborative infrastructure for peaceful cooperation among nations.

The idea that a just global peace would prevail with the emergence of democratic nations surfaced in modern times in Immanuel Kant's profound essay titled *The Perpetual Peace*, which epitomized classical liberal ideals regarding human nature and the future of humanity. The drive toward international justice and world peace was attempted twice by two liberal presidents, first Woodrow Wilson in 1917 which led to the founding of the League of Nations, an organization that ironically betrayed its founding principles when it was used by the two imperial powers of the day to justify the colonialization of the Near East after the U.S. Congress failed to ratify the treaty. The second attempt by Franklin Roosevelt was more successful, as the United Nations brought a semblance of stability to the international order and indeed facilitated the decolonization of former European colonies. The subsequent failure of the United Nations to uphold its mandate of implementing international law and ensuring human dignity across the globe stems from the selective application of international law by the permanent members of the Security Council through the use of the veto power, and the frequent violations of the rules of international laws and treaties by the five victors of World War II, most notably the United States and Russian Federation.

THE SHIFT TO POLITICAL REALISM

An important factor behind the inability of the United Nations to apply international law and to ensure more equitable relationship relates to the paradigm shift in American thinking, leading to the rise and the gradual domination of international relations by political realism. The major shift in strategic thinking toward the Middle East took place as a result of a paradigmatic shift in the conceptualization of the role of the United States from one rooted in classical liberalism to an opposing vision of U.S. involvement in world politics anchored in political realism. The shift was dramatic and profound as the purpose of the U.S. involvement in the world shifted from one based on the optimistic liberal view of humanity and on the liberal values of freedom, equality, and justice for all, to one framed in the pessimism of political realism about human nature and seeing international relations as merely a political game nations play. The shift coincided with the arrival of European emigres during WWII, most notably that of the founders of American political realism: Hans Morgenthau, George Liska, and Nicholas Spykman.[1] Saturated with the European experience of nationalism and realpolitik, they rejected American idealism and declared ethical values to be irrelevant to international politics, while they acknowledged the power of ethical values for restraining political ambition.[2] Up until the end of WWII, American thinkers were, to a great extent, under the influence of the liberal tradition. Albeit imperfect and with some serious lapses, liberal values guided American political thinking both at home and abroad and were at odd with the pessimistic outlook of European realism and its obsession with power politics. For them, realism's frame of reference was peculiar to "European-formed" thinking.[3]

Political realism framework began to dominate the U.S. approach to international relations and foreign policy after WWII, as the American foreign policy specialists were gradually schooled in political realism and quickly internalized the imperial European approach to international politics. The influence of political realism was not confined to any particular political party, a few leading liberals continued to lean toward international liberalism as late as 1970s, as was the case of President Jimmy Carter and his National Security Advisor Zbigniew Brzezinski. Kissinger led the argument against the promotion of democracy in the MENA region, even dismissing it as an ineffective way for dealing with the rise of religious extremism. He consistently refused to connect the radicalization of the region with the repression and atrocities committed by Arab dictators toward their populations in the name of modernization and stability. He was content with working with autocrats and tyrants to maintain stability in the Middle East and elsewhere. Brzezinski, on the other hand, saw the link between repression and terrorism more clearly. He believed, for instance, that "bin Laden and al Qaeda as isolated in time, products of the Soviet-Afghan war, not an evolving decades-old movement of Sunni militancy that has become ever more lethal and anti-Western under the Middle East's post–World War II dictatorships."[4] For his part, Kissinger openly expressed caution against the development of democracy in Middle Eastern countries like Iraq but had no issue with its invasion by North Atlantic armies. He continued to express doubts even with the recent democratic push in the MENA region insisting that no democracy should be expected until "a secular middle class [which] can emerge strong enough to insist on full representative democracy."[5] The realist's cynical dismissal of democracy and human rights as a possibility for Middle Eastern politics ignores the fact that the region experienced democratic rule as early as 1919 in Egypt and 1949 in Syria and Lebanon. One can still encounter voices within the foreign policy establishment who believe that the United States should promote democracy and human rights in the Middle East, such as the voice of Daniel Benjamin, the director for counterterrorism in the National Security Council during the Clinton administration, but these are few and far between. Benjamin made a crystal-clear case for promoting democracy in the Middle East to fight terrorism and radical extremism in a book titled The Age of Sacred Terror.[6] But even this idea was deployed to expand U.S. hegemony in the Middle East by the neoconservative actors that dominated the Bush administration in 2003.

The real politics approach goes far in dealing with the MENA region, long before the rise of Islamist militancy and was clearly manifested in the modernization theory school that dominated the international relations debate on MENA in the early 1950s through the late 1970s, and later in the neoconservative thinking that dominated American foreign policy since the 1980s.

MODERNIZATION AND DEVELOPMENTALISM

Modernization theory developed the basic narrative that continues to dominate the international relations community and foreign policy circles toward the Middle East. According to its advocates, there is one path to modernization for all societies regardless of their culture, religion, and history, which is the path through which Europe achieved its modernization. This Eurocentric understanding of modernization and progress guided the thinking of all modernization theorists, including W.W. Rostow, Gabriel Almond, and Daniel Lerner, who often emphasize two elements: (1) the need for all cultures to go through cultural secularization and a religious disenchantment and (2) the priority of economic development over political democratization. These points provided the justification for downplaying the importance of advancing human rights and promoting democracy that one encounters in the policy advocated by the dominant views on international relations.

The economic development argument has become the bedrock upon which neoliberalism advanced its economic interests in the MENA region with the full collaboration of the most corrupt leaders in the Arab world, from Ali Saleh of Yemen to Hosni Mubarak of Egypt and Hafiz Assad of Syria, to Ben Ali of Tunisia.

Regardless of ideologies, theories, and intentions, the reality of the Middle East is increasingly shaped by contradictory aims and goals that have led to the deterioration of the sociopolitical conditions of the region, thereby arresting the declared efforts of pursuing liberal democracy. Secularism and liberalism have become synonymous with imposition and corruption at the popular level of Middle Eastern society, as every authoritarian and tyrannical regime in the region is associated with these labels and supported by world powers. Secularism is no more associated in the popular imaginary with liberty, equality, and human rights but is often equated with the police states that rule Arab society and the aloof and disengaging political elites, and with political and administrative corruption. Even the proponents of modernization theory who were evidently interested in the modernization of Arab and Middle Eastern societies justified supporting Arab Junta and autocrats, thereby favoring order over democratization in the name of creating an Arab culture that is a carbon copy of the West. This, however, changed with the advent of neoconservative politics, with a new emphasis on nation-building and social engineering. Rather than advancing liberalism and democracy, modernization theory recipes led to the rise of terrorism committed by violent extremists who hijacked Islam and used it to justify violence against their adversaries. By the turn of the twenty-first century, it became obvious that the policy of keeping Middle Easterners in check by empowering autocrats had imposed a terrible cost not only for Muslim societies but also for the entire globe. This realization was interestingly announced by George W. Bush in his remarks at the twentieth anniversary of the National Endowment for Democracy in 2002, few months after the invasion of Iraq.

In his remarks he made during the twentieth anniversary of the National Endowment for Democracy in 2002, right after the invasion of Iraq, Bush had the following to say:

> Sixty years of Western nations excusing and accommodating the lack of freedom in the Middle East did nothing to make us safe—because in the long run, stability cannot be purchased at the expense of liberty. As long as the Middle East remains a place where freedom does not flourish, it will remain a place of stagnation, resentment, and violence ready. for export. And with the spread of weapons that can bring catastrophic harm to our country and to our friends, it would be reckless to accept the status quo.[7]

The realist approach to politics succeeded by the late 1980s in transforming liberalism and creating a new form that turned liberal ideology into an instrument for domination and imposition, giving birth to neoliberalism. This new ideology that promotes free enterprise on a global scale reduces the idea of liberty to financial liberalization and the opening of world markets to free capital movement and has caused serious declines in the overall social and economic standing of the majority in the Middle East and South America while creating financial elites thriving on Rentier economies. The social and economic transformation that began in the early 1970s, right after the peace treaty between Egypt and Israel, was disastrous for the Middle Eastern countries, except the Gulf countries that benefited from the rise of petroleum prices.

BUILDING MENA OLIGARCHY

The push to liberate the MENA countries from European colonialism did not bring truly independent states but vassal states that continued to move within the orbit of former European powers. The formula was simple: provide security advice, protection, and support to Arab autocracy in exchange for facilitating the national interests of global powers in the protected countries. Arab autocrats and military dictators were also required to push for social secularization and economic liberalization of their countries. The collaboration created a win-win situation for elites across the board, and MENA populations benefited initially in the middle of the twentieth century before corruption and inequality began to set in as early as the late sixties. Eventually, MENA elites used their creative energy to construct an indigenous form of colonialism, that is, an internal colonialism, whereby they placed their interests and the interests of their foreign patrons above those of the populations they controlled.

Less than a decade after their independence, most MENA countries came under autocratic governments. Even in countries where a semblance of democratic governance was established (Egypt, Syria, and Iran), Western democracies did nothing to protect or nurture the fledgling Middle Eastern democracies but instead were eager to recognize the military dictators who overran them as long as they continue to appease their international patrons. European colonial rule was replaced by a form of internal colonialism that adopted the same brutal approach to control the populations they governed in the same manner European colonial rulers governed the region. Ironically, rather than making the world safe for democracy as liberal theorists advocate, the neoliberal order that was established in the late 1970s strove to make the world safe to transnational corporations and the free and unregulated movement of capital around the world and in the MENA region, entering into partnership relation with the region autocratic rulers and devised policies that help them stay in power despite strong opposition and frequent uprisings.

Three case studies give us insights into how European centers of power protect and support MENA dictatorships, one involves a program set by the European Union (EU) under pressure from civil society organizations. The other implicates neoliberal NGOs embroiled in setting oligarchy networks in Jordan and Morocco.

A. *The European Neighborhood Policy (ENP)*

The implementation of the ENP in Egypt illustrates how European bureaucrats provide vital support to MENA autocrats. The policy was developed under pressure from European civil society organizations to promote democracy around the world, particularly in East and Southern Europe in the MENA region. The policy was set in 2001 with the aim to encourage public participation to ensure political accountability. The EU signed an agreement with the Egyptian government in 2004 to promote civil society organizations in 2004. The agreement was a precondition set by the European parliament for all trade relations that increased between European countries and Egypt and was designed to link improved trade relations with democratic steps and programs that advance the democratic process. The promotion of democracy intent was expressed "as a set of arrangements that will foster public participation in the reform process, the objectives of which are defined in advance as 'catching up with globalization.'"[8]

After years of negotiation and planning, the democracy-promotion project was reduced to providing financial support to NGOs that were either marginally involved in promoting democracy and civil society or were set by individuals close to the Egyptian Junta. The EU democracy-promotion effort did not help Egyptian civil society to assume a more constructive role in enhancing human rights and curtailing autocratic corruption. One of the programs sponsored by EU centered around "combating the culture of police officers' impunity in a context marked with four decades of entrenched authoritarianism."[9] The program consisted of training sessions conducted by El-Nadim for the rehabilitation of victims of violence. Evidently, El-Nadim itself was registered as an independent NGO by cohorts of the military establishment that became, after the peace treaty with Israel, preoccupied with setting up business jointventures.[10]

The Arab Spring that broke out in 2010 pushed the EU to develop a new version of ENP by advancing a threefold strategy: building deep democracy, securing economic development, and facilitating people-to-people contacts.[11] The new strategy continued to place emphasis on achieving democratic transformation by supporting civil society organizations, but it began, this time around, to emphasize the "people-to-people" principle, as it moved away from its earlier approach of over relying on state institutions. By then, the complex trajectory that emerged as the Arab Spring began to unfold with the rising of the religoius tone of the revolution, and many Western leaders began to gradually withdraw their support, commencing with the Obama administration. The ENP was once again reassessed by the middle of 2013 as the counterrevolutionary forces in Egypt, Yamen, and Syria succeeded in overcoming the democratic forces. Indeed, the lack of clear and principled commitment to deep democratization gave autocratic regimes the opportunity to invigorate the role of violent extremist groups.[12]

The European leadership decided to distance itself from the forces of change and to take more pragmatic posture. The new posture, referred to as "more-for-more," meant that the EU would not deal with the Arab Spring countries in accordance with a uniform approach but that the EU would deal with each country in accordance with actual development on the ground, effectively keeping the door open to renewing cooperation with autocratic regimes.[13] The new regulations conditioned positive support to partner countries on their commitments to "the principles of democracy, the rule of law and respect for human rights and fundamental freedoms."[14] In actuality, the EU prioritized the stabilized authoritarianism as the favored course of action. This perplexing approach to nurturing fragile democratic movements resulted, as Jan Wouters observed, from prioritizing two other objectives above democratic formation in the MENA region: first, creating a buffer zone "against Islamic extremism and illegal migration, and second as a guarantee of the bloc's own economic and security interests, including a continuous flow of oil and maintaining a modus vivendi with Israel."[15]

B. Exclusivist Social Entrepreneur Networks (SENs)

The interworking of SENs illustrates the efforts to align SENs' interests with those of the MENA authoritarian regimes. Several transnational organizations have shown interest in MENA countries, most notably Jordan, Morocco, and Tunisia. The neoliberal groups are based in various Western countries and include Ashoka (United States), Synergos (United States), the Schwab Foundation (Switzerland), and the Skoll Foundation (United Kingdom), to groom authoritarian elites in Morocco and Jordan "to respond aggressively to the triple threat of globalization, markets, and democratization."[16] Neoliberal SENs' activities reveal the formation of selective and exclusive networks of entrepreneurs who are practically coopted to promote the interests of the autocratic regimes of these countries. The networks distinguish from what we normally expect in public programs is their closed and long-term membership of the operators within those networks, and their connectedness to authoritarian state power. The NGOs engage in financial support channeled toward skill development through fellowships and awards. What is peculiar here is the goal of cultivating closed networks put together through a selective process. All recipients of the grants are identified through personal recommendations of highly placed individuals. Social entrepreneurs receive stipends for a specific period (two to three years) or a cash prize and become fellows for life, allowing the participation of those who can attend meetings and training sessions along with social elite groups.[17]

Neoliberalism insistence on freeing the corporate world from governmental regulations often interpreted that neoliberal organizations and groups assume an anti-statist approach. On closer examination, we can observe high collaboration with the state. The state is indeed seen as a central actor in neoliberal literature and strategy. This is particularly evident in the MENA region where neoliberal organizations not only abandoned their support for open society and democratic governance but are ironically busy supporting authoritarian regimes. Several studies conducted in the post Arab Spring period have established the interconnection between neoliberalism and authoritarianism and have coined the term "authoritarian neoliberalism" to describe this new reality.[18] In a recent study published in *Globalizations*, Ian Buff concluded that neoliberalism "seek to marginalize, discipline and control dissenting social groups and oppositional politics rather than strive for their explicit consent or co-optation."[19] Similarly, Jessop rejected in a study published in 2019 the idea that the state has lost its relevance under neoliberalism and cited two youth empowerment programs in Jordan sponsored by neoliberal groups as examples of the increasingly "authoritarian statism" tendencies of neoliberalism.[20]

The King Abdullah II Award for Youth Innovation and Achievement (KAAYIA) and the Oasis500 are two youth empowerment programs that were set by Jordan's King in 2007 and 2010 consecutively. KAAYIA was launched in 2007 during the World Economic Forum Middle East and North Africa (WEFMENA) that was held in Jordan, while the Oasis500 was introduced in 2010 evidently to provide more extensive support to select youths who receive KAAYIA. An extensive study published in 2021 concluded that the selective empowerment strategy, rather than contributing to a broad approach to socioeconomic development, has deepened inequalities within the Jordanian society.[21] The programs do not address the fundamental issues of youth unemployment, poverty, and underdevelopment and completely ignore social and political issues that inhibit youth empowerment.[22] The study also revealed:

"[E]ntrepreneurs who express critical views on political and social issues and come close to pushing the regime's red lines" are penalized by being denied future participation in elite initiatives.[23]

C. Supporting Military's Stronghold on Egyptian Civil Society

The blatant and most sticking example of international support of authoritarian regimes in the MENA region can be found in Egypt. For four decades since the Camp David peace agreement between Egypt and Israel, the United States continued to provide multibillion foreign aid to the Egyptian armed forces. And throughout these decades, the Supreme Council of the Armed Forces of Egypt has been the chief custodian of this foreign aid. The Council has grown to become a state within the state and to dominate every aspect of the Egyptian economic and political life. Acting under the leadership of the president, since the military coup of 1952, the council. The Council has created countless economic and financial corporations that increasingly dominate every economic sector of the Egyptian society, from tourism to consumer goods to energy. Despite a clear evidence that the military rule of Egypt has led to a constant deterioration of the education, economic, and political life in the country, Western democracies continue to extend unwavering support, with the exception of a few years in the mid-2000s when American and European governments became weary about the deterioration of social and economic conditions and the fear that the trajectory would inevitably lead to a failed state similar to those created in Somalia, Iraq, Lebanon, and Syria.

The coup led by Abdelfattah al-Sisi in 2013 against the first elected government since the mid-twentieth century was welcomed with open arms by the United States and European leaders and several of their regional allies. Indeed, the elections brought to power a coalition of unexperienced moderate and radical Islamic groups was unacceptable to many people in Egypt and was alarming for most political leaders in Europe and the United States. The coming of Islamist groups to power was expected, even foreseen, by most political observers of Egyptian politics given the fact that the military regime crackdown hard on all forms of opposition, including liberal political parties. Only religiously motivated opposition groups were able to withstand the iron-fist policy adopted by the police state. Sisi assured his supporters, foreign and local, that his coup was intended to restore democracy and allow for fresh elections to give Egypt another chance at having a more inclusive governing coalition. Instead, Sisi moved in collaboration with the Military Council to consolidate power and crack down harder on all opposition groups, liberally oriented opposition included. Rather than apply pressure on his government to open up the political space, Western allies decided to extend financial support leading to the accumulation of national debt, beyond the ability of the Egyptian state to even service the debt without further impoverishing an already exhausted Egyptian economy.

In the decade that succeeded the military coup, Egypt is today on the brink of economic collapse that could make the 2011 popular uprising that brought the Islamist forces to power a picnic. Egypt's annual deficit has approached $44 billion, or 12% of its $360 GDP.[24] The national debt has quadrupled since 2010, increasing over 100% between 2017 and 2020, and the total debt is predicted to rise to $557 billion by 2026.[25] The ratio of the national debt-to-GDP is now 91.6%.[26] What makes the matter worse is that the steep rise in national debt is far greater than the increase in GDP growth. The military leadership is so corrupt and incompetent to the extent of having no plan to grow the economy or even limit economic deterioration and prevent economic collapse. Rather than using the opportunity of having access to staggering lending facility by the IMF and World Bank to build a stronger manufacturing and agricultural industries, the al-Sisi government has been spending huge loans on luxurious infrastructure with no prospect of generating any additional revenue. Examples of reckless governmental spending include over $58 billion to build a new administrative capital in the desert outside Cairo, weapons acquisitions that placed the country among the world's top five arms purchasers and an $8 billion expansion of Suez Canal capacity with an insignificant increase in transit dues (less than 0.035% increase in overall canal revenue).[27]

Meanwhile, the internationally empowered ruling elites continues to spend lavishly on infrastructure project, while the citizens of Egypt are squeezed between stagnating incomes and rising household expenses. Wage and salary expenditures have been flat for years while the cost of living climbs rapidly with staggering inflation,[28] and military-controlled companies under no legal obligations to share their operation date with the public squeezing out private sector enterprises, further leading to deterioration in economic conditions.[29] The Egyptian household's stagnant income has further lost purchasing power due to the rising taxation, including a new VAT tax that has a particularly negative impact on middle- and lower-class income.[30]

The complacency of global financial institutions, most notably the IMF and World Bank, is clear and quite transparent to specialists in the fields, including World Bank economists. Alia al-Mahdi, professor of economics at Cairo University, placed the responsibility for the deterioration of the Egyptian economy squarely on the Sisi government and implicitly on the IMF that allowed the wasteful spending of billions of dollars on infrastructure projects: "The government should have channeled this spending to production projects that can generate revenues, overspending on infrastructure projects has contributed to the financial crisis we suffer from now."[31] Ishac Diwan, a former senior World Bank official, went further to accuse the IMF of using the loan to provide political support to the Sisi government and to prevent necessary political reform from taking place in Egypt: "the combination of the IMF's stamp of approval, and very liquid international markets after 2016, have allowed Egypt to borrow a lot so as to delay necessary reforms."[32]

GLOBAL JUSTICE IS ESSENTIAL FOR GLOBAL PEACE AND STABILITY

Egypt is moving steadily toward a complete economic collapse and political disorder, and unless there is a serious change of attitude and approach on the part of Western powers, it might soon join the growing list of failed states in the Middle East. The ramification of such collapse will be felt across the world and not only in the Arab region, for Egypt is the largest Middle East country with a population that exceeds 100 million. The collapse of a state as large as Egypt would destabilize the countries of the Mediterranean basin and beyond. Reversing the current deconstructive geopolitical game in the Middle East is a must to prevent a disaster with far-reaching ramifications. The short-sighted approach to global governance has to change, and the unwavering support of authoritarianism in the MENA region must be replaced with serious and more robust support for democratization and civil society. The current approach is neither morally acceptable nor politically sustainable. It not only hurts MENA but also feeds into global authoritarian powers.

Perhaps the most important step for realigning the foreign policy of key Western democracies toward the MENA region is to give up the irrational commitment to hard-core secularization of Arab and Muslim society and the recognition that the cultural reform necessary for generating internal commitment to democratic rule must draw from the Islamic values that place human dignity at the core of the Islamic faith. Indeed, social reform in MENA was led, in the mid-nineteenth century, by Islamic reformers. These were inspired by the achievements of historical Islamic rationalism in a manner unlike that which inspired European modernization. Islamic reformist movements were later challenged and pushed aside by populist movements grounded in various forms of nationalism and Salafism, and they were able to do so precisely because of the marginalization of Islam by autocratic regimes in the postcolonial states, most of whom were supported by Western democracies. Islam is important because cultural transformation presupposes deep religious values, and Islam nurtures the values necessary for democratic rule, most importantly the values of equality, religious freedom, justice, and ethic and social pluralism. Political groups that espouse extremist and exclusivist interpretations of Islam are closely linked to MENA autocratic regimes that justify oppression by reference to terrorism.

Like all religions, Islam takes a variety of shapes and forms. It has historically served as both the source of social renewal and reform and the ground of stagnation and close-mindedness. These two manifestations of religion can be found today in the MENA region. The inception of modern Islamic reform coincided with the European colonial expansion into Muslim territories in Asia and Africa in mid-nineteenth century. Muslim reformers were inspired by the achievements of historical Islamic rationalism in a manner similar to the inspiration the Enlightenment reformers received from the rational idealism movement that emerged in Europe in the late Middle Ages. Islamic reformist thought made initially a great impact on Middle Eastern society through the works of rationalist scholars, including Syed Ahmed Khan, Jamal al-Afghani, Muhammad Abdu, Abd al-Rahman al-Kawakibi, Rasheed Rida, Muhammad Iqbal, and Said Nursi. Islamic reformist ideas continued to make inroads into Muslim societies through the work of Al-Tayib Ibn Ashur, Malik Bennabi, Ali Shariati, Ismail Faruqi, Fazlur Rahman, Rashid al Ghannouchi, Mohammed Abed al-Jabri, and others.

The Muslim reformists were challenged and later marginalized by populist movements grounded in various forms of nationalism and Salafism. The migration of Muslims to Western countries in the wake of European colonialism, which later increased with the rising repression of Muslim dictatorships under conditions enhanced by the rise of neoliberal globalism, has been associated with the upswing of Muslim reformist ideas, influenced by the new experiences of Western Muslims and the rapid advancement of modern globalism. The presence of sizable Muslim communities in Western societies under conditions of open debate provides great opportunities for a meaningful exchange of ideas and a new attempt at a creative synthesis of Islam and Western scholarship that could potentially help to generate new thinking about world peace and global pluralism.

GLOBAL JUSTICE PRESUPPOSES THE PRIMACY OF HUMAN DIGNITY

Social reform presupposes a religious reform of a sort, as religion was and remains the foundation of any profound social change. The West should stop dealing with Islam in a wholesale fashion and recognize that Islam has also been the source of inspiration for Muslim reformers, not violent extremist movements, distinguished by a literalist reading of the Islamic text. After all, Islamic extremism has been generated and empowered by the autocratic regimes supported by Western powers. These literalist and fundamentalist Muslims have chosen to work with MENA autocrats to further marginalize reform-minded Muslims and to silence all critical voices in the MENA region. Islam lays strong emphasis on human dignity and individual choice and is essential for promoting democracy and human rights in Muslim society, as many reform-minded Muslims do.

Islamic extremism is closely linked to MENA autocratic regimes that favors the growth of fundamentalism in societies to further suffocate public debates and to use extremist outburst to gain international support and justify their iron-fist treatment of their populations. This vicious circle of autocrats generating extremism, which in turn justifies authoritarianism, is a dangerous game. It is the very game that produced the sectarian government in Iran that is working hard to transform the MENA region into a block ruled by religious autocracy.

The current approach is not only morally hazardous but politically unsustainable. The rise of both extremism and authoritarianism undermines freedom and democracy not only in the MENA region but also throughout the world. We already started to see a shift toward the autocratic regimes in Russia and China. The corrupt autocratic rules are also responsible for an unending migration of people from the South to the North as economic and security conditions continue to deteriorate.

There is also an urgent need to distinguish the secularization of the state and of society. The first is desirable and has wide support among different societies and religious communities. The latter is troublesome particularly when it is done through undermining freedom, democracy, and human rights. The best approach to deal with MENA and other communities whose binding values are grounded in religious commitment is to adopt John Rawls' distinction between political and social liberalism.[33] These differentiations allow for the creation of a pluralist and democratic state while allowing the diverse world cultures to maintain under conditions of social pluralism.[34] This approach has also been advocated by Islamic liberals since the 1980s and was documented in the work of Leonard Binder, Islamic liberalism. The distinction of social liberalism was also adopted by Western Muslim scholars, including Abdullahi An-Naim in his Islam and the Secular State.[35]

NOTES

1. Keith I. Shimko, "Realism, Neorealism, and American Liberalism," *The Review of Politics*, 54, no. 2 (1992): 282.

2. Hans Morgenthau, *Politics among Nations* (New York: Alfred A. Knopf, 1947), 163.

3. Ibid., 281–287.

4. Timothy Mitchell, "McJihad: Islam in the U.S. Global Order," *Social Text*, vol. 20, no. 4 (2002), 1–18, p. 7. Project MUSE muse.jhu.edu/article/38471.

5. Ibid., 8.

6. Daniel Benjamin and Steven Simon, *The Age of Sacred Terror* (New York: Random House, 2003), 415.

7. Remarks by the U.S. president at the twentieth Anniversary of the National Endowment for Democracy, United States Chamber of Commerce, Washington, DC, January 29, 2002. https://georgewbush-whitehouse.archives.gov/news/releases/2003/11/print/20031106-2.html (accessed August 29, 2020).

8. Michelle Pace (ed.), *Europe, the USA and Political Islam Strategies for Engagement* (New York: Palgrave Macmillan, 2011), 19.

9. Ibid., 20.

10. Ibid., 22.

11. Shimaa Hatab, "Deepening Democracy or Stabilization? European Neighborhood Policy (ENP) and the "Arab Spring,"" *Review of Economics and Political Science*, 4, no. 1 (2019): 20–37. See also P Bauer, "European-Mediterranean security and the Arab spring: Changes and Challenges," in *Arab Spring Challenges for Democracy and Security in the Mediterranean*, ed. P. Bauer (New York: Routledge, 2015), 1–18.

12. The Assad regime let loose a large number of extremist groups it imprisoned in the wake of the Iraq war who later formed DAESH.

13. EU Parliament Com. "Proposal for a regulation of the European parliament and of the council establishing a European neighbourhood instrument. Brussels," available at: www.europarl.europa.eu/ meetdocs/2009_2014/documents/com/com_com(2011)0839_/com_com(2011)0839_en.pdf (accessed 25 July 2016).

14. Ibid.

15. Jan Wouters, S.D. "The European Union and Consular Law, Leuven Centre for Global Governance Studies," (2013), available at: http://fletcher.tufts.edu//media/Fletcher/Microsites/VCCR/ WP107-Wouters-Duquet-Meuwissen.pdf (accessed 20 June 2018).

16. Thomas G. Weiss and Rorden Wilkinson, *International Organization and Global Governance* (London and New York: Routledge, 2014), 120.

17. Nadine Kreitmeyr, "Neoliberal Co-optation and Authoritarian Renewal." *Globalizations*, 16, no. 3 (August 9, 2018): 289–303.

18. See for example Brencht De Smet and KoFenraad Bogaert. "Resistance and Passive Revolution in Egypt and Morocco," in *States of Discipline: Authoritarian Neoliberalism and the Contested Reproduction of Capitalist Order*, ed. C. B. Tansel (London: Rowman & Littlefield International, 2017). 211–233. Also, Ian Bruff and Cemal Burak Tansel. "Authoritarian Neoliberalism: Trajectories of Knowledge Production and Praxis." *Globalizations* 16, no. 3 (2019): 233–244.

19. Bruff and Tansel. "Authoritarian Neoliberalism," 234.

20. Beste İşleyen and Nadine Kreitmeyr, "Authoritarian Neoliberalism' and Youth Empowerment in Jordan," *Journal of Intervention and Statebuilding*, 15, no. 2 (2021): 244–263; see also C. B. Tansel, ed. *States of Discipline: Authoritarian Neoliberalism*

and the Contested Reproduction of Capitalist Order (London: Rowman & Littlefield International, 2017).

21. İşleyen and Kreitmeyr, "Authoritarian Neoliberalism and Youth Empowerment in Jordan," 244–263.

22. Ibid., 251–253.

23. Ibid., 254.

24. "GDP per capita, PPP (current international $)," The World Bank, accessed December 9, 2021, https://data.worldbank.org/indicator/NY.GDP.PCAP.PP.CD; and Aaron O'Neill, "Egypt: Trade balance from 2010 to 2020," Statista, August 5, 2021, https://www.statista.com/statistics/377970/trade-balance-of-egypt. See also Robert Springborg, Follow the Money to the Truth about Al-Sisi's Egypt, Project on Middle East Democracy (POMED) (January 7, 2022).

25. Aaron O'Neill, "Egypt: National debt from 2016 to 2026," December 1, 2021, https://www.statista.com/statistics/531560/national-debt-of-egypt/

26. Central Bank of Egypt, "Egypt Government Debt to GDP," Trading Economics, accessed December 9, 2021, https://tradingeconomics.com/egypt/government-debt-to-gdp

27. Robert Springborg, Follow the Money to the Truth about Al-Sisi's Egypt, Project on Middle East Democracy (POMED), January 7, 2022. See also Mustafa Hosny, "Big fish in a shrinking pond: How an Armed Forces company is building a fish farming monopoly," Mada Masr, April 15, 2021: https://www.madamasr.com/en/2021/04/15/feature/economy/big-fish-in-a-shrinking-pond-how-an-armed-forces-company-built-a-fish-farming-monopoly/

28. "Egypt's Draft Budget Supportive for Debt Reduction," *Fitch Ratings*, May 11, 2021, https://www.fitchratings.com/research/sovereigns/egypts-draft-budget-supportive-for-debt-reduction-11-05-2021.

29. Sisi set "Tahya Mysr" fund and pushed private entrepreneurs to contribute to it by placing their companies under the supervision of the fund which he has complete and unfettered control over it. See "Sisi calls to increase resources of Long Live Egypt Fund," Egypt Independent, September 6, 2021, https://www.egyptindependent.com/sisi-calls-to-increase-resources-of-long-live-egypt-fund. See also Yezid Sigh, Retain, Restructure, or Divest? Policy Options for Egypt's Military Economy. Carnegie Endowment for International Peace, 2022. https://carnegieendowment.org/files/Sayigh_Egypt_Military_Economy_FINAL.pdf.

30. Ibid.

31. "How IMF loans keep Sisi afloat as Egypt sinks deeper into debt." Middle East Eye, 28 January 2023.

32. Ibid.

33. John Rawls, *Political Liberalism* (New York: Columbia University Press, 2005), 12.

34. See also chapter 10 of my recent book, *Islam and the Trajectory of Globalization* (Routledge: New York and London, 2022).

35. *Islam and the Secular State: Negotiating the Future of Shari'a* (Cambridge, MA: Harvard University Press, 2008).

REFERENCES

Abdu, Muhammad. *Al-Islam wa al-Nasraniyyah ma'a al-Ilm wa al-Madaniyyah* (Cairo: Dar al-Manar, 1367 AH).

Afghani, Jamaluddin. "Lectures of Teaching and Learning," in *An Islamic Response to Imperialism Political and Religious Writings of Sayyid Jamal ad-Din al-Afghani*, ed. Nikki R. Keddie (Berkeley: University of California Press, 1968).

Ahmad, Aziz. "Sayyid Aḥmad Khān, Jamāl al-dīn al-Afghānī and Muslim India," *Studia Islamica*.

Asad, Talal. *Formations of the Secular Christianity, Islam, Modernity* (Stanford, CA: Stanford University Press, 2003).

Bauer, P. "European-Mediterranean security and the Arab spring: Changes and challenges", in *Arab Spring Challenges for Democracy and Security in the Mediterranean*, ed. P. Bauer (New York: Routledge, 2015), 1–18.

Binder, Leonard. *Islamic Liberalism* (Chicago, IL: University of Chicago Press, 1988).

Brown, Judith M. *Modern India: The Origins of an Asian Democracy* (Oxford: Oxford University Press, 1994).

Brown, L. Carl. *International Politics and the Middle East: Old Rules, Dangerous Game* (Princeton: Princeton University Press, 1984).

Bruff, Ian and Cemal Burak Tansel. "Authoritarian Neoliberalism: Trajectories of Knowledge Production and Praxis." *Globalizations* 16, no. 3 (2019): 233–244.

Calhoun, Craig, et el. (eds.), *Rethinking Secularism* (Oxford: Oxford University Press, 2011).

Dalacoura, Katerina. *Islam, Liberalism, and Human Rights* (London: I.B. Tauris, 2007).

De Smet, Brecht, and KoFenraad Bogaert. "Resistance and Passive Revolution in Egypt and Morocco," in *States of Discipline: Authoritarian Neoliberalism and the Contested Reproduction of Capitalist Order*, ed. C. B. Tansel (London: Rowman & Littlefield International, 2017).

Ehteshmi, Anoushiravan. *Globalization and Geopolitics in the Middle East: Old Games, New Rules* (London: Routledge, 2007)

El-Karanshawi, Shaimaa. *Egypt Court Approves Moderate Islamic Party* (Almasry Alyoum, February 20, 2011).

Esposito, John L., *Tamara Sonn, and John O. Voll, Islam and Democracy after the Arab Spring* (Oxford: Oxford University Press, 2016).

Hasan, Farhat. "Conflict and Cooperation in Anglo-Mughal Trade Relations during the Reign of Aurangzeb," *Journal of the Economic and Social History of the Orient*, 34, no. 4 (1991): 351–360.

Inglehart, Ronald F. "Changing Values in the Islamic World and the West," in *Values, Political Action, and Change in the Middle East and the Arab Spring*, eds. Mansoor Moaddel and Michele J. Gelfand (Oxford: Oxford University Press, 2017).

İşleyen, Beste and Nadine Kreitmeyr, "Authoritarian Neoliberalism' and Youth Empowerment in Jordan," *Journal of Intervention and Statebuilding*, 15, no. 2 (2021): 244–263.

Kivimäki, Timo. "Democracy, Autocrats and U.S. Policies in the Middle East," *Middle East Policy Council* (Washington, DC), XIX, no. 1 (Spring 2012): 64–71.

Kreitmeyr, Nadine. "Neoliberal Co-optation and Authoritarian Renewal." *Globalizations, Routledge*, 16, no. 3 (August 9, 2018).

Mahmood, Saba. "Religious Freedom, the Minority Question, and Geopolitics in the Middle East," *Comparative Studies in Society and History*, 54, no. 2 (2012): 418–446.

Malik, Hafeez. "Sir Sayyid Ahmad Khan's Role in the Development of Muslim Nationalism in Indo-Pakistan Subcontinent," *Islamic Studies*, 5, no. 4 (1966).

Price, Richard N. "The Psychology of Colonial Violence," in *Violence, Colonialism and Empire in the Modern World*, eds. Philip Dwyer and Amanda Nettelbeck (New York: Palgrave McMillan, 2018).

Shimko, Keith I. "Realism, Neorealism, and American Liberalism," *The Review of Politics*, 54, no. 2 (1992): 282.

Smith, Adrian. Alison Stenning, and Katie Willis (ed.), *Social Justice and Neoliberalism Global Perspectives* (London & New York: Zed books, 2008).

Smith, S. "Positivism and Beyond," in *International Theory: Positivism & Beyond*, eds. K. Booth et al. (Cambridge: Cambridge University Press, 1996).

Streets, Heather and Martial Races, *The Military, Race and Masculinity in British Imperial Culture*, 1857–1914 (Manchester: Manchester University Press, 2004), 39.

Supriyanto, Abdi. "Islam and (Political) Liberalism: A Note on an Evolving Debate in Indonesia," *Journal of Indonesian Islam*, 3, no. 2 (2009).

Waever, O. "The Rise and the Fall of the Inter-Paradigm Debate," in *International Theory: Positivism & Beyond*, eds. K. Booth et al. (Cambridge: Cambridge University Press, 1996).

Weiss, Thomas G. and Rorden Wilkinson, *International Organization and Global Governance* (London and New York: Routledge, 2014), 144.

Wilford, Hugh. *America's Great Game: The CIA's Secret Arabists and the Shaping of the Modern Middle East* (New York: Basic Books, 2013).

Wouters, Jan S.D. "The European Union and Consular Law, Leuven Centre for Global Governance Studies" (2013, available at: http://fletcher.tufts.edu//media/Fletcher/Microsites/VCCR/ WP107-Wouters-Duquet-Meuwissen.pdf (accessed 20 May 2023).

Conclusion

Justice as a principle of order rises high in the hierarchy of values in all cultures and philosophies, even though the systems people construct for its implementation continue to be subject of fierce contestation. This is because justice, like beauty, is an intrinsic human value that people sense before they begin to articulate. Human beings possess a sense of justice as they have a sense of beauty. However, as soon as we move away from the shared sense of justice, which we feel deep in our being, the consensus over justice begins to disappear, and disagreements about the details of what constitutes justice emerge. As we saw earlier, different individuals and cultures do entertain different meanings of justice even when they initially agree on its general concept. People seem, for instance, to agree with Aristotle's expression of justice as "treating equal people equally and unequal unequally." However, differences immediately emerge when we realize that Aristotle was not referring here to differences in competence but in social status. Treating people differently because they belong to different social classes invokes outrage as it deeply conflicts with modern sensibility, despite the fact that the two most revered Greek philosophers took it for granted that an aristocrat and a layperson should never be treated equally. Our modern association between the notion of justice and that of equal dignity continues to be grounded in faith and not rationality. No modern philosopher has succeeded in grounding the value of equality in rational argument, and the most vigorous attempt undertaken by John Rawls in his widely acclaimed work, *A Theory of Justice*, produced a nuanced argument that only few in the high echelon of moral philosophy could fully grasp.

Throughout the book, the notion of equal justice is located within the monotheistic traditions that historically challenged the ancient conception of society as a hierarchical and stratified social enterprise, and the various chapters managed to bring new insights into the notion of justice beyond the nation state, thereby contributing the debate over global justice. In order to engage the current debate on the meaning and conditions of global justice, the authors of the chapters that comprise this volume managed to relate the work advanced by Islamic rationalism on the question at hand and traced the various values that constitute the notion of global justice, or justice beyond the confines of national interests. Global justice, we argue, is an ancient concept as old as the monotheistic tradition itself. It reemerged in the post-Soviet period at the end of the Cold War that dominated international thought throughout the twentieth century. At the core of global justice is the idea that all human beings have intrinsic values and that they should be treated with equal dignity. This notion has been known in Western literature for at least three centuries and has been repeatedly emphasized by the Enlightenment philosophers. From Spinoza to Hobbes, through the work of Kant and John Stuart Mill, and in most recent times through the writings of Rawls and Habermas, the intrinsic worth and dignity of all humans have been emphasized. Yet despite the theoretical acceptance of the notion of equal dignity of all people with remarkable clarity, the idea remained, for the most part, confined within the boundaries of the nation state and has often been reduced to the notion of civic rights.

Long before the Enlightenment, Islamic rationalists have for centuries struggled to ground justice in public ethics and demanded that the powerful people in society are not above the law but are socially accountable. They insisted that the exercise of justice cannot be limited to ethnic and religious boundaries as they contemplated the prophetic models and echoed the pronouncements that permeate the Islamic normative sources. The former followed a long line of exemplary individuals who came over the centuries to reiterate the monotheistic call to speak truth to power and to reject injustice. Islamic rationalists developed a set of values and practices that made it possible to push justice beyond the confines of religious and ethnic communities. The universal applicability of justice was also embraced by early modern philosophers at the level of theory, but the application of the principle was subverted by the advocates of nationalism and the idea of the moral inequivalence of religious communities. The ideas presented in this volume challenge national and ethnic limitations imposed on the exercise of justice and call for the development of a globally inclusive model of equal justice.

The call to develop an inclusivist model of justice is shared by the contributors to Islam *and the Drive to Global Justice*, and the contributions they produced focused mainly on exploring the contradictions between the deeply held values by the populations of the MENA region and the failure of MENA states to translate the values sacred to Muslim societies to public relations institutions. The irony today is that the communities that led historically to advancing the ideas of equal justice and social accountability allow today outrageous injustices to take place in their midst. The discussion in the various chapters has shed light on the gap between the Islamic values emphasized in the Qur'an and was developed over the centuries by Islamic rationalist scholars and jurists into political relations and institutions.

The deliberations on the question of global justice brought several important threads for ensuring that justice is not only experienced among the citizens of world powers but is also extended to all humanity. Contrary to the cry of anti-globalization actors who blame the current predicaments of European states on pluralism and multi-culturalism, global justice is the only way to prevent the mass migrations of large number of people from the countries of the South to the North that skyrocketed in the last few decades. Such mass migrations are bound to upset the internal balance in both the North and the South. Anyone who studied issues of migration knows that those who leave their homeland in search of a safe heaven and the opportunity to make a living in a foreign country do not do that out of sheer ambition or in pursuit of a more luxurious lifestyle, but because of the extreme poverty and lack of personal security in societies ruled by autocratic and authoritarian governments supported by the powerful nations of the North. If we look at the countries that have produced the waves of migrants in the last two decades, we find that all of them are ruled by corrupt and incompetent regimes that put the corporate interests of foreign powers before that of their own people. The list is long and includes countries like Afghanistan, Egypt, India, Mexico, Nigeria, Somalia Syria, Yamen, and a host of Latin American dictatorships. The common denominator of all these countries is a corrupt regime supported by outside powers.

The above observation points us not only to the need to search for the root causes of the rising migration, which lies in subverting the local interests of less-developed societies for the benefit of dominant world powers, but also to the need to ground political systems in the universal values at the heart of modern moral sensibilities, including the values of equal justice for all. The United States took the lead in setting the United Nations Organization to overcome the cynical pursuit of realpolitik and to replace it with the rule of international law, but the United States was the first to break international law and the UN rules itself by acting in violation of the Security Council and the UN General Assembly to advance its national interests and those of its close allies. Soon, other world powers followed through, reducing international law and UN resolutions to nonbinding suggestions implemented selectively by global powers and applied against developing weak nations. We argued in the preceding chapters against the selective application of international law, pointing out that supporting tyrannical regimes who carry favors to world powers has been a major cause for the massive migration from the countries of the South and for the rise in the number of failed states in Africa, Asia, and South America in the last three decades.

The challenge the international order faces today stems partially from the complexity of the notion of justice, as it combines both intuitive and ideational elements. At the level of intuition, justice remains a universal element that speaks to the idiosyncratic nature of individual experiences and the spontaneous outburst of human emotions. The generalization and universalization of the experience of justice require that it develops into a rational and intellectual construct that generates broader consensus in society. The fragmentation of humanity into unequal groups and the segmentation of justice have served to justify treating different peoples in accordance with different sets of values, thereby justifying the application of double standards and unfair practices. Europe succeeded toward the end of the Middle Ages in breaking out from the ancient regime by embracing a new set of ideas that gave new meanings to the values of freedom, equality, and justice. The new intellectualization brought by the Enlightenment scholars successfully deconstructs the ideas of the divine right of kings, the infallibility of the pope, and the sinfulness of wealth creation. By doing so, the Enlightenment underscored the benefits of disobeying tyrants, holding public officials accountable and subjecting the church to values grounded in the revealed text.

The world is once again in need of new ideas that liberate developing societies from the tyrannical dictates of major world powers and reconnect humanity with the transcendental values that allowed it in the past to build cooperative and justice-based societies. For that to happen, a new construct should be introduced and debated to mend the internal friction developing in Western society, expand the application of justice into the global society, and reject the strategies employed by few powerful nations to subvert international law and justify the exploitation of the rest of humanity.

Index

Abderrahmane, Aisha (Bint al-Shati'), 133
Abderrahmane, Taha, 126, 127, 144, 145, 148, 150
Abduh, Muhammad, 38, 104, 115, 118, 119, 134, 137, 139, 147
Abraham, the Prophet, 9, 10, 14, 15, 18, 28, 44, 46, 104, 130, 141, 181
Abrahamic faith, 14, 44, 46, 130, 141
Abu Bakr (First Caliph), 18
accumulation of meanings, 60
Adam, 41, 42, 55
aesthetic, 57–63, 65–73, 75–77, 87, 88, 90, 133
al-Afghani, Jamal al-Din, 220, 224
Afghanistan, 4, 166, 171, 173, 181, 185, 186, 229
Afsaruddin, Asma, 55, 61, 74, 121, 123
Akif, Mehmed, 119
al-Bukhari, 45, 54, 118, 119
al-Shatibi, 115, 122
al-Qurṭūbī, 69–71, 75
al-Tabari, 37, 42, 46, 49–54, 56, 68, 69, 71, 72
An-Na'im, Abdullahi Ahmed, 155, 161
Arab society, 4, 48, 193–97, 199–207, 212
Arab Spring, 95, 97, 100, 173, 194, 214–16, 222, 224
Aristotle, 11–13, 26, 28, 227
Asharite, 19, 71

Augustine, St., 16, 17, 27, 29
authoritarian, 94, 95, 114, 121, 126, 134, 136, 163, 172, 174, 198, 212, 215, 216, 222, 229; leaders, 172, 173; neoliberalism, 216, 224; regimes, 4, 94, 116, 143, 166, 172, 180, 187, 191, 198, 215–17, 221
authoritarianism, 93, 119, 123, 209, 213, 215–17, 223, 225

beautification, 63, 65–68, 70–72
beauty, 3, 35, 58, 63–72, 128, 143, 227
belief and disbelief, 3, 57–63, 66–72
Ben Badis, Abdelhamid, 201
Bennabi, Malik, 134, 167, 169, 220
Bin Achour, al-Tahir, 134
Bush, George, 173, 176, 188, 191, 211, 212, 222
Byzantium, 40, 50

capitalism, 24, 79, 80, 82, 127, 159–61, 167–70, 175
Central Intelligence Agency (CIA), 173
Christian, 23, 30, 48, 92; Christian churches, 119, Christian philosophy, 148, 149; Christian theology, 83; Christian values, 17
Christianity, 10, 14, 16–18, 74, 94, 115, 131, 136, 177, 224; Roman Christianity, 17

Christians, 36, 38, 47, 50, 103, 110, 195, 196
church, 48, 84, 86, 107, 119, 133, 146, 177, 196, 204, 206, 207, 230
civil dialogue, 3, 31
civilization, 4, 25, 79–81, 84, 90, 110, 126, 145, 147, 159; human, 127; Islamic, 96, 98, 110, 113, 115, 125, 141, 143, 147; modern, 26
civilizational ethos, 125, 126
civil society, 94, 97, 99, 202, 214, 215, 217, 219
coercion, 38, 94, 107, 108, 113, 115, 119
Cold War, 171, 172, 175–78, 188, 193, 228
colonialism, 52, 80, 85, 86, 89, 93, 126, 134, 135, 137, 147, 161, 213, 220, 225
colonialization, 209
communication, 73, 76, 126, 145, 193, 209
communism, 114, 160, 172
compassion, 9, 11, 37, 44, 47, 81, 87
conflict, 13, 44–46, 55, 57, 88, 94, 96, 98, 157, 178, 188, 191, 205–7, 209, 224, 227
constitution, 18, 22, 25, 27, 29, 110, 112–14, 120, 121, 127, 137, 138, 155, 174, 179, 181
cosmopolitanism, 3, 80, 91, 95
covenant, 15, 18, 22, 23; dhimmi covenant, 23; peace covenant, 23; Saini covenant, 15
critical thinking, 127, 199

democracy, 5, 13, 25, 26, 29, 98, 121, 123, 126, 127, 157, 164, 168, 169, 171, 172, 174–77, 179, 180, 184–86, 188, 189, 210–13, 215, 217, 221–25; liberal democracy, 171, 174; Muslim democracy, 189, 191
Descartes, 141
discourse, 1, 3, 18, 20, 31, 43, 47, 80, 92, 93, 96, 99, 127, 135, 137, 138; academic, 84; civil, 47; Islamic, 67, 74, 78; legal, 85, 86; orientalist, 88, 95; Qur'anic discourse, 31; religious, 133, 135
disenchantment, 142, 211
disparity, 1, 2, 39, 43, 183
distinction between crime and sin, 105, 106
double standards, 2, 126, 172, 187, 192, 230
Durkheim, Emile, 80, 83, 91

Egypt, 5, 15, 19, 27, 29, 38, 58, 73, 77, 93, 97–99, 111, 113, 115, 134, 137, 147, 173, 185, 186, 194, 211–15, 218, 219, 222–24
Empire, 107, 130, 225; Byzantine, 119, 123; Islamic, 51; Ottoman, 86, 97, 99, 110, 112–14, 121, 122; Roman, 11, 16, 84
equal dignity, 2, 3, 9–12, 14, 15, 17–19, 22–25, 45, 183, 227
equity, 43, 44, 88; inequity, 183
ethics, 2–4, 9, 11, 16, 31, 35, 69, 72, 75, 77, 120, 125, 127, 132, 136–39, 143–46, 150, 167, 169, 172, 180, 189, 191; bioethics, 141 ethical paradigm, 188; ethics of dignity, 11, 14; ethics of duty, 14; Greek, 10, 12, 14; Grego-Roman ethical order, 3; Islamic, 9, 10, 20, 24, 149; Kantian ethics, 14; Nicomachean, 12, 26; public, 10, 16–18, 228; religious ethics, 74, 87; transcendental, 9, 10, 17, 26
ethnicity, 18, 23, 45, 194
Eurocentrism, 17, 84, 91, 94, 211
Europe, 4, 5, 12, 14, 16, 17, 25, 53, 83, 84, 87–89, 92, 94, 96, 98, 99, 114, 115, 127, 131, 133, 135, 138, 146, 148–50, 159, 161, 164, 177, 179, 210; European colonialism, 86, 90, 209; European realism, 210; European scholarshiip, 16, 80
expansionism, 178

faith, 3, 16, 19, 22, 25, 28, 39, 51, 62, 86, 110, 112, 121, 123, 125, 129, 137, 138, 140, 142, 144, 145, 148, 161, 166, 169, 177; Abrahamic, 14, 44, 46; dynamics of, 128; interfaith, 76; monotheistic, 48; orthodox, 129; tradition, 6, 33, 127–29, 139, 141
Faruqi, Ismail, 220
al-Fassi, Allal, 134, 137
Fazlur Rahman, 104, 117, 119, 123, 139, 142, 144, 162, 168, 170, 220
female imamship, 133, 136, 148
foreign policy, 2, 4, 171–79, 181, 183–87, 189, 191, 210, 211, 219
France, 25, 112, 114
freedom, 5, 9, 15, 16, 22, 28, 52, 96, 101, 103, 112, 113, 115–19, 121, 122, 129, 138, 142, 144, 156, 162, 164, 167, 170, 171, 173, 174, 178, 182, 196, 202, 210, 212, 215, 221, 230; religious, 219, 225
Fukuyama, Francis, 180, 189
fundamentalism, 203, 207, 221
fundamentalist, 155, 221

gender, 31, 39–43, 45, 54, 55, 93, 103, 116, 194, 202, 204
al-Ghannouchi, Rashid, 164, 165
global, 28, 32, 89, 119, 123; economy, 176; Global Age, 148, 150; global challenges, 1; Global North, 52, 53; global power, 2; Global South, 52, 172; governance, 219, 222; justice, 1, 4, 10, 26, 125, 127, 155–62, 164–70, 179, 228, 229; market, 126; order, 1, 2, 7, 26; peace, 2, 5;society, 26
globalization, 4, 90, 95, 126, 145, 151, 187, 189, 222
globalizing, society, 10; world, 31, 57
Goethe, Johann Wolfgand von, 129, 146, 150
Greco-Roman, 10, 11, 14
Greek, 10–14, 24, 108

Habermas, Jurgen, 79, 94, 95, 98, 99, 146, 150, 228
hadith, 38, 42, 45–47, 106, 107, 117–19, 122, 148, 164, 195; Ahl al-Hadith, 106; hadith literature, 45, 52, 119, 122, 124; prioritized hadiths, 106, 132
Hamka, 4, 156–69
Hebrew prophets, 15
Hegel, G.W.F., 10, 11, 16–18, 27, 28
hermeneutics, 3, 43, 74, 76, 77
Hodgson, Marshall, 28, 86, 87, 91, 96
Hourani, George, 143, 147, 150, 151
humanity, 2, 9, 10, 14, 16–20, 26, 28, 61, 73, 77, 125–28, 130, 131, 141, 144, 157, 161, 183, 209, 210, 229, 230
human rights, 1, 9, 17, 36, 101, 116, 127, 130, 136, 142, 146, 155, 157, 158, 161, 175, 176, 179, 209, 211, 212, 215, 221, 224

Ibn ʿAjība, Ahmad, 68–72, 75, 76
Ibn al-Khattab, Umar, 53
Ibn Ashur, Muhammad al-Tahir, 115, 122, 123, 220
Ibn Battuta, 88
Ibn Hazim, 56
Ibn Hisham, 27, 29
Ibn Qayyim al-Jawziya, 162, 170
Ibn Rushd, 141, 144
Ibn Sina, 141
Ibn Taymiyya, 163
idealism, 3, 24, 26, 125, 141, 143, 188, 192; American, 210; German, 11; rational, 2, 3, 9, 11, 13, 15, 17, 19, 23–25, 27, 79, 81, 86, 99, 145, 151, 175, 187, 192, 220; transcendental, 2
imperialism, 85, 89, 224
inclusion, 194, 195, 197, 199, 200, 202, 204
India, 25, 28, 29, 58, 61, 62, 119, 120, 123, 136, 224, 229
inequality, 10, 12, 13, 26, 39, 40, 45, 158, 167, 184, 213

intellectual history, 101
International Law, 26, 55, 116, 117, 122, 123, 132, 138, 177, 209, 210, 229, 230
International Relations, 2, 174, 175, 188, 189, 191, 210, 211
interpretation, 31, 40, 41, 46, 55, 56, 60–62, 68, 69, 73, 76, 88, 103, 104, 106, 108, 112, 114, 123, 124, 129, 132, 135–37, 143, 144, 157, 166
interreligious tensions, 3, 57
Iqbal, Muhammad, 128, 131, 137, 139, 140, 142, 144, 146, 148, 151, 220
Iran, 9, 93, 161, 166, 169, 223
Iraq, 4, 5, 23, 113, 166, 171, 173, 181, 194, 195, 198, 204, 205, 211, 212, 217, 222
Islam, 1–3, 9, 12, 16–20, 23, 24, 26–29, 31, 41, 44, 45, 49, 51–53, 55, 58, 60, 62, 67, 68, 73–77, 91, 93, 95, 96, 98–100, 103, 104, 107, 108, 112, 115, 119, 121–23, 125–28, 131, 134–36, 139, 142, 145–51, 155–57, 160–62, 164–70, 180, 181, 183, 186, 187, 189–92, 203–5, 207, 212, 218–20, 223–25, 228; Sheikh-ul Islam, 110
Islamic, 5, 9; contractualism, 86, 87; ethics, 9, 10, 20, 22, 24; law, 20, 23, 43, 97, 99, 101, 116–18, 122–24, 160, 168, 169, 181, 204; legal doctrine, 90; patterns of civility, 90;philosophers, 17; philosophy, 19, 74, 76, 141, 148, 149; rationalism, 2, 9, 10, 14, 15, 17, 19, 20, 24, 26, 219, 220, 228; scholars, 1, 15, 16, 73, 107, 118, 157; scholarship, 73, 78; society, 3, 97, 98; Sufism, 138; symbols, 57; traditions, 1, 3, 15, 79, 117, 125, 126, 140, 142, 144; values, 1, 5, 179, 219, 229
Islamophobia, 135
Islamosphere, 117, 119, 121, 125, 127, 131, 133, 134, 136, 137

Israel, 187, 213–15, 217; Israeli Zionist movement, 199
Israelites, 15, 42
Izetbigovic, Ali, 144, 149

al-Jabri, Mohammed Abed, 139, 144, 147, 150, 220
Jewish, 15, 18, 22, 48, 196, 204
Jews, 22, 23, 36, 38, 47, 71, 103, 196, 205
justice, 1, 2, 4, 9–13, 15–17, 19, 20, 22, 23, 27, 29, 31–36, 38–40, 43–46, 49, 51–53, 55, 67, 75, 76, 79, 93, 95, 97, 101–3, 111, 120, 127, 157, 169, 179, 180, 183, 184; concept of, 9, 12, 31, 179, 182–84; definition, 184; economic, 35, 36; equal, 9, 22; global, 10, 26, 125, 127, 154–61, 165–67; international, 209; political, 181; principles of, 64; social justice, 33, 34, 37, 129, 132, 143, 144, 160, 161

Kalam, 17, 19, 69, 75, 76
Kamali, Mohammed Hashim, 116–18, 123
Kant, Immanuel, 9, 11, 14, 27, 29, 141, 209, 228; Kantian philosophy, 24
al-Kawakibi, Abd al-Rahman, 160, 220
Kemalism, 108
Khan, Sayyid Ahmad, 119, 224, 225

Latin Christendom, 16, 17, 79, 84
law, 9, 13–17, 19–24, 26, 27, 29, 43, 46, 61, 83, 86, 87, 90, 92, 97–99, 101–3, 107, 108, 110–16, 120, 122–25, 132, 138, 155, 160, 164, 165, 168, 169, 174, 181–83, 190, 192, 201, 209, 210, 215, 222, 225, 229, 230; criminal, 104; custoian of, 3; modern civil, 123; rule of, 17; transcendental, 16
liberalism, 29, 114, 126, 156, 167, 170, 171, 175, 176, 178, 179, 184, 186, 188–90, 192, 212, 213, 216, 221–25

liberty, 105, 108, 112, 118, 122, 126, 130, 143, 150, 161, 173, 179, 192, 204, 212, 213

Majlis Ulama Indonesia, 157
management of diversity, 198, 200, 202
Manifest Destiny, 177
Maqasid (sharia objectives), 115, 122, 123
marginalization, 166, 194, 198, 199, 219
maslahah, 4, 157, 162, 165
al-Massiri, Abdelwahab, 141, 149
materialism, 24, 141, 160, 169
Mecca, 38, 47, 48, 51, 60
Medina, City of, 18, 19, 22, 23, 27, 28, 48, 50, 102, 105
MENA (Middle East and North Africa), 4, 5, 156, 167, 210–17, 219–21, 228
Middle East, 4, 96, 97, 100, 121, 123, 134, 147, 150, 171–73, 181, 184, 185, 187, 188, 191, 203, 206, 207, 210–13, 216, 219, 220, 223–25
military coup, 172, 194, 217, 218
modernism, 24, 120, 123, 186
modernization, 5, 24, 113, 114, 121, 172, 184, 210–12, 219
monotheism, 11, 58, 104
Montesquieu, 114, 121, 123, 124
moral agency, 10, 15, 18, 20, 42
Mosaddegh, Mohammad, 173
Moses, Prophet, 15, 64, 96
Mu'tazili, 67. *See also* Mutasilites
Muhammad, Prophet, 15, 18, 22, 47, 49, 60, 68, 102, 103, 122, 144, 186
Muhammadiyah, 134, 157
multiculturalism, 1, 2
Muslim feminist, 39, 41, 43, 133
Muslim jurists, 21, 42, 105, 107, 115, 129
Muslims, 15, 18, 22, 23, 32, 43, 45–49, 51–53, 57, 59–62, 66, 74, 75, 78, 91, 92, 94, 103–5, 108, 110, 111, 115–17, 131, 132, 136, 140, 143, 144, 156, 160, 162, 164, 180, 186, 187, 193; cities, 91; community, 106; exegtes, 54; feminism, 43; intellectuals, 91, 155, 158, 167; leaders, 111; Muslim rule, 47; society, 24, 43, 97, 111, 157, 184; theology, 124; traditions, 97; women, 43, 55; world, 113–15, 122, 134, 144, 172, 184, 186
Muslim scholars, 2, 18, 20, 36, 37, 43, 44, 49, 52, 58, 62, 127, 132, 155, 157, 164, 165, 221
Mustafa Kemal (Atatürk), 113
Mutazilite, 19, 20

Nasr, Abu Zayd, 73, 76
Nasr, Seyyed Hossein, 77, 144, 146, 148, 149
neocolonialism, 126, 135
neoconservatives, 176, 177
neoliberalism, 126, 167, 170, 175, 176, 179, 189, 192, 212, 213, 216, 222–25
Nicomachean Ethics, 12, 26, 28
Nursi, Said, 220

oppression, 33, 35, 38, 46, 49, 60, 79, 89, 95, 135, 220
orientalism, 38, 117, 125, 227, 230
orientalists, 23, 80, 85, 135, 148, 150
Ottoman, 93, 97, 108, 111–13; constitution, 121; empire, 86, 97, 99, 110, 113, 114, 122; parliament, 113, 169; reform, 113, 120, 121, 123; society, 110; Waqf, 99

Pakistan, 28, 29, 101–3, 115–17, 122, 123, 146, 151, 173, 186, 203, 207, 225
patriarchy, 39, 101
peace, 2, 5, 13, 20, 23, 31, 36, 44–46, 49–55; global, 2, 5, 209, 219; peacebuilding, 205–7; perpetual, 174, 188, 191, 209; Roman, 13
People of the Book, 46, 47, 201
Persia, 19, 40; Persian culture, 54; Persians, 13; Persian territories, 23
philosophy of religion, 128

Plato, 11, 12, 24, 26, 28, 29
political Islam, 3, 125, 131, 134, 168, 169, 203, 207, 222
polygyny, 43, 44
postcolonial, 4, 80, 84, 91, 93–95, 97, 98
postmodern, 24, 120, 123, 126
power, 1–5, 9–22, 24–26, 28, 29, 39, 48, 51, 80–83, 86, 89–92, 94–97, 100, 106, 110–13, 120, 121, 123, 126, 127, 130, 133, 135, 136, 140, 142, 148, 166, 171, 173–78, 180–84, 194, 198, 199, 201, 209, 210, 212–14, 216–24, 228–30
public sphere, 3, 144, 148, 186, 197
public value, 10, 16

Qur'an, 44, 52, 58, 105, 128, 129, 131, 132, 142, 144, 182, 195
Qur'anic: aesthetics, 57; ethics, 51; prescriptions, 39; text, 2; verses, 31, 35, 40–42, 45; vision, 39

rational idealism, 3, 9, 13, 15, 17, 19, 21, 23–25, 27, 29
rationalization, 79, 82, 83, 85, 140
Rawls, John, 129, 157, 167, 170, 184–86, 221, 223, 227, 228
al-Razi, Fakhr al-Din, 37, 38, 47, 48, 53–55, 65
realism, 3, 14, 19, 24, 129, 143; Greek, 24; Grego-Roman, 2; moral: political, 5, 210; rational, 24
reciprocity, 12, 13
reform: in jurisprudence, 161; reformism, 203
relations: mutual relations, 85; socioeconomic relations, 70
religious: communities, 2, 31, 36, 44, 202, 221, 228; ethos, 89; freedom, 22, 52, 112, 196, 202, 219, 225; pluralism, 4, 62, 74, 78, 148, 149, 203; reformation, 16; society, 2, 23; values, 1, 161, 219
Rida, Muhammad Rashi, 38, 118, 119, 220
Roman, 2, 10, 11, 13, 14, 16, 17, 23, 26, 83, 84, 111, 146

Roosevelt, Franklin D, 172, 209

Safi, Louay, 79, 81, 88, 94–99, 126, 145, 151, 173–75, 184, 187–89, 192
Sahriati, Ali, 220
secularism, 1, 98, 126, 141, 142, 145, 148, 155, 212, 224; authoritarian, 134; full, 141, 149; partial, 141; radical, 142
Security Council, 209, 211, 229
selectivity, 1
sensory experiences, 58, 59, 62, 63, 66
Shah, Mohammad Reza, 173
shari'a (*also sharia and shariah*), 3, 86, 87, 91, 93, 96, 97, 99–101, 103–15, 118, 119, 122, 123, 125, 129, 132–35, 144, 145; classical, 132, 133, 138; hermeneutics of, 3, 43; modern, 132, 133; thik sharia, 135; thin sharia, 133
shura, 4, 154, 157, 162, 163, 165
slavery, 107, 108, 119
Smith, Dorothy E., 39, 56
social accountability, 19
Soroush, Abdolkarim, 62, 139, 144, 147
spiritualism, 3, 125, 127, 138–40, 148, 167, 169
spirituality, 3, 16, 77, 125, 127, 129, 138–40, 143, 148
Sunna (*Prophetic tradition*), 38, 52, 69, 104, 106
Syria, 5, 19, 54, 111, 113, 134, 173, 181, 185, 186, 194, 198, 205, 211–13, 215, 217, 229; Greater, 134

Tanzimat (*Reorganization*), 122
Taylor, Charles, 137, 142, 146, 148, 149, 151
theology, 28, 30, 74–77, 83, 84, 117, 119, 124, 131
transcendental: ethics, 9, 10, 13–15, 17, 24–26, 28, 40, 43; ethos, 4, 25; faith, 3; idealism, 2; law, 16; morality, 114, 214, 216, 218, 220; truth, 3; values, 2, 10, 230

truth, 3, 12, 14–16, 19, 24, 27, 36, 40, 50, 58, 59, 62, 63, 66–68, 70, 72, 75, 108, 130, 137, 139, 146, 150, 182, 201, 223, 228
Turkey, 108, 111–13, 120–22, 186

U.S. foreign policy, 4, 171, 172, 185, 187, 191
U.S. invasions, 4, 171
ulama (*religious scholars*), 110, 112, 134, 157, 168, 169
underdevelopment, 119, 123, 158, 216
United Nations, 161, 166, 172, 177, 209, 210, 229
United States, 4, 25, 61, 111, 114, 136, 171–73, 176–79, 187, 191, 204, 209–11, 215, 217, 229
universal, 1–3, 9, 11, 13–15, 17, 19, 21, 23, 25–27, 29, 31, 32, 58, 61–63, 66, 67, 72, 74–76, 78, 94, 126, 129–32, 161, 165

universalization, 2, 9, 11, 14, 15
utilitarianism, 3, 125

Virgil, Roman Poet, 17, 27, 29

waqf, 3, 80, 87–90, 92, 93, 97–99
war, 44, 47, 49–52, 60, 113, 117, 147, 158, 171–78, 183, 188, 191, 211, 222, 228
Weber, Max, 30, 80, 82–84, 88, 90, 94, 96–98, 100
Western: colonialism, 80, 89, 161; complacency, 215, 217, 219, 221; culture, 127; democracy, 164, 174, 175, 213, 219; exceptionalism, 91; institutions, 5; liberal thought, 95, 157, 161; societies, 25, 107, 220, 230; world, 108, 114, 183
Westphalia, 3, 80, 85, 86, 92–94, 96, 100
wisdom, 11, 18, 115, 183

About the Contributors

EDITOR

Louay Safi is a professor of political science and Islamic philosophy at Hamad Bin Khalifa University (HBKU), Qatar. He published extensively on issues such as globalization, political development, democracy, human rights, and Islamic and the West. He is the author of twenty-four books and numerous papers, including *Islam and the Trajectory of Globalization* (Routledge 2022), *The Quranic Discourse* (Praeger 2009), and *Tensions and Transitions in the Muslim World* (University Press of America, 2003).

CONTRIBUTORS

Muhammed Abu-Nemir is a professor of international peace and conflict resolution at American University. He is the founder and president of Salam Institute for Peace and Justice and the co-founder of *Journal of Peacebuilding and Development*. He has worked for over three decades in a number of conflict areas, including Middle East, Chad, Niger, Nigeria, Mindanao, and Sri Lanka, on issues related to conflict resolution and intercultural and interreligious dialogue; forgiveness and reconciliation; and evaluation of peacebuilding programs. His most recent book is *Evaluating Peacebuilding and Interfaith Dialogue: Methods and Frameworks* (2021).

Asma Afsaruddin is a professor of Middle Eastern Languages and Cultures at the University of Indiana, Bloomington. Her scholarships cover a wide range of issues, including Islamic religious and political thought, contemporary Islamic movements, gender roles, and Islam in modern society. She is the author and editor of eight books, including the award-winning *Striving in the Path of God* (Oxford University Press, 2013) and *The First Muslims: History and Memory* (Oneworld, 2008), translated into Turkish, Malay, and Bosnian. She was inducted in 2019 into the Johns Hopkins Society of Scholars in recognition of the scholarly and professional distinction she has achieved in her field.

Mustafa Akyol is a senior fellow at the Cato Institute's Center for Global Liberty and Prosperity, where he focuses on the intersection of public policy, Islam, and modernity. Since 2013, he has also been a frequent opinion writer for *The New York Times*, covering politics and religion in the Muslim world. He is the author of *Reopening Muslim Minds: A Return to Reason, Freedom, and Tolerance* (2021).

Khairudin Aljunied (PhD SOAS, London) is a professor at the University of Malaya and a senior fellow (previously Malaysia Chair of Islam in Southeast Asia) at the Alwaleed Centre for Muslim-Christian Understanding, Georgetown University. He is the author of several books, including *Muslim Cosmopolitanism: Southeast Asian Islam in Comparative Perspective* (Edinburgh University Press), *Hamka and Islam: Cosmopolitan Reform in the Malay World* (Cornell University Press, 2018), and *Islam in Malaysia: An Entwined History* (Oxford University Press, 2019).

Mohammed Hashas (PhD, Habil.) is a lecturer in the Department of Political Science at Luiss University of Rome. He is a scholar of Islam, contemporary Islamic thought, contemporary Moroccan thought, and Islamic thought in Europe. He is the author of *The Idea of European Islam* (2019) and *Intercultural Geo-Poetics* (2017) and the coeditor of a couple of works on contemporary Arab-Islamic thought.

Armando Salvatore is the Barbara and Patrick Keenan Chair in Interfaith Studies and a professor of Islamic and Interreligious Studies at McGill University. His most recent single-authored book is *The Sociology of Islam: Knowledge, Power and Civility* (Wiley Blackwell, 2016). He is the chief editor of *The Wiley Blackwell History of Islam* (Wiley Blackwell, 2018) and *The Oxford Handbook of the Sociology of the Middle East* (Oxford University Press 2022).

Farid Senzai is an assistant professor of political science at Santa Clara University, where he teaches courses on U.S. foreign policy and Middle East politics. He is a former fellow of the Institute for Social Policy and

Understanding (ISPU), a research associate at the Brookings Institution, and a research analyst at the Council on Foreign Relations.

Abdulkader Tayob is a professor of Islamic Studies, Religion, and Public Life and holds the chair in Islam, African Publics, and Religious Values at the University of Cape Town, South Africa. He has published on Islam in South Africa, modern Islamic thought, and Islam and the history of religions. He has led several research initiatives and projects and convened numerous workshops and conferences.

www.ingramcontent.com/pod-product-compliance
Lightning Source LLC
Chambersburg PA
CBHW050326020526
44117CB00031B/1811